The
Assessment
of Social Research

Guidelines for
the Use of Research
in Social Work
and Social Science

F. E. PEACOCK PUBLISHERS, INC.

ITASCA, ILLINOIS

The Assessment of Social Research

Guidelines for the Use of Research in Social Work and Social Science

TONY TRIPODI
PHILLIP FELLIN
HENRY J. MEYER
THE UNIVERSITY OF MICHIGAN

Acknowledgements

This book is a product of the interaction of its authors, each of whom recognizes but cannot adequately acknowledge the sources in his own career from which the ideas in the book derive. Some sources are indicated by references to the literature but the direct and indirect contributions of our colleagues and students are equally appreciated though less apparent except to us and to them. Our thinking about the assessment of social research has been particularly stimulated by associations with: David Fanshel and Samuel Finestone, Columbia University; Ernest Greenwood, University of California at Berkeley; James Bieri, University of Texas; Martin McCarthy, St. Louis University; Edgar F. Borgatta, University of Wisconsin; and our present colleagues at The University of Michigan: Edwin J. Thomas, Rosemary Sarri, Eugene Litwak, and Irwin Epstein. Naming them does not exonerate them from their influence but we hope they will forgive us for any untoward consequences they find in this book for which they bear no responsibilities.

We are most grateful to Fedele F. Fauri, Dean of the School of Social Work, The University of Michigan, for material facilitation of our work, and, even more, for fostering the intellectual climate among his faculty that sustained our enthusiasm during the preparation of the book. Robert D. Vinter, Associate Dean, has made a special contribution to that climate.

We thank the following graduate assistants for their help: Roslyn Weinberger, Elizabeth MacIntyre, Anne Springer, Ben Hemke, Carol Wortman, John Ford, Tai K. Shin, and David Dillman. We appreciate also the suggestions and constructive reactions to earlier versions of the text by students in our classes on research methods.

Among the administrative and secretarial staff of the School of Social Work to whom we express our deepest appreciation, we particularly thank Roy Gaunt, Administrative Assistant to the Dean, and Marian Iglesias, Dianne Etzel, Sande Smith, and Betty Ring, all of whom helped to prepare the manuscript.

The consent of authors and publishers to reprint materials is gratefully acknowledged here, and specifically recognized where the materials are reproduced.

We thank F. E. Peacock, our publisher, and his associates, Thomas LaMarre and Joyce Usher, for helpful advice and constant encouragement.

Members of our families and friends assisted in editing portions of the manuscript, and in other less tangible ways. In particular we appreciate the contributions of Carol Lee Tripodi, Phyllis Fellin, Suzanne Meyer, Sheldon Rose, Irwin Epstein, and Roni Newman.

Contents

Introductory Statement
To the Student and the Teacher

The reading and use of scientific research is an increasing obligation of social workers and other professional persons. This book is written for consumers of the literature of empirical research in social work and the social sciences. There is no precedent for a textbook on research consumption. Therefore, a note about some features of the book may be helpful.

The reader of this book may find some concepts and terms from the vocabulary of social research that are unfamiliar to him if he has not previously studied research methods. For such readers we have included brief explanations as part of the relevant exposition of topics and we have given specific references to sources from which more extensive explanations may be obtained. Furthermore, we have identified technical terms and concepts in the index so the reader may readily return to locations in the book where they are explained or their meanings made evident by the context. Most of the major concepts recur as the text develops and as examples of research are discussed. The student can expect to gain a firmer sense of their meaning as he proceeds but he will find it helpful if he keeps at hand an elementary book on research methods, such as one of those mentioned on page 16.

To aid the teacher using this textbook, we have included discussions of the literature from which our approach and perspective on classifying, evaluating, and utilizing research have emerged. The student may omit these sections, if he wishes, without losing the continuity of the presentation. The teacher may, however, find an examination of our sources useful for elaborating points in the text and for stimulating his own ideas about the topics discussed.

The six research articles reprinted in Part II of the book were selected because we consider them to be examples of good studies. Our detailed assessments of three of them are not intended as critiques but as illustrations of how one may gain maximum benefit by careful and thoughtful examination. It is necessary to be critical of even the best research but criticism is not the end but the first step toward appreciating what research can contribute to our understanding and make available for our use. This is the pervading theme we would have those who use the book appreciate and make part of their conscious equipment as professional practitioners.

In Part II of this book we apply guidelines for the assessment of social research to specific research studies. Our narrative assessments illustrate at considerable length how a reader might examine various features of a research study in the framework of the guidelines discussed in Part I. The studies reproduced in Part II were chosen because they are worthy of serious assessment. Our purpose is not to find fault with the research so as to minimize its contribution. On the contrary, the aim is to show that careful assessment extends the contributions of the research by engaging the research reader creatively in the problems with which the researcher has grappled. When we note what the researcher "might" or "should" have done, we are not criticizing him or saying that he should have done a different study. We are taking his purposes and achievements seriously so as to advance our own understanding and stimulate our own thinking.

PART I

Guidelines for the Classification, Evaluation and Utilization of Social Research

Chapter 1

Consumption of Research:
An Introduction

The Purpose of This Book

Research is the application of systematic procedures for the purposes of developing, modifying, and expanding knowledge that can be communicated and verified by independent investigators. When the knowledge obtained by research is about the observable world—that is, about phenomena that independent observers can apprehend—it is called empirical research. Because science (both natural and social) is more closely identified with empirical research than any other knowledge-seeking enterprise, empirical research is often referred to as scientific research. This book is about empirical research relevant for social work. Such research is typically reported in the professional journals of social work and the social and behavioral sciences and in monographs and books.

Characteristic of empirical research in the social sciences and social work is the use of a variety of available methods, such as sampling techniques, in order to obtain relatively unbiased observations of human behavior in different social situations. In addition to methods for producing standardized observations, the methodology of social research is concerned with logical alternatives for reaching degrees of certainty in conclusions that constitute additions to knowledge. Empirical research is thus characterized by *purpose* (i.e., to answer questions, to reduce ignorance) and *method* (i.e., standardized procedures of observation and logical procedures for reaching conclusions). A typical research study contains these interrelated aspects of the research process: problem formulation, research design, data collection, analysis of data, and the conclusions of the study (Selltiz *et al.*, 1959). Problem formulation and research design involve the articulation of the precise problem to be investigated and the specification of the logical approach to answer the questions posed for study. The sampling procedures are indicated, and methods of gathering data relevant to the research problem are considered. Data are collected and analyzed by quantitative and qualitative devices, and there is a consideration of the extent to which conclusions can be made regarding tentative answers to the major questions of the investigation.

Most books about empirical research, including those for social workers, are designed to help the reader learn how to conduct research. They are focused primarily on the production of research. This book, in contrast, is focused on consumption of research. Its aim is to increase the sophistication of the reader of research reported in the literature. The more one learns about doing research the more sophisticated he is likely to become in reading research already done. Likewise, the more one becomes efficient in reading research the more likely he is to understand how to do research. Nevertheless, there are different objectives and skills for the research producer and the research consumer. This book seeks to enhance the skills of research consumption.

In the years since World War II, along with the increased use of research in the development of technology in modern society, research has received increasing emphasis in the profession of social work. Social work educators have observed that trends include more research conducted by professionals within the field itself and a greater influence of the social sciences in both substantive and methodological contributions (Fanshel, 1962a, 1962b; MacDonald, 1960). In spite of this increasing production of knowledge through research, the typical social work practitioner has usually not been well trained either to produce or to consume empirical research. In undergraduate college or in the graduate schools of social work, social work students will rarely have achieved more than an elementary knowledge of research methods in courses that usually are about doing research. Yet educational objectives for instruction in research, according to the Council on Social Work Education (1965), are designed to help the social work student:

Understand the nature and function of social work research and its relationship to the advancement of professional knowledge and improvement of professional practice.

Understand the relationship of research to the helping and problem-solving tasks of social work, and strengthen habits of disciplined thought and performance.

Become familiar with the application of principles of scientific inquiry to social work practice and to the prevention, treatment, and control of social problems.

Develop capacity to undertake or participate in studies and research, and to evaluate and use the results of research in social work practice.

The critical evaluation of research reports and a consideration of the ways in which research findings can be utilized are skills which are regarded as increasingly necessary for social workers (Francel *et al.*, 1968). The importance of developing skills in assessing research studies is also reflected in the opinions of students in graduate schools of social work. From a study concerned with the learning of research skills in five schools of social work, it was concluded that students characterized the topic of reading and analyzing research reports as that portion of research teaching which was most useful for social work practice (Goldstein, 1967).

In keeping with the intent to facilitate learning how to consume empirical research reports, this book is written primarily for persons studying to become social workers. However, it is not a textbook on research methods, and it is not intended to replace existing texts which explain and illustrate elementary principles of research. The student will find this book more useful if he already has had some exposure to research concepts, or if the book is used concurrently with standard research methods texts in a beginning course on research. Social work practitioners and social work educators who need to assess and codify knowledge from research for their own purposes are also among those for whom the book is intended. Our aim is to assist the research reader—whether a social worker, a psychologist, a sociologist, or in some other discipline—to read research more usefully, and perhaps even more pleasurably.

LEARNING HOW TO CONSUME RESEARCH REPORTS

The Plan of this Book

To become a proficient consumer of research, the research reader must learn how to assess published studies and he must have practice in doing so. Assessment of research requires standards for judging how well a study has been done and how useful it can be. We refer therefore to *evaluation* and *utilization* as crucial features of assessment and these, in turn, are facilitated by the *classification* of a study in terms of its purposes and research methods. The development of criteria for classifying, evaluating, and utilizing research that appears in the social work and social science literature is the prime objective of those who would learn to consume research. Following this introductory chapter, the next section of this book consists of chapters proposing criteria and guidelines for classifying, evaluating, and utilizing research.

Criteria and guidelines become meaningful, of course, by their use. Understanding the criteria for classifying, evaluating, and utilizing research, the reader needs to face specific research reports so as to gain proficiency in applying the criteria. This is always a creative, not a mechanical, process and one that is mastered only by practice. To facilitate such practice, the last section of this book consists of three chapters—one for each type of research we have distinguished—in which two research articles are reproduced. In each chapter the first research report is assessed in detail following the criteria previously developed. A second research report is presented as it appears in the literature, followed by sets of leading questions so that the reader may practice for himself the application of the criteria for assessment.

A Supplementary Learning Aid

In keeping with the principle that the research reader can only learn to consume research effectively by reading and assessing research as reported in the literature, we have prepared a book of readings, *Exemplars of Social Research* (Fellin, Tripodi, and Meyer, 1969), which includes published studies of different types of research. The selections for this reader, as well as for the last section of the present book, have been made from journals of social work, psychology, and sociology. Moreover, bibliographies of additional research articles are included so that students and instructors of courses in research can have a ready source of studies to assess. The consumer of research should be equipped, after his guided tour through the studies we have selected, to pursue his own directions of interest in the literature. Our selections have been made from social work, sociology, and psychology because these are the fields of our own greatest experience and also because their substantive content is a major source of knowledge for social workers. However, we believe that the principles and guidelines for assessment that are developed can be applied to research reports from other disciplines.

SHOULD A RESEARCH REPORT BE READ AT ALL?

As previously noted, our concern in this book is with the assessment of reported empirical research relevant to social work. We will not develop guidelines for assessing publications of historical and bibliographic research. Furthermore, the classification scheme and the guidelines we subsequently develop will not apply directly to articles that discuss research strategies and methods without presenting empirical data, or those that present portions of data from one or several research investigations to support theoretical propositions or practice principles, or to essay reviews of one or more research studies. Exclusion from consideration in this book does not imply that such literature is not valuable for the social worker. On the contrary, knowledge from these and other sources about a topic of relevance to the practitioner is most important. The more the research reader knows about a topic of interest the more he will gain from reading research that bears on the topic.

The classification and assessment schemes which are developed are in general meant for use in reading research reports devoted to a single investigation. Such reports normally include information on the problem formulation, research design and data collection, and data analysis and conclusions of the research which is being reported. But, should an article, or research report, of empirical research be read at all?

This may seem to be a trick question in a book devoted to assessing published research. Assessment begins, however, with a decision that an article or monograph deserves the time and energy its reading will require. The practitioner is in a familiar dilemma: he must read the study to know if it is worth reading! He risks wasting time or overlooking something useful. The title of the research report may help him decide whether to read it but often the title will not tell him anything about the quality of the research. Not all titles are reliable indicators of the content of a research report. The title, *Girls at Vocational High* (Meyer *et al.*, 1965), does not reveal that this is a field experiment on casework and group counselling. "The 'Hang Loose' Ethic and the Spirit of Drug Use," (Suchman, 1968) is a title that may not imply that research is being reported. The titles, "Scapegoats, Group Workers, and Pre-emptive Intervention," (Shulman, 1967) and "Epilepsy and Social Adjustment" (Morgan, 1967) do not reveal that the latter reports a research study and the former does not. Fashions in titles for research reports vary, but readers soon become familiar with the practices of journals they find most pertinent to their interests. Even when titles—as they usually do—indicate a general subject-matter area, e.g., drug use, illness, delinquency, etc., the peripheral relevance of a research study to the practitioner may not be evident. Subtitles, abstracts or head-notes preceding the article may be helpful, but often there will be no other way than a cursory, first reading to decide whether or not to undertake more careful reading. Of course, a colleague who has read the study may offer helpful information.

Having a cursory, first knowledge of a research report, what basis does the practitioner have for deciding whether it is worthwhile for him to go further? We may note a number of reasons that the practitioner may keep in mind as he answers this question for himself:

1. The practitioner may be currently, or persistently, faced with a particular problem in his practice on which the research seems to bear. For example, he faces clients with excessive anxiety and the research appears to deal with effectiveness of different ways of treating the problem (as in Paul, 1966 and 1967). Or, he is an administrator of a large professional staff and the subject of the research is supervision (as in Scott, 1965). In short, the subject matter of the research may have direct relevance to an immediate problem of the reader's practice.

Having a specific practice problem, like any other felt need, can be a stimulus for problem-solving research behavior. The practitioner with such a problem need not—indeed, should not—wait for the chance appearance on his desk of a pertinent research study. He should examine the literature on the topic to see if studies have been made that will be useful to him. Articles reviewing the state of research on a particular question may be especially helpful in these circumstances. Also, there may be books that collect major research studies on a problem or area. Use should be made, also, of publication of abstracts, such as *Abstracts for Social Workers, Psychological Abstracts*, and *Sociological Abstracts*.

2. The practitioner may choose to study the research, even if it does not apparently bear on a current practice problem, because it seems likely to supply knowledge about his practice

area where he might face problems or have questions. Such questions may be about client characteristics, social situations, or new approaches to practice or about other factors that affect his work. If he counsels persons with marital problems, for example, he may find relevant an experiment with differential assignment of caseworkers to marriage partners (as in Pollak, 1963). Or, if he works with groups of delinquents, he may want to know what was learned in a study of street corner gangs (as in Jansyn, 1966). In short, the subject matter of the research may be relevant to the reader's area of practice, if not to a specific problem he currently faces.

3. The practitioner may read a research report peripheral to his area of practice, or entirely outside it, because he believes it to be important to social work as a profession and to him as a professional social worker. He may want to "be informed," or "keep up with what is going on." (Some research studies become widely publicized and knowing them is an unavoidable expectation of the professional social worker. Some of these "classics" will have been on reading lists when the practitioner was in social work school, and he may want to get around to reading them at last!) Some studies that seem far from the practitioner's own area may be provocative and stimulating and, in an indirect fashion, offer useful knowledge. It is not the purpose of this book to promote knowledge for its own sake, but one answer to the question, "Why should I read a research study?", may be, simply: "Because it interests me." This is not the sort of usefulness we propose guidelines for, but the double meaning of a title of an old article by Abraham Flexner comes to mind: "The Usefulness of Useless Knowledge."

TYPES OF EMPIRICAL SOCIAL RESEARCH

Based on the objectives of the investigation and the use of different strategies and methods, empirical research studies can be classified into three broad groupings: experimental, quantitative-descriptive, and exploratory (Weinberger and Tripodi, 1968). Experimental studies have the general purpose of producing empirical generalizations, i.e., verified hypotheses. Such studies attempt to establish cause-effect relationships by minimizing the influence of variables other than those specified in the hypothesis being tested through the use of such devices as random assignment of subjects to experimental and control groups. The field experiment conducted by Paul (1966) is an example of an experimental study. He was interested in assessing the relative efficacy of insight-oriented psychotherapy as compared to systematic desensitization with regard to the treatment of college undergraduates who had interpersonal performance anxiety ("stage fright"). Students who had shown evidence of anxiety and who were motivated for treatment were assigned randomly to three different treatment groups (desensitization, insight, attention-placebo therapies) and to an untreated control group. Five experienced psychotherapists worked individually with each student in each of the treatment groups for five interviews over a six-week period. Individuals were evaluated both prior to and subsequent to the experiment on anxiety scales, frequencies of symptoms related to anxiety, and on physiological indicators.

There are a variety of quantitative-descriptive studies which have a range of objectives from the production of facts to the determination of correlations among selected variables and the testing of hypotheses through approximations to rigorous experimental designs. An example of one variation of quantitative-descriptive studies is the cross-cultural study by Bacon, Child, and Barry (1963). They selected a sample of 48 societies for which there was sufficient ethnographic material available so that comparative ratings of types of crime and child rearing practices could be made by independent judges. The researchers were interested in seeking correlates of crime as a function of different family structural and household arrangements in different societies.

Unlike experimental and quantitative-descriptive studies, exploratory studies have as their major purpose the articulation of concepts and the development of hypotheses. While a variety of research techniques (such as procedures for interviewing and participant observation) may be used, less concern is devoted to the systematic application of research procedures to describe accurate quantitative relations among variables. An example of an exploratory study is the study by Bonjean (1963) who attempted to refine the concept of community leadership. In a community in North Carolina he located influential persons by using a method which involves ranking of community leaders. He used sociometric devices to determine whether the leaders could be regarded as forming a group, and then differentiated three types of leaders. Using available documents, demographic information, and information from interviews, he developed a series of hypotheses pertaining to leadership type and the variables of social class, status, and power.

RESEARCH FOR SOCIAL WORK

All of the above strategies in social research can be used in research for social work, which is the use of systematic procedures in the seeking of knowledge relevant to the goals of social work practice (Greenwood, 1957). The goals of social work range from the development of social welfare programs and services in society to the enhancement of the social and psychological functioning of individuals, groups, and communities. Areas of practice within social work are designated typically as social casework, group work, community organization, and administration and policy development. Examples of selected areas of knowledge derived from research that can be construed as relevant for social work practitioners are as follows: the location of specific kinds of clientele who could use the services of social welfare programs; the relative efficacy of varying approaches in psychotherapy; the development of hypotheses for managing hyper-aggressive children in residential treatment centers; the development of devices for determining the influential persons in a community; the accumulation of demographic information necessary for social planning; and the development of theories pertaining to the influence of different kinds of groups or organizations on individuals.

We have already noted that research has received increasing emphasis in social work. More funds have become available for research through public and private auspices, and the number of persons completing doctoral dissertations in schools of social work has increased from twenty during the academic years 1949–52 to ninety-two during a comparable period of time in 1959–62 (Shyne, 1965). Another indication of the increasing production of research for social work is provided by a content analysis of selected social work periodicals (Weinberger and Tripodi, 1968). A systematic review of 1,894 articles from 1956 through 1965 indicated that the relative percentage of research articles increased from 13.8 percent in 1956–60 to 20.2 percent in the period from 1961 through 1965. It was concluded further that research studies concerned with producing empirical generalizations have increased, which is an indication that more sophisticated research techniques are being used in seeking knowledge for social work.

As a result of increasing research endeavors and a concern for systematizing knowledge for social work, articles which review research studies in specified areas of social work have appeared more frequently in the professional literature. Illustrative of this trend is the book, *Five Fields of Social Service: Reviews of Research* (Maas, 1966), which attempts to review critically research in social work and related disciplines for the purpose of deriving knowledge which can be used for social work. Research studies applicable to the following areas of social work are reviewed: family services, public welfare, child welfare, neighborhood centers, and social planning.

The desire to synthesize and transmit knowledge from research which may increase the quality of social work practice is also apparent in the publication in 1965 of the journal, *Abstracts for Social Workers*, by the National Association of Social Workers. It contains abstracts of articles from more than 200 journals in social work and related disciplines. Its function is to summarize reports on all aspects of knowledge available in professional literature and related social science publications which may be used by social workers.

AVAILABLE GUIDELINES FOR ASSESSING EMPIRICAL RESEARCH

In spite of the availability of texts concerned with the methodology of research inquiry, there is very little in the professional literature which deals with systematic procedures for assessing research findings. Research texts such as *Research Methods in Social Relations* (Selltiz *et al.*, 1959) and *Social Work Research* (Polansky, 1960) do not include the topic of evaluation of research; and the text by Goldstein (1963), *Research Standards and Methods for Social Workers*, contains only sixteen pages directly concerned with the evaluation and utilization of research. Although the monograph on *Guidelines for Evaluative Research* (Herzog, 1959) provides some useful criteria on what an administrator can expect from evaluative research studies, it is not concerned directly with the assessment of research. Furthermore, the few articles regarding the evaluation of research which appear in professional journals are typically brief and highly schematic (Anderson, 1954; Caplow, 1958; Goldstein, 1962; Knop, 1967).

Published guidelines for evaluating research are devoted primarily to research which has the purpose of producing empirical generalizations, and often seem to carry the implication that all research studies are to be evaluated solely from the perspective of absolute certainty. On the basis of our experiences in teaching research at several graduate schools of social work, we have observed that when some students learn to uncover the flaws of published research studies, they conclude immediately that no research is useful. This is particularly likely to occur when students apply criteria for evaluating experiments to exploratory studies which have different purposes than those of verifying hypotheses. Thus, studies may be evaluated without taking account of their specific purposes and methods. This minimizes the possibility of differential assessment and appreciation of different sorts of usefulness from different types of studies. It also increases the likelihood that conclusions from different kinds of research studies will be regarded as equivalent.

Social scientists have been interested, particularly since the 1950's, in developing general guidelines for applying the findings of their disciplines to fields working with practical social problems (Likert and Lippitt, 1953; Merton, Broom, and Cottrell, 1959; Gouldner, 1965; Lazarsfeld *et al.*, 1967). During the same period, social work educators were concerned with the ways in which content from the social sciences could be used to expand the knowledge base of social work (Kahn, 1959; Bartlett *et al.*, 1964). Moreover, in recent years efforts have been made to develop more systematic criteria for utilizing knowledge from the social sciences for social work. Significant publications in this regard are *Behavioral Science for Social Workers* (Thomas, 1967a), "Social Work and Social Welfare" (Meyer *et al.*, 1967), and *Social Science Theory and Social Work Research* (Kogan, 1960a). However, these works do not deal typically with the evaluation of research *per se*, which we regard as prerequisite to the appropriate utilization of social science knowledge for social work.

In his study of 308 professional social workers in New York City, Rosenblatt (1968) concluded that professional social workers should use research findings to a greater extent than was evident. While approximately 30 percent of his respondents indicated they would read more research articles if they had the time to do so, only 9 per cent of his respondents reported that they actually read research reports. A practitioner's published response to this study reinforced the idea that research findings should be used more often for practice (Franks, 1968), but the implication was that criteria for evaluating and utilizing the findings of research are not standardized and not readily available.

MAJOR ASSUMPTIONS AND SOURCES OF GUIDELINES
FOR ASSESSING EMPIRICAL RESEARCH

Since the essential reason for developing principles for classifying, evaluating, and utilizing research is to facilitate the use of research findings for social work, it is appropriate to delineate our major assumptions regarding knowledge. We endorse the position of Eaton (1958) who postulates that knowledge of a particular phenomenon is not absolute although it can be approximated by relative degrees of certainty through the scientific approach. In this context, then, social research can be regarded as the use of systematic procedures in an attempt to reduce uncertainty in the understanding of human behavior. In addition to the idea of relative degrees of certainty in approximating knowledge, we believe that it is important to consider forms of knowledge. In concurrence with Greenwood (1960) and

Thomas (1967a), we view knowledge as being comprised of concepts, hypotheses, empirical generalizations, and theory.

Essentially, concepts are verbal symbols of ideas abstracted from experience, while hypotheses are predictive statements of relationship between two or more concepts. The following hypothesis specifies the relationship between the concepts of socio-economic class and the receipt of psychotherapy for mental patients: mental patients of low socio-economic status are less likely to receive psychotherapy than mental patients of middle socio-economic status. Empirical generalizations are hypotheses that have withstood refutation in a number of research studies. Theory consists of an interlocking set of hypotheses that are logically related, and it seeks to explain the inter-relations among empirical generalizations.

Different approaches in social research are dependent upon the form of knowledge sought, which ranges from the clarification of concepts to the testing of hypotheses derived from theory. In view of this, we believe that the potential utility of research could be enhanced if consumers of research would consider the form and the degree of relative certainty of the knowledge that is to be utilized from research studies.

The interrelated processes of classification, evaluation, and utilization can be viewed with respect to their relations to knowledge. In the assessment of research, one classifies the research by the types of information sought by the investigator and by the procedures that the researcher uses to seek knowledge. In addition, the research is evaluated with respect to the extent to which uncertainty is reduced in accordance with the purposes of the investigator. Finally, depending on the state of knowledge that is produced, the findings of research are applied to social work practice. Prior to application, however, there is the consideration of the specific aspects of social work practice to which the research findings may be applied.

We employ the criteria developed by Gouldner (1957) and Thomas (1964, 1967a) in our development of principles for utilizing research. These criteria involve considerations of *content relevance, knowledge power,* and *referent features. Content relevance* refers to subject matter and the levels of human arrangements to which the subject matter is applied. The levels range from individuals to organizations and societies. *Knowledge power* refers generally to the extent to which selected propositions are valid and relatively more predictive of social phenomena than other available hypotheses. *Referent features* include notions such as the degree to which variables are operationally accessible and can be manipulated easily by a practitioner. Thomas (1964) cites the example of "group size" as a variable which has a referent, number of persons in a group, which is accessible and can be manipulated in the context of group work. In addition, such notions as the cost and ethical suitability of manipulating variables are relevant to discussions pertaining to the utilization of knowledge.

With respect to the evaluation of research which seeks to verify hypotheses, we incorporate Campbell and Stanley's (1963) concepts of internal and external validity. *External validity* is concerned with the extent to which results can be generalized *beyond* the specific context in which the research is conducted; while *internal validity* refers to the degree of control of extraneous influences *within* the specific context of the research. These concepts are particularly relevant in the assessment of experiments and in approximations to experimental design because they serve to broaden the perspective of evaluators of research. Experiments ideally can maximize both internal and external validity with a resultant increase in the relative certainty of the research conclusions. However, due to constraints from the social situations in which research is conducted, the ideal is rarely achieved; consequently, much social research involves the use of survey methods with contrasting groups as alternatives to experimentation. The näive evaluator might assume that experiments are *ipso facto* more likely to lead to a greater degree of relative certainty, but this is not necessarily true. Using the notions of internal and external validity, one might conclude, for example, that a particular survey approach had a high degree of external validity, i.e., generalizability, with a moderate degree of internal validity. On the contrary, an experiment may have a low degree of external validity with a high degree of internal validity. The point is that we do not assume that certain research designs and procedures *per se* are always superior to other research approaches. Such an assessment should be specific to the purposes of the research and to the manner in which the study is conducted. We further would ascribe to the viewpoint of Hirschi and Selvin (1967) who regard evaluation of research in terms of constructive criticism so that a reviewer of research should consider alternative approaches which could improve on the research investigation of a specific study.

Procedures for conducting exploratory studies are less systematic than those for conducting quantitative-descriptive and experimental studies, especially since the chief goals of exploratory studies are the refinement of concepts and the development of hypotheses. Consequently, criteria for assessing exploratory studies are more difficult to systematize. Illustrative of the need for more systematic procedures for exploratory research is the appearance of *The Discovery of*

Grounded Theory by Glaser and Straus (1967). These authors propose strategies for developing theories through comparative analyses of qualitative data, and they provide some useful ideas. For our objective of developing criteria for assessing exploratory research, the discussions by Riley (1963) on case studies, Katz (1953) on field studies, and Selltiz *et al.* (1959) on exploratory studies are also most provocative. Gouldner's article on "Explorations in Applied Social Science" (1965) is also instructive with reference to the potential utilization of results from exploratory studies, for he believes that the applied social scientist is more likely to use the concepts than the verified hypotheses of the social sciences.

In order to learn principles for assessing research studies, we assume that the discussion and articulation of general guidelines are not sufficient. We believe that the application of general criteria of assessment to specific research studies is necessary. It is also assumed that skills in assessment will develop through experience in actually assessing research studies. A further consideration for social workers in regard to developing skills in assessment is that social workers should evaluate research from the social sciences as well as research conducted under social work auspices. This is important since much substantive content of social work is derived from the social sciences. In light of these considerations, we believe that the inclusion of studies from sociology and psychology in this book and in the supplementary book of research studies, *Exemplars of Social Research*, will be helpful to students and instructors.

We selected research articles from a systematic review of all articles included in four social work journals spanning the years 1956 through 1965 (Weinberger and Tripodi, 1968). Approximately 172 research studies were located and classified as experimental, quantitative-descriptive, or exploratory studies. To locate research studies from sociology and psychology journals we reviewed approximately 15 journals, principally from the years 1960 through 1967. More than 100 studies were selected, and they were also classified as to the type of research approach used. Our final selections of articles for this book and for *Exemplars of Social Research* were based on our judgments using the following guidelines:

1. The studies should be exemplary of major research approaches as articulated in the classification scheme of Weinberger and Tripodi (1968).
2. The group of studies should include a variety of research methods, e.g., participant observation, cross-cultural method, etc.
3. Approximately one-half of the articles should be from social work journals, one-fourth from psychology journals, and one-fourth from sociology journals.

4. The studies should be of reasonably good quality, and should be illustrative of general issues regarding the assessment of research.

5. The findings of the group of studies should represent a diversity of substantive areas which are potentially relevant to a variety of social work activities: social casework, group work, community organization, administration, and further research for social work.

Recognizing that social work students usually have limited experience in using concepts of research and statistics, we include throughout this book references to specific bibliographic sources in the context of discussions which presume familiarity with research concepts. For an overview of methodology in social research, we recommend several texts as general references. *Research Methods in Social Relations* (Selltiz *et al.*, 1959) provides a lucid description of the process of research and is geared appropriately to students who have had no previous preparation in research or statistics. Our scheme for classifying research studies is derived primarily from that text. *Social Work Research* (Polansky, 1960) includes discussions of various aspects involved in the production of research for social work, while *Guidelines for Evaluative Research* (Herzog, 1959) presents clearly key research concepts to be considered in research which attempts to evaluate the effectiveness of treatment programs for bringing about psycho-social changes in individuals. For students with a background in sociology either *Sociological Research: A Case Approach* (Riley, 1963) or *Methods in Social Research* (Goode and Hatt, 1952) is recommended. *Foundations of Behavioral Research* (Kerlinger, 1967) and *Research Methods in the Behavioral Sciences* (Festinger and Katz, 1953) are excellent in their coverage of research methods used in psychology and social psychology. An elementary text in statistics which includes illustrations appropriate to social work and sociology is *Social Statistics* (Blalock, 1960), while *Statistical Methods for the Behavioral Sciences* (Edwards, 1961) includes examples from psychological research, especially in regard to experimentation.

The Use of Guidelines for Assessment of Empirical Research

The next three chapters of this book develop criteria and suggest guidelines for the classification, evaluation, and utilization of empirical research by research readers. In order to develop and present these guidelines it is necessary to treat the subject matter of assessment as though it consisted of separate operations to be followed in sequence. However, this is not our intent and the research reader using the guidelines will discover for himself that all aspects of assessment must be related and considered together when an actual research study is read. One does not first classify, then evaluate, and finally utilize a research study. Being aware of these different aspects will alert the reader to questions that help him reach a reasoned assessment of a study as a whole.

Likewise, the questions proposed as guidelines for the research reader as he assesses a study are not to be considered exhaustive and they are not to be applied mechanically. Consuming research is an active and a creative process for the reader. As he gains experience by reading more research and assessing it, he will develop his own version of the guidelines and his own way of bringing them to bear as he adapts them to the particular character of a particular study he is reading. The guidelines we suggest are intended to stimulate the reader in this direction. The process of generating one's own guidelines from the principles of assessment that are offered in Chapters 2, 3, and 4 should become evident when the studies presented in the last three chapters of this book are assessed.

Chapter 2

Classification
Of Research

DEVELOPMENT OF A CLASSIFICATION SYSTEM

The purpose of this chapter is to present a system for classifying empirical social research studies. Our primary objective is to provide a framework which can be used for locating different types of studies that the research reader wishes to evaluate and utilize. However, a classification system may have additional functions:

1. A device for teaching different types of research methods.
2. A scheme for systematizing research knowledge within a discipline in order to document trends over periods of time.
3. A system for differentiating the particular forms of knowledge sought in research investigations.

A typology of research studies should contain categories which are distinct from each other and to which research studies can be assigned uniquely. For example, a study assigned to the category of experimental research should be distinct from a study which is assigned to the category of exploratory research. Furthermore, it is assumed that research typologies should have reliable categories such that different persons should be able to read a research study and independently assign it to the same category. To facilitate understanding and use of a classification system, the following requisites are necessary: specification of the criteria used for classification; definitions of the categories in the system; presentations of examples for each category; and a demonstration of the reliability of the system.

In our review of the literature in the social sciences and in social work, we did not find a system for classifying research that satisfied the above requirements. Indeed, most of the typologies in text books on research had to be inferred since they were not presented systematically so they could be used for classifying research. Nevertheless, we were guided by the literature in our quest for a classification scheme; and our classification system, in the final analysis, is essentially a reorganization of ideas derived from the works of previous authors.

Research classifications in sociology and psychology are based primarily on research methods, which include different logical approaches for the design of research investigations and the choice of a variety of techniques such as the construction of questionnaires and rating scales. The classifications range *from* a consideration of several methods for achieving a single purpose *to* a consideration of the use of one method for accomplishing a variety of purposes. For example, Campbell and Stanley (1963) discuss different types of research design that could be employed in the pursuit of empirical generalizations; and Hyman (1955) considers the use of survey procedures for testing hypotheses, for describing characteristics of a phenomenon, and for seeking quantitative relations among designated variables.

There are two general kinds of research classification schemes that have been articulated for social work. One kind of typology is based on substantive considerations, and the other is based primarily on the research methods linked to the level of knowledge at the researcher's disposal. Greenwood's (1957) typology is illustrative of the first approach. He identifies different substantive categories such as administrative information, social work philosophy, and practice theory which includes principles of diagnosis and treatment. An illustration of the second approach is provided by Kahn (1960) who discusses several kinds of research studies in terms of the state of available knowledge about the research problem and the research methods that appear to be most appropriate for the solution of the problem. Using the distinctions posited by Selltiz et al. (1959), he specifies the following main categories of research: formulative exploratory, descriptive-diagnostic, and experimental. The categories of the classification system of Selltiz et al., are: formulative or exploratory studies, descriptive studies, and studies testing causal hypotheses.

To develop the classification system used in this book, we first reviewed the literature in search of a comprehensive system that appeared to be reliable. Since we were unable to locate a system which had actually been used systematically for classifying research studies, we tried several typologies for a content analysis of research studies reported in social work periodicals (Weinberger and Tripodi, 1968). We used the typologies of Kahn (1960), Selltiz et al. (1959), Greenwood (1957), and Festinger and Katz (1953). It became clear that the categories were overlapping so that research studies could not be classified uniquely within any particular category. Further, it was observed that different labels were used by different research text books for classifying the same study. In view of these considerations, we arbitrarily selected the typologies posited by Kahn (1960) and by Selltiz et al. (1959) to be used as a general frame of reference. Then we revised and modified the categories as we tested the extent to which independent reviewers could read research studies and classify them in the same way. We followed this procedure in reviewing all of the articles in four social work journals from 1956 through 1965. Hence, the classification scheme evolved from the nature of the articles themselves and their distinctions from each other. A reliability test was made for the specific classification of research articles in the journal, *Social Casework*, for the years 1963 and 1964, and two independent reviewers agreed 98 percent of the time in their use of the general categories of research which were developed for our purposes: experimental, quantitative-descriptive, and exploratory studies (Weinberger and Tripodi, 1968).

Following the same procedure, the classification scheme was used by the three authors of this book for selecting and classifying research articles from sociology and psychology journals. Although no systematic reliability tests were conducted, it appeared that such a system could be used reliably in that the authors were able to agree in their classifications of studies selected for this book and for the reader, *Exemplars of Social Research* (Fellin, Tripodi, and Meyer, 1969). The final procedure involved a comparison of the classification scheme with other typologies in order to revise it where necessary so that it would be sufficiently comprehensive to be applicable to the ranges of empirical social research.

In subsequent sections of this chapter the classification system will be presented in detail. First, the basic criteria for conceptualizing distinctions within the system will be considered. Following this, definitions and examples within each of the three major categories—experimental, quantitative-descriptive, and exploratory studies—will be presented. Limitations of the typology and typical problems in using the system will be discussed, and the guidelines for classifying research studies will be provided. The chapter will conclude with an illustration of an application of the classification system in a study which reviews trends in research for social work.

An Overview of the Classification System

This classification system is based on the conclusion that research studies should be categorized both in terms of the major purposes of research with respect to the seeking of knowledge and in terms of the various types of empirical methods employed to achieve such purposes. It will be recalled from Chapter 1 that forms of knowledge can be identified as concepts, hypotheses, empirical generalizations, and theories. It is to be emphasized that this typology is restricted to empirical research, which includes the use of systematic observations and standardized procedures which can be independently reproduced (Greenwood, 1957). Furthermore, reports of empirical research that can most usefully be subjected to the classification scheme are those which present a single investigation. Where more than one study is reported in the same article or book, each study can be separately classified. The typology is not applicable to non-empirical research, such as documentary or bibliographic studies. Likewise, the classification system is inapplicable to essay reviews of one or more research studies; it is not useful with articles that primarily attempt to develop practice implications or to support theoretical arguments, even though research findings may be cited; and it does not apply to methodological papers whose purpose is the development, exposition, or criticism of research strategies or issues.

As previously indicated, the classification distinguishes three major categories: experimental, quantitative-descriptive, and exploratory studies. These major categories are divided into nine sub-types.

Major type: Experimental Research

The category of experimental studies is the category which can be most easily specified. Experimental studies have the primary objective of verifying research hypotheses in the quest for empirical generalizations. Although there is a variety of empirical methods and examples of experimentation in the literature, we chose to use the strict interpretation of experiments as delineated by Campbell and Stanley (1963, pp. 183–204). The distinguishing features of empirical methods used in experimentation include the experimental manipulation of one or more independent variables, the use of control groups, and the employment of randomization procedures to assure that the experimental and control groups can be regarded as equivalent. These features can be illustrated by a hypothetical research study which has the purpose of testing the hypothesis that emotionally disturbed delinquents who receive tranquilizing drugs are less likely to engage in criminal activities than emotionally disturbed delinquents who do not receive tranquilizing drugs. In this hypothesis it is presumed that the receipt of tranquilizing drugs will reduce the frequency of engaging in criminal activities. The presumed causal variable is the *independent variable* of the hypothesis, while the presumed effect is the *dependent variable*. The research study uses several procedures. Emotionally disturbed delinquents are defined and identified. A group of delinquents are located by the use of sampling methods to obtain a representative sample of the population of emotionally disturbed delinquents (*see* Chein, 1959, for a discussion of sampling methods). There might be 200 delinquents identified for the study. These delinquents are then assigned randomly to either an experimental or a control group. Random assignment is a procedure based on probability theory which assures that each delinquent has an equal chance of being assigned to either the experimental or the control group; it is that feature of experimentation which enhances the internal validity of the experiment by increasing the likelihood that experimental and control groups are initially equivalent with respect to potentially relevant variables. Those delinquents assigned to the experimental group receive tranquilizing drugs, while those assigned to the control group do not; hence, the independent variable of receiving tranquilizing drugs is manipulated by the experimenter. Measurements are made on the dependent variable of engaging in criminal activities over specified periods of time, and the relative frequencies for the experimental and control groups are compared.

SUB-TYPES: FIELD AND LABORATORY EXPERIMENTS. Experimental studies are differentiated by the setting in which they take place, and sub-types can be identified as field experiments and laboratory experiments. *Field experiments* involve the manipulations of independent variables in a natural setting as in the example above. *Lab-*

oratory experiments include the creation of artificial situations in which independent variables are manipulated by the experimenter. A typical laboratory experiment concerned with the effects of group influences on individual judgments might involve the use of volunteer subjects at a college who are randomly assigned to experimental and control groups which have been created for the first time in a relatively isolated situation. The experimental and control groups are structured so that individuals in each group participate in some common task. Members of both the experimental and control groups are asked to make judgments prior to and subsequent to their group participation. During the course of the experiment, the experimental group might receive contrived information from the experimenter that their initial judgments were discrepant from those of other members in the group, while the control group would not receive any information from the experimenter. The final judgments of members of the experimental group would be compared with the judgments of the control group members.

Laboratory experiments are frequently used in the testing of hypotheses related to various sociological and psychological theories. On the contrary, field experiments are frequently employed in studies which seek to evaluate the efficacy of various programs or techniques for helping people. In general, laboratory experiments are more likely than field experiments to have the purpose of seeking empirical generalizations for refining and modifying theories of behavior.

Major type: Quantitative-Descriptive Research

The category of quantitative-descriptive studies is similar to that of experimental studies in that both seek quantitative-descriptions among specified variables. Quantitative-descriptions are obtained through the use of measuring devices to describe relationships among variables; hence, statistical concepts such as correlation, proportions, and so forth are employed. A hypothetical example of a quantitative-description is that the percentage of lower class families who participate in community activities is significantly smaller than the percentage of middle class families who participate in community activities. With respect to the empirical methods employed, quantitative-descriptive studies differ from experimental studies in that they do not use randomization procedures in assigning subjects to experimental and control groups. In addition, they do not employ the experimental manipulation of independent variables.

Quantitative-descriptive studies cover the entire range of purposes in seeking forms of knowledge, and they include a variety of research designs and data collection techniques. Accordingly, we have classified these studies into four sub-types which form a hierarchy of research objectives within the major type: hypothesis testing studies, program evaluation studies, studies describing characteristics of populations, and studies seeking to identify relations among variables.

SUB-TYPE: HYPOTHESIS TESTING. Studies which have the purpose of testing hypotheses employ research methods which are essentially approximations to experimentation, and this sub-type can be regarded as a transition from experimental to quantitative-descriptive studies. Campbell and Stanley (1963) refer to these approximations as "quasi-experiments," and they discuss a variety of research designs which have been used by researchers. For example, one approach for testing the hypothesis regarding the use of tranquilizing drugs by emotionally disturbed delinquents and their subsequent criminal activities might involve a selection of a group of emotionally disturbed delinquents who have received tranquilizing drugs and a comparison of that group with a contrasting group of emotionally disturbed delinquents who have not received tranquilizing drugs. Comparisons might be made with regard to the frequency of criminal activities in both groups. Unlike an experimental study, randomization procedures are not employed. Hence, the investigator would attempt to demonstrate by statistical methods that the experimental and control groups are similar with respect to potentially relevant variables which could influence the frequency of criminal activities observed.

SUB-TYPE: PROGRAM EVALUATION RESEARCH. Program evaluation studies may or may not have the underlying objective of testing explicit hypotheses; their major purpose is to attempt to measure the effects of programs of social intervention. Usually, however, hypotheses are implicit. For example, in a study that seeks to evaluate the effects of the antipoverty program on unemployment rates in a specific community, the implicit hypothesis might be that unemployment will be reduced, as a function of the antipoverty program in that community. These studies may also employ research methods which are approximations to experimentation.

SUB-TYPE: POPULATION DESCRIPTION. Research which seeks to describe accurately some characteristics of designated populations are typically represented by survey studies which are conducted at one or more periods of time. As a hypothetical example, a national sample may be obtained by probability sampling techniques, and the 2,000 or more persons in the sample may be asked their opinions concerning prospective candidates for president, their attitudes toward a program such as Medicare, and the like. These studies have the purpose of answering specific questions in regard to quantitative-descriptions of a designated population, and they strive to obtain samples which are representative of the population so that external validity, i.e., generalizability, is maximized.

SUB-TYPE: SEEKING VARIABLE RELATIONSHIPS. Studies which seek quantitative relations among variables explore the relations among a series of variables for a specific population. The investigator systematically collects information on a variety of variables, which are defined sufficiently so they can be measured (see Selltiz et al., 1959, pp. 144–98, for a discussion of measurement). For example, information on family income, age, ethnic group, and other variables may be obtained; the investigator then determines whether there are any significant correlations among these variables.

Major type: Exploratory Research

The category of exploratory studies is distinguishable from the category of quantitative-descriptive studies in that the major purpose is to refine concepts and to articulate questions and hypotheses for subsequent investigation. A variety of data collection procedures may be used, but less attention is devoted to the accurate description of quantitative relations among variables. Accordingly, representative sampling is of less importance than is the selection of a range of cases to stimulate ideas. In addition to quantitative data, researchers may use qualitative data in narrative form which may be derived from their observations of a particular phenomenon.

Exploratory studies typically include a great deal of information for a single case or for a small number of cases. For example, detailed quantitative and qualitative information may be accumulated in a clinical study of one individual's response to psychotherapy over an extended period of time. This is different from many quantitative-descriptive studies which may include brief information from a large number of respondents. We have classified exploratory studies into three sub-types.

SUB-TYPE: EXPLORATORY-DESCRIPTIVE RESEARCH. The sub-type of combined exploratory-descriptive studies is intended to serve as a transition between quantitative-descriptive and exploratory studies. The primary purpose of these studies is to refine and develop concepts and hypotheses. Both quantitative and qualitative-descriptions of the phenomenon being studied are included in the research. For example, a study of the political system in a particular community may include quantitative-descriptions of the voting patterns of community residents and unstandardized impressions of the ways in which political leaders attempt to influence the voters in the community.

SUB-TYPE: RESEARCH USING SPECIFIC PROCEDURES. Studies which use specific data collection procedures to develop insights and ideas typically employ devices such as content analysis in an attempt to systematize qualitative material. Comparisons are made, and then hypotheses are developed. For example, it may be hypothesized from a review of case records in a particular agency that parents of retarded children are more likely to seek contacts with caseworkers than are parents of emotionally disturbed children.

SUB-TYPE: EXPERIMENTAL MANIPULATION. Studies which experimentally manipulate independent variables to demonstrate ideas can be regarded as clinical studies or demonstrations of social action programs. Their essential purpose is to demonstrate the plausibility of using specified treatment methods or programs to accomplish some particular goal. These studies are distinguishable from experiments in that they do not use randomization procedures or experimental and control groups. They are different from quantitative-descriptive studies in that they typically involve the study of one case with little attention devoted to the problem of external validity. For example, an experimenter may be interested in using techniques of learning experiments to change the behavior of a patient. He uses the techniques on a single patient, and he observes systematically the changes in the patient's behavior over a period of time.

In summary, the classification system is based on a combination of the purposes of the research and the methods used to accomplish those purposes. Variations of purpose and method provide a basis for the distinguishing characteristics of the types and sub-types. In the sections that follow we present the major assumptions behind each research approach for seeking knowledge, more elaborate definitions of each category, and abstracts of research literature representative of each category. The purpose is to clarify the classification system more precisely.

EXPERIMENTAL STUDIES

Since the purpose of experimentation is to provide evidence that bears directly on the extent to which hypotheses may be refuted, it is instructive to consider some underlying ideas that contribute to the methodology of experimental studies. If the meaning of experimental studies is better understood, efforts toward classification of research will be facilitated.

As indicated in Chapter 1, a hypothesis is a statement which predicts the relationship between two or more variables. The formulation of the research hypothesis is of primary importance in experimentation. If a hypothesis is inadequately conceived, the research procedures of experimentation may not be applicable. Consequently, research educators have developed criteria for judging whether or not hypotheses are stated in a form which is amenable to research. Goode and Hatt (1952, pp. 68–71) have specified several guidelines for determining the potential researchability of hypotheses. These criteria are as follows:

1. The hypotheses must be conceptually clear.
2. Hypotheses should have empirical referents.
3. The hypotheses must be specific.
4. The hypotheses should be related to available techniques.
5. The hypotheses should be related to a body of theory.

Essentially, these criteria are derived from the assumptions of scientific method pertaining to the necessity of operationalizing concepts in such a way that they can be measured. It is believed that measurement will allow for systematic comparisons of observations and for reliable communication. The central notion pertains to the necessity for specifying the empirical referents of the concepts being investigated. Empirical referents refer to direct or indirect objects in the physical world which are potentially observable through the senses of man. For example, a variable such as education can be operationally defined by an indication of either the years of education completed in particular kinds of school systems or by the construction of tests of knowledge which are reflective of expected achievement for certain grade levels. Greenwood (1960, pp. 58–63) discusses in considerable detail the virtues and defects of operational definitions, and his discussion is recommended for an introduction to this subject.

Having specified the hypothesis to be investigated, the experimenter then faces the problem of designing his study so that evidence pertaining to the tentative acceptance of the hypothesis can be accumulated. Hypotheses for experimentation typically imply a cause-effect relationship between one or more independent variables and one or more dependent variables. For example, it might be predicted that the independent variable of group counseling will affect the dependent variable of anxiety.

Criteria for the verification of hypotheses which posit cause-effect relationships are essentially extensions of John Stuart Mill's *A System of Logic* (Nagel, 1950), which is a systematic theory regarding the nature of proof. Although such criteria have been discussed in many volumes on philosophy and research methods, we find the discussions by Selltiz *et al.* (1959, pp. 80–127), regarding the types of evidence for inferring a causal relationship between two variables sufficient for our purposes here. They summarize three major types of evidence that are necessary for testing hypotheses about causal relationships:

> 1. The assumed causal variable, the independent variable, should be associated with the dependent variable in the manner predicted by the hypothesis.
> 2. Changes in the dependent variable attributed to the independent variable should occur in time sequence so that the independent variable is prior.
> 3. Other variables, which might influence the dependent variable, should be ruled out as possible causes of observed changes in the dependent variable.

The third criterion above has been further specified by Campbell and Stanley (1963, pp. 175–76) who have delineated factors in the design of experiments which seek to provide evidence for the testing of hypotheses pertaining to human subjects. It will be recalled from our introductory chapter that Campbell and Stanley provide two key concepts for interpreting the validity of research studies concerned with causal inferences. These are the notions of internal validity and external validity.

Internal validity refers to the control of extraneous variables in the specific context of experimentation. Campbell and Stanley consider in detail the extraneous factors which are related to internal validity. Included in their discussion are such factors as the effects of testing and instrumentation, biases in the selection of different respondents for comparison groups, maturational and historical influences occuring while the experiment is in progress, variables that have influenced the subjects in the past, statistical artifacts, and the loss of subjects during the research. They also discuss factors which need to be controlled with respect to *external validity,* which refers to the generalizability of the results from the experiment to other populations in other settings. In particular, they provide a thoughtful discussion pertaining to the effects of experimenters *per se* on experimental subjects, as well as a consideration of the problems of bias in the selection of respondents for experimentation.

The design of experiments is built around the sources of evidence necessary for testing hypotheses. In addition to the consideration of ideal requirements for the design of research, experimenters must consider what is practically possible. Problems of manpower, financial auspices, ethics, and the securing of permission to conduct studies within different communities and organizations are types of constraints that typically render ideal experimental designs impractical. Thus, the research reader will observe in the literature numerous studies that depart from ideal experimental designs. These studies are more properly considered quantitative-descriptive studies that are approximations to experiments. Kerlinger (1967, pp. 275–408) and Kahn (1960, pp. 59–67, offer detailed discussions regarding experimental designs and approximations to experimentation.

In our classification system a research study must have several requisites before it can be classified as experimental. *There must be an explicit or implicit hypothesis that is being investigated.* An explicit hypothesis is one that is specified in the formulation of the problem for research. As alluded to earlier in the chapter, implicit hypotheses are those which are not articulated precisely in the formulation of the problem; however, they are implicit in the overall research study. In the evaluation of a tutorial program devised to increase the reading skills of students, for example, hypotheses might not be specifically stated, but the research design may involve the random assignment of students either to an experimental group for tutoring or to a control group which does not receive tutoring. In addition, measurements of reading skills may be obtained from both groups before and after the experimental group receives tutoring. The implicit hypothesis is that tutoring will increase the reading skills of students. A second requisite for studies to be classified as experimental is that the *variables in the hypotheses of the study must be operationally defined so that measurement is possible.* This is necessary so that quantitative-descriptions among variables can be ascertained in order to provide evidence for establishing an association between the independent and dependent variables. A third requisite is that *the independent variable must be manipulated by the experimenter.* This is done in experimental studies to assure that the independent variable (sometimes called the experimental variable) occurs prior in time to the dependent variable. The fourth requisite is that *one or more control groups must be employed* to provide a basis for contrasting the results obtained in the presence of the experimental variable to those results obtained in the absence of the experimental variable. The fifth requisite is that *randomization procedures must be employed in the assignment of subjects to experimental and control groups.* This is a minimum requirement for experiments; it provides some assurance of the equivalence between experimental and control groups, and it provides the basis for the use of tests of statistical inference in the interpretation of results. The student is referred to Edwards' text on *Experimental Design in Psychological Research* (1960, pp. 13–27) for a discussion of the importance of randomization in the execution and interpretation of experiments.

Based on the foregoing discussion, experimental studies may be defined in the following manner:

Experimental studies are empirical research investigations which have as their primary purpose the testing of hypotheses concerned with cause-effect relationships. All of these studies use experimental designs which include control groups, randomization procedures, and the manipulation of independent variables in order to control pertinent factors to as great a degree as possible. Relevant variables are specified so they can be described quantitatively. These studies may employ rigorous sampling techniques to increase the generalizability of the experimental findings.

Two sub-types of experimental studies noted earlier are (1) laboratory experiments and (2) field experiments. Both types must satisfy the requirements of the definition for experimental studies. The chief distinction between laboratory and field experiments is the degree of control maintained by the experimenter in the setting in which the experiment is conducted. Since there is an artificially created environment by the experimenter in laboratory experiments, the possibility for the control of influential variables other than those postulated in the hypothesis is increased. The field experiment which takes place in the natural environment poses relatively more obstacles in experimental control. Field experiments may be used for testing hypotheses linked to theory and for testing hypotheses which are relatively more pertinent to practical situations, while laboratory experiments are used predominantly in testing theoretical propositions. The student is referred to Kerlinger (1967, pp. 379–87), French (1953, pp. 98–135) and Festinger (1953, pp. 136–72) for detailed discussions regarding the conduct of laboratory and of field experiments. Definitions and examples of laboratory and field experiments are presented below.

Laboratory Experiments

Laboratory experiments are experimental studies in which the investigator creates an isolated situation in an artificial setting with hypothetically constructed variables. Relationships among variables are tested by the manipulation of one or more independent variables and by the control of the potential influence of variables which are extraneous to the hypothesis being tested.

"An Experimental Study of the Observational Process in Casework" by Roger Miller (1958) is an example of a *laboratory experiment*. The investigator began the formulation of his research problem by reviewing Reik's (1948) theoretical model of the observational process in interpersonal communication. In particular, he considered Reik's conceptualization of clinical observation in therapeutic interviews which is based on the concept of the observer's active or passive attention. Active attention is regarded as the selection of specific kinds of information in the interview, and passive attention is conceived as "free-floating" in the sense that equal attention is presumably devoted to all perceived information. The concept of the direction of the observer's attention in therapeutic interviews is also discussed; the observer may direct his attention internally toward his own responses, or it may be directed externally toward the explicit content of communication. According to Miller (p. 98), Reik's theory is suggestive of the following hypothesis: "The adequacy of the observer's conscious psychological comprehension is said to be positively related to the extent to which he uses free-floating attention and the extent to which his attention is directed internally."

In order to test the hypothesis, Miller designed an experiment. All subjects in the experiment were shown the same film of an actual interview. The purpose of this was to create a hypothetical situation in which each observer would view the client as a "common client" so that comparisons could be made with respect to attention and understanding. The independent variable of attention was assumed to be manipulated by the use of three experimental groups which were given different kinds of information with respect to what they were to observe in the film. Members in the *process group* were told to write detailed reports on all they had observed to see how accurately they could perceive the client; members of the *diagnostic group* were told to be prepared to write a summary report of the most important information observed, rather than a detailed report; and members of the *empathic group* were told to develop impressions about the client in a natural manner as the interview in the film progressed. The process group was presumed to observe by active and external attention, which was predicted to lead to the lowest level of understanding. On the contrary, the empathic group was presumed to observe by "free-floating" and internal attention, which was predicted to lead to the highest level of understanding. It was further hypothesized that the diagnostic group would be intermediate in understanding in comparison to the other groups.

The dependent variable of psychological understanding was operationalized by the extent to which the rank orderings of descriptive statements made by the experimental subjects were similar to the rank orderings of descriptive statements made by a group of five "expert" clinicians. These descriptive statements were comprised of brief phrases, and the subjects were asked to order these statements in 11 groupings which ranged from a group of most descriptive statements to a group of least descriptive statements.

Fifty-four casework students at a graduate school of social work were randomly assigned to the three experimental groups. Comparisons were made among all groups on a discrepancy score, which indicated the discrepancy of rankings in the experimental groups as compared to the panel of experts. As predicted, it was found that the greatest discrepancy occurred in the process group, while no differences were observed between the other two groups.

Field Experiments

Field experiments are experimental studies which involve the manipulation of one or more independent variables in a natural setting in order to determine causal relationships. These studies may attempt to control the influence of environmental constraints on the relationship between independent and dependent variables. They do not rely exclusively on natural conditions of the environment in that the independent variables are manipulated by the experimenter. Field experiments typically have less rigorous control features than laboratory experiments.

An example of a *field experiment* is "An Experiment in Prevention through Social Work Intervention" by Meyer, Borgatta, and Jones (1967). The research was generated from a concern of Youth Consultation Service: "how to serve effectively the adolescent girl with types of problems that got her into difficulties at school and elsewhere" (p. 364). Youth Consultation Service (YCS) is a nonsectarian, voluntary social agency in New York City, which offers casework and group work services to adolescent girls between the ages of 12 and 25 with characteristic problems such as out-of-wedlock pregnancy, chronic truancy and home management. Social workers in the agency believed that services were frequently offered too late in the lives of the adolescent girls for such services to be effective. In view of this, it was assumed that preventive services offered to girls at earlier ages might facilitate treatment which would decrease the extent to which girls would be involved in serious difficulties in later stages of their lives.

The researchers devised an experiment in order to evaluate the effectiveness of a program of preventive services. The implicit hypothesis was that the provision of services by YCS to adolescent girls would result in improved school performance and social behavior. The research design first involved the selection of a group of adolescent girls who could be considered as having potential problems. A high school in New York City, referred to as Vocational High, agreed to cooperate in the research. The researchers reviewed each student's prior school records for four classes entering the high school in four successive years. The records were used to detect problems that each student might have had in school or at home, and approximately one-fourth of the students were identified as having potential problems. These students were randomly assigned either to an experimental group or to a control group. As a result of randomization, 189 girls were included in the experimental group, while 192 girls were included in the control group. To assure that the randomization procedures were effective, the experimental and control groups were compared on data obtained from the school records such as socio-economic characteristics and family background and on a battery of attitude questionnaires and personality tests. The experimental and control groups were essentially equivalent with respect to those variables.

The girls in the experimental group were referred to YCS. In general, the reason for referral was explained to the girls as an opportunity to discuss problems which high school girls usually have. The girls were not required to participate in the experiment, and three percent of the 189 girls in the experimental group had no service contacts with a social worker at YCS. Girls in the experimental group participated in a median number of 16 casework interviews or group counseling sessions.

The investigators chose several criteria in an attempt to operationalize dependent variables relevant to the effectiveness of the treatment program. Dependent variables included data related to school performance, delinquent behavior, attitudes, personality changes, and friendship patterns. School performance criteria included truancy, suspensions, drop outs, academic grades, and the receipt of honors and awards. Delinquent behavior included the relative incidence of out-of-wedlock pregnancy and getting into trouble with the police. Two measures of personality, the Junior Personality Quiz and the Make A Sentence Test, were used to observe changes in behavior such as shyness, aloofness, and lack of confidence. The girls' attitudes toward help, general feelings about life, and future plans were estimated through a series of questions developed by the investigators.

Comparisons were made between members of the experimental group and members of the control group on the dependent variables included in the study. Although the girls in the experimental group were less likely to be truant than the girls in the control group, there were no significant differences observed on other criteria of school performance such as grades, completion of school, and so forth. The girls in the experimental group increased in self-control and orderly behavior to a greater extent than the girls in the control group. However, the researchers concluded that there were no significant differences between the experimental and the control groups on practically all other criteria which they considered indicative of success.

QUANTITATIVE-DESCRIPTIVE STUDIES

The category of quantitative-descriptive studies includes research investigations having various purposes with respect to the seeking of knowledge. These purposes fall into two general classes: (1) the testing of hypotheses, and (2) the description of quantitative relations among specified variables. Hypotheses subject to testing are *either* (1a) those which posit cause-effect relationships *or* (1b) those hypotheses which simply state the existence of a measurable relationship among two or more variables. Hypotheses which posit cause-effect relationships have been discussed in the previous section on experimental studies. An example of the second type of hypothesis is as follows: There is a significant association between the variables of "slum conditions" and of "mental illness," i.e., there is likely to be *either* a greater *or* a lesser incidence of mental illness for those persons who live in slums than for those persons who do not. The hypothesis merely states the existence of an association between the two variables. It does not predict the direction of the relationship; it does not state that living in the slums is the cause of mental illness, nor does it state that mental illness causes people to live in the slums.

The second general purpose—that of describing quantitative relations among specified variables—can be subdivided into two separate objectives. The first objective (2a) is that of measuring a series of specific variables in order to answer specific questions posed by the research study. One may survey a specified population concerning its social welfare needs, which might include questions regarding family composition and size, use of day care facilities, availability of day care facilities for different ethnic and religious groups of the population, and so forth. The purpose is to describe accurately the relationship among those variables presumed to be important. The second objective (2b) is to *search* for relationships among designated variables in order to articulate more precise hypotheses for subsequent investigation. For example, a researcher may be interested in identifying the social correlates of heart disease. The investigator may not know which variables are relevant for the research, and his approach may be to specify as many variables as possible for inclusion in the study. He selects a population of patients with heart disease and a corresponding population without heart disease. He then attempts to discern the correlation among all of the social variables, such as ethnic group and family income, with heart disease in order to locate significant clues for further research. The student is referred to Blalock's *Social Statistics* for an excellent discussion of correlation, association, and the strength of relationship between variables (1960, pp. 225–41, pp. 273–325).

As discussed previously in relation to experimentation, studies which seek to test hypotheses concerned with cause-effect relationships ideally attempt to provide evidence regarding the time order of independent and dependent variables, the association of independent and dependent variables, and the ruling out of other factors that could be responsible for the observed relationships between the independent and dependent variables. Since experimentation may not be feasible, alternatives to experimentation may be devised in quantitative-descriptive studies. The experimental features of randomization and the manipulation of independent variables are typically not included in quantitative-descriptive studies. In such studies it is assumed that the use of various alternative devices might approximate experimentation.

Approximations to experimentation may include such devices as matching or the use of an experimental group as its "own control." To obtain experimental and control groups the researcher might select a group exposed to the independent variable, for example, a group of children enrolled in a pre-school program. He then seeks a *contrast group* of similar children who are *not* enrolled in the program. He does this by specifying the characteristics of the experimental group such as proportions of males, average age, etc., and by seeking to *match* the children in the contrast group with those in the experimental group with respect to characteristics presumed to be relevant for the study. Another alternative might be to use an experimental group as its *own control*. The members of the experimental group are compared to themselves with respect to their performance at two different time periods. For example, the independent variable might consist of a program to increase the verbal utterances of autistic children. Prior to the program the verbal utterances of the children are described and measured in order to establish a "base-rate" of speech. The program is introduced, and the rate of speech is determined for the subjects in the research; their subsequent rate of speech is compared to their base rates of speech. These and other alternatives which are described in detail by Campbell and Stanley (1963), have a lesser degree of internal validity than do experimental studies; the reason for this is that quantitative-descriptive studies have a lesser degree of control over potentially relevant variables. Nevertheless, quantitative-descriptive studies, particularly in the study of natural phenomena, may be the only approaches which are possible for the investigator.

All other quantitative-descriptive studies have the essential objective of accurately describing the associations among variables, but without regard to cause-effect relationships. These studies rely on basic assumptions which are concerned primarily with the establishment of associations among variables. These assumptions involve the concepts of measurement, reliability, validity, and the refinement of statistical associations in order to estimate the extent to which an association is spurious. An underlying assumption is that the variables are operationally defined so that they can be measured. As in experimental studies, the data used as indicators of the variables are assumed to be both reliable and valid. Reliability refers to the extent to which the measurements are free from error due to chance fluctuations and biases involved in the collection of data; it refers to consistency in measurement procedures, and to the reproducibility of measurements. Validity is an indication of the extent to which the measurement corresponds with the concept being measured. For example, a valid measurement of intelligence might be an I.Q. test score which corresponds with one's concept of intelligence. For an extensive discussion of the concepts of reliability and validity, the student is referred to Selltiz *et al.* (1959, pp. 154–86).

Using statistical techniques of association, an investigator may observe that two or more variables are associated. However, it is possible that the association is *spurious*. Procedures for identifying spurious associations have been elaborated by survey methodologists such as Hyman (1955) and Hirschi and Selvin (1967), and these procedures have been employed in quantitative-descriptive studies. A spurious association is one which can be explained by another variable introduced into the statistical analysis of data. For example, a survey of a population in a designated community may uncover an association between church attendance and delinquency: those who attend church show smaller proportions of adjudicated delinquency than those who do not attend church. For the same population, it is noted that there is also a strong association between family income and delinquency. The investigator may use family income as an approximation to a statistical control in a more refined analysis of the data. He may divide his population into two sub-groups of lower income and of higher income families. Then, he discerns the association between church attendance and delinquency for each income sub-group. If he finds that there is no significant association between church attendance and delinquency for each income sub-group, he might infer that the association between church attendance and delinquency for the total population studied is *spurious* because it is explained by family income, which occurs prior in time to church attendance.

The primary research technique used in quantitative-descriptive studies is that of survey methods, as described by Hyman (1955) and Moser (1958). A particular population is selected, and a sampling plan is employed in order to obtain a representative sample or samples of that population at one or more periods of time. Data collection procedures, typically questionnaires or scheduled interviews, are constructed, and they contain variables considered to be relevant for the investigation. Data are collected, tabulated, and analyzed. The primary problem for the researcher is the extent to which he can provide evidence concerning the description of relations among attributes of the population being studied. In order to achieve accuracy, the investigator attempts to reduce errors due to such sources as sampling fluctuations and interviewer bias.

In our classification system a research study must have several requisites before it can be classified as quantitative-descriptive. The first requisite is that *the study must not be classifiable as an experimental study.* The second requisite is that *the study must include variables which are amenable to measurement and, hence, quantitative-descriptions.* There must be provisions for the systematic collection of data for the purpose of accurately describing relations among variables. Thirdly, *the study must have one of the following purposes pertaining to the seeking of knowledge: the testing of hypotheses or the accurate description of quantitative relations among variables selected for inclusion in the research.*

We may define quantitative-descriptive studies in the following way:

Quantitative-descriptive studies are empirical research investigations which have as their major purpose the delineation or assessment of characteristics of phenomena, program evaluation, or the isolation of key variables. These studies may use formal methods as approximations to experimental design with features of statistical reliability and control to provide evidence for the testing of hypotheses. All of these studies use quantitative devices for systematically collecting data from populations, programs, or samples of populations or programs. They employ personal interviews, mailed questionnaires, and/or other rigorous data gathering devices and survey sampling procedures.

Four sub-types of quantitative-descriptive studies are identified according to the primary purpose of the investigation. As indicated earlier, these sub-types are (1) hypothesis testing studies, (2) program evaluation studies, (3) population description studies, and (4) studies that search for variable relationships. All of these sub-types must satisfy the requirements for the definition of quantitative-descriptive studies. Hypothesis testing studies include explicit hypotheses which guide the research inquiry. Typically, the hypotheses are derived from theory. In the testing of cause-effect relationships, formal methods such as the use of contrast groups and matching procedures may be used to approximate experimental design. Investigators may use purposive sampling procedures in seeking to "test" hypotheses concerned only with the association between independent and dependent variables. For example, one community may be selected purposively due to its reported high incidence of crime. The investigator may wish to demonstrate in that community that his hypothesis pertaining to different types of gangs for different types of criminal activity is plausible.

Studies which seek to evaluate programs are similar to studies which seek to test hypotheses. However, in program evaluation studies, the hypotheses may be implicit rather than explicit, and the hypotheses are typically not derived from theory. Program evaluation studies frequently originate from practical concerns, and they are all concerned with the evaluation of a program or a technique. On the contrary, hypothesis testing studies, as defined here, do not include such evaluative purposes. Program evaluation studies and field experiments may have the same objectives with respect to program evaluation; their chief distinction is in regard to the research procedures employed to achieve the purposes of the study. Hence, those program evaluation studies that contain the requisites for experimental studies would be classified as field experiments. The student is referred to Suchman (1967) who discusses a variety of research designs which have been used in evaluative studies.

Studies which seek to accurately describe characteristics of populations are typically geared to answering specific questions posed by the investigators. These studies usually contain the use of survey procedures, and they have the purpose of describing simple facts about selected populations, organizations, or other collectivities. These studies often employ the same procedures as do research studies which seek to discover quantitative relations among specified variables. The primary distinction is that of the researcher's purpose. In a study which seeks quantitative relations, the investigator attempts to discover correlations among the variables he includes in the survey. These correlations are then used to form the basis of hypotheses for future research investigations. Contrary to population description studies, the researcher is not likely to use such discovered relationships to serve as answers to specific questions which may have guided the research inquiry.

Definitions and examples for each of the four sub-types of quantitative-descriptive studies are presented below.

Hypothesis Testing Studies

Hypothesis testing studies are those quantitative-descriptive studies which contain in their design of research explicit hypotheses to be tested. The hypotheses are typically derived from theory, and they may be either statements of cause-effect relationships or statements of association between two or more variables without reference to a causal relationship.

"Group Levels of Aspiration in United Fund Campaigns" by Zander and Newcomb (1967) is an example of a *hypothesis testing study*. The investigators began their study by considering the general relation of a sub-group in an organization with respect to the setting of goals for the organization by that particular sub-group. Since it was believed that the goals established for United Fund community campaigns are usually established by a committee or sub-group, Zander and Newcomb regarded financial canvassing in United Fund campaigns as an example of a situation in which a sub-group in an organization could be studied. In particular, they were interested in the relationship of repeated goals and repeated performances. They employed the concept of group aspiration level, which is the goal to which a group aspires, in considering the official goals established by the United Fund. Having articulated their assumptions about the nature of goal-setting, they then derived several interrelated hypotheses for study. One major hypothesis was that "committees with more failing campaigns, compared to those with more successful campaigns (a) fix their future goals at a greater distance above past levels of performance, and (b) change the levels of their goals a smaller amount from one year to the next" (p. 158).

They obtained the basic data for their study for the years 1961 through 1964 from directories and pamphlets published yearly by the United Community Funds and Councils of America. Included in those documents were items of information such as names of communities raising funds, goals of campaigns for each community, amounts of money raised, and monies raised in previous campaigns. The investigators selected 149 communities which were of similar size in that they had populations which ranged between 55,000 and 140,000 people.

A successful campaign was defined as one in which the amount of funds raised were greater than or equal to the goal set by a committee in a particular community, while a failure was defined as a campaign in which the amount of funds raised were less than the desired goal. The dependent variable of "fixing goals at a greater distance above past levels of performance" was operationally defined as the *discrepancy* between prior level of performance with respect to number of dollars collected per capita and the new goal. The dependent variable of "changing the level of goals" was determined by an index which reflected the direction and amount of shifting in goals for raising funds from one year to the next.

The investigators divided the 149 communities into five different types with respect to successes and failures in annual United Fund campaigns. These types ranged on a continuum from communities with four successes and no failures to communities with no successes and four failures. The number of communities in each type ranged from 27 to 37. The discrepancies between prior level of performance and new goals were examined for each of the five types. Those communities which were successful in fund raising showed a smaller discrepancy between prior performance and the setting of new goals than communities which were not successful. In addition to this analysis, the investigators examined the relationship between successful communities and the shifting of goals. Consistently successful communities tended to shift their goals upwards, and consistently failing communities tended to maintain their goals. Thus, the investigators concluded that evidence from this study was in support of their hypothesis.

Program Evaluation Studies

Program evaluation studies are those quantitative-descriptive studies which are concerned with seeking the effects of a specific program or method of helping. Such programs may contain a variety of objectives pertaining to health, education, and welfare. Hypotheses may not be explicitly stated, and they frequently are derived from the objectives of the program being evaluated rather than from theory. Such studies may employ a variety of procedures to approximate experimental design.

"Rehabilitation of Former Mental Patients: An Evaluation of a Coordinated Community Aftercare Program" by Northcutt, Landsman, Neill, and Gorman (1965) is an example of a *program evaluation study*. The investigators briefly described a program in a metropolitan Florida county which was attempting to facilitate the post hospital adjustment of former mental patients. A plan was developed in which the services offered by social and health agencies could be coordinated to assist patients and their families. An organization, the Mental Health Resource Council, was created to achieve more efficiently the goal of providing coordinated services. In addition to an employed staff, professionals from the community participated in making recommendations for specific agency services for patients who were on trial visits from mental hospitals. Referrals for services were made to agencies in the community by the staff of the Mental Health Resource Council. The council was interested in evaluating the effectiveness of the program, and it posed the following hypothesis:

A program designed to coordinate services to patients returning to the community following hospitalization for mental illness is more effective in facilitating their post hospital adjustment than is a community program in which there is no designated coordinating service for this purpose (p. 571).

The design of the research involved the comparison of an experimental county in which the coordination program was operative with a contrast county which had no program for coordinating services to patients returning from state hospitals. The county with no coordination program was selected as a contrast county due to its presumed similarity to the experimental county with respect to population characteristics, economic structure, and mental health resources. During the third year of the program, all patients who returned from state hospitals to either the experimental or the contrast county were interviewed. The interviews took place approximately one year after the patients returned to the communities. Information was collected for a one-year period for 147 patients in the experimental county and for 122 patients in the contrast county. The data obtained in the interviews consisted of a variety of information about the patients: socio-economic characteristics; employment records; diagnoses and psychiatric history; information on the receipt of community services and medical care; and information on selected areas of adjustment concerning employment, friends, and hospital status.

In an attempt to demonstrate the equivalence of patients in the experimental county to patients in the contrast county, the investigators made comparisons with respect to variables that might influence the patients' rehabilitation. The patients were found to be similar on 20 out of 25 characteristics. The patients in the contrast county were more likely to be Negro and to be unmarried than the patients in the experimental county. On the contrary, patients in the experimental county were more likely than patients in the contrast county to be accepted in community organizations and to be active in community organizations.

The two counties were compared on 19 variables of post hospital adjustment, and no significant differences were observed for 16 of the variables. Patients in the experimental county tended to have more friends and to be more accepted by community organizations, while patients in the contrast county tended to show a higher level of performance in their jobs. Compared to the experimental county, a greater percentage of patients in the contrast county received services from community agencies. Thus, it was concluded that the findings of the study failed to support the research hypothesis.

Population Description Studies

Population description studies are those quantitative-descriptive studies which have as their primary function the accurate description of quantitative characteristics of selected populations, organizations, or other collectivities. These studies frequently use survey procedures. They usually employ sampling methods to claim representativeness, and they contain a large number of variables. Some of these studies are descriptive of characteristics of designated populations such as roles, functions, needs, attitudes, and opinions.

"Professional Functions and Opinions of Social Group Workers" by Main and MacDonald (1962) is an example of *a population description study*. The researchers were interested in describing job activities of social group workers and their opinions concerning job assignments and professional preparation for social group work. In particular, they wanted to describe the various functions of social group workers who were employed in agencies which provided direct services to groups. Main and MacDonald chose to restrict their population to 164 group workers who were members of the Group Work Section of the Chicago Area Chapter of the National Association of Social Workers in 1960.

An interview schedule was used in an attempt to obtain spontaneous responses from the group workers to questions regarding their job responsibilities. Graduate students in social work were used as interviewers, and approximately 92 percent of the group workers participated in the study. The investigators were careful in confining their findings to a description of group workers who were members of the particular organization being studied. Several of their major findings are summarized below.

The majority of respondents were thirty years of age or older, and most of the respondents had 10 years or more experience in social work. Fifty-four percent of the group workers were women, and 96 of the 151 respondents had master's degrees in social work. Approximately two-thirds of the group workers were employed in agencies which provided direct services to groups such as settlements and neighborhood centers. More than one-half of the workers employed in such agencies identified themselves as supervisors. However, there were no distinctions among administrators, supervisors and practitioners with respect to their reported job functions of direct service, staff development and supervision, and general administration. Essentially administrators were involved in direct services, and practitioners were engaged in administrative activities. Nevertheless, as noted by the researchers, the relative amount of time actually devoted to each job function was not included in the study.

Forty-three of the 151 respondents were not involved directly in the practice of group work; they were employed in such jobs as community organization, education, research, and social casework. The majority of respondents believed that, if there were a sufficient supply of funds and of trained group workers, group workers should be used primarily in direct service activities. In addition, approximately one-third of the respondents believed that recent graduates of schools of social work should have more training concerning direct services with groups. However, the majority of respondents aspired to be administrators rather than practitioners.

Variable Relationship Studies

Studies searching for variable relationships are those quantitative-descriptive studies which are concerned with the finding of variables pertinent to an issue or situation and/or the finding of the relevant relations among variables. Usually neither *a priori* hypotheses nor specific questions are formulated to guide the research. Survey procedures may be used, and a large number of potentially relevant variables are included in such studies. Often there is an interest in seeking variables with predictive value.

"The Decision by Unmarried Mothers to Keep or Surrender Their Babies" by Meyer, Jones, and Borgatta (1956) is an example of *a study searching for variable relationships*. The investigators were interested in studying the extent to which background characteristics of unmarried mothers served by a social casework agency were associated with the decisions to keep their babies or to surrender them for adoption. In addition to locating predictive variables, Meyer *et al.*, were interested in extracting factors which could uniquely summarize and describe the interrelationships of variables related to background characteristics and agency contacts.

The researchers selected a social agency which provided services to unmarried mothers, and chose all active cases of unmarried mothers who made final dispositions regarding their babies during a six month period of time in 1954. For their initial analyses, 100 cases were obtained. Background characteristics such as age, race, financial status, and family composition were derived from the case records. The authors indicated that 40 of the unmarried mothers gave up their babies for adoption and 60 kept their babies. Sixty-two percent of the 52 white girls surrendered their babies, while only 17 percent of the 48 Negro girls gave up their babies.

The investigators noted that the group of eight Negro girls who relinquished custody of their babies was too small to permit the statistical identification of background variables which were predictive of the unmarried mothers' decisions. Their analyses of background characteristics of the white girls revealed seven variables which were predictive: religion, education, marital status of putative father, age, employment status, financial status, and socio-economic status. Combinations of these variables were tried out, and it was discovered that a white girl with two or more of the following characteristics was likely to surrender her baby: non-Catholic, attended college, putative father is single, and the mother is under age 18. Using these items, the researchers classified 83 percent of the cases accurately.

Meyer *et al.*, applied the same predictive test to another sample of 175 closed cases for which decisions were recorded for the years 1952 and 1953 and for several new cases in 1954. They achieved 77 percent accuracy in predicting the decisions of white mothers. Simply predicting that all of the Negro mothers would keep their babies, the investigators classified 84 percent of the cases correctly.

Utilizing all of the 223 cases at their disposal, the investigators explored the interrelationships of 28 variables, of which 19 were used in a factor analysis. Factor analysis is a statistical technique which allows for the identification of a smaller number of factors which could account for the interrelationships of most of the variables used in the analysis. Five factors were extracted in the factor analysis, and it was believed that these factors constituted distinctions that were descriptive of the agency's caseload. Only two of the factors were related to the decision to surrender babies. These factors were identified as social class and casework ratings of the unmarried mothers' appropriate handling of the social situation regarding her decision. The analysis also indicated that the factor of social class was that single factor which showed the strongest association with the decisions of unmarried mothers. Thus, the following hypothesis was suggested: "the higher the social class, the more likely the girl is to surrender the baby" (p. 108).

EXPLORATORY STUDIES

Exploratory studies have the major purpose of developing ideas and hypotheses. These studies are less definable than experimental and quantitative-descriptive studies, which include procedures to provide evidence for the association of variables and for the verification of hypotheses. Essentially, exploratory studies are based on the assumption that through the use of relatively systematic procedures relevant hypotheses pertaining to a particular phenomenon can be developed. In addition, it is assumed that measurement devices can be developed, and the feasibility of experimentation and approximations to experimentation can be assessed.

The logical strategy of exploratory studies consists of providing a framework which may facilitate the process of deriving pertinent questions in the investigation of a phenomenon. The process of discovery is not articulated sufficiently so that a researcher can follow a prescribed set of rules; indeed, such a creative process does not necessarily follow orderly rules of logic. Nevertheless, research methodologists have described several guidelines for structuring investigations in such a way that the likelihood of discovery may be enhanced. These guidelines are usually applied to three general categories: *sources of information, types of data,* and *the use of data.*

Sources of information include reviews of the published literature, "the experience survey" which involves the interviewing of those people who are closest to or are reputed to be knowledgeable about the particular area of inquiry (Selltiz *et al.*, 1963, pp. 53–59) , and the location of available records (Webb, Campbell, Schwartz, and Sechrest, 1966, pp. 53–111) .

Types of data included in exploratory studies may be both quantitative and qualitative. In addition to the use of quantitative data, much emphasis is also devoted to the methods for accumulating such qualitative data as narrative information from unstructured interviews and from the researcher's observations. In particular, the method of participant observation has been a primary tool for anthropologists and sociologists who have studied various types of communities and subcultures (see Riley, 1963, pp. 68–75, for a discussion of the advantages and limitations of participant observation) . The investigator lives in the community, and he interviews and observes people in a variety of social situations. In such studies, a great volume of data may be collected over a period of time for very few behavioral units. By unit we are referring to the intended target of inquiry, which may be individuals, groups, organizations, or communities.

Regarding the use of data in exploratory studies, guidelines have primarily involved the researcher's proper attitude and suggested procedures for categorizing and analyzing large amounts of quantitative and qualitative data. Katz (1953) indicates that in exploratory studies of a community the investigator should delimit his area of inquiry with respect to what he is to observe. This may be done through the investigator's previous hunches or theoretical notions. In addition, Katz notes that the researcher should be receptive to new information and be flexible in the use of his research procedures. He also suggests some relatively systematic procedures concerning the interviewing of community leaders and other key informants. The interviewer seeks out leaders who are presumed to view the community differently. Having interviewed one leader, he then seeks to make comparisons with another leader. He continues the process of comparing responses of a number of leaders until no more ideas are manifest. The notion is that the investigator seeks discrepancies and divergent opinions in order to stimulate his conceptualizing of the phenomenon.

A problem for researchers in exploratory studies is that of information overload. The investigator may not be able to assimilate large volumes of qualitative data; hence, he inevitably needs to resort to some device to categorize or code the data into manageable chunks of information. Content analysis (Berlson, 1954, pp. 488–522) is a procedure which provides a set of rules for casting narrative data into manageable categories amenable to quantitative-descriptions. The assumption in such a procedure for exploratory studies is that the process of forming categories and of subsequently using them for quantitative-descriptions will eventuate in researchable hypotheses. A more recent device is the "constant comparative method of qualitative analysis" of Glaser and Strauss (1967, pp. 101–15). They principally describe steps in a process which is assumed to lead to the development of theoretical ideas. Their chief idea is that of alerting the researcher to making a continuous comparison of similarities and differences among incidents which are assigned to a set of categories. For example, categories of various group behaviors might be tentatively designated by the researcher, and he might make comparisons of three-minute group discussions which are regarded as incidents to be categorized. Each incident is compared with every other incident, and impressions of similarities and differences are noted. In addition, new categories are formed as are necessary to classify the incidents. As many categories as possible are devised. Comparisons are made continuously among categories until there is theoretical saturation, i.e., no new categories can be formed. The researcher then stops categorizing, and he writes down his ideas; from these impressions he derives hypotheses for further testing.

Another device for developing ideas is that of clinical studies or demonstration programs. For example, the investigator may identify a relatively new treatment technique which he believes would be useful in practice, but he may be unclear as to what the consequences of such a technique might be. He may devise an exploratory study to determine the potentialities of his technique. In order to do this, he manipulates the independent variable in a field setting, and he observes the effects of the technique on the participants in the research. His purposes are to determine the feasibility of implementing the technique, to clarify the independent variable, and to locate possible dependent variables to be used in subsequent experimentation.

In essence, exploratory studies have the primary goal of developing, clarifying and modifying concepts and ideas in order to provide researchable hypotheses for further study. This primary goal can be sub-divided into three subordinate purposes:

1. The relatively detailed quantitative and qualitative-description of a particular phenomenon.

2. The development of ideas through the systematic use of a specific data collection procedure.

3. The systematic observation of the potential effects of an independent variable as it is manipulated for a small number of behavioral units in clinical and/or demonstration studies.

In our classification system a research study should have several requisites before it can be classified as exploratory. *It should not be classifiable as either an experimental or a quantitative-descriptive study.* However, there is one exception to this. *Searching for variable relationship studies* has the primary purpose of specifying hypotheses and locating associations among variables, which is a goal of exploration; such studies exclusively use quantitative procedures for describing quantitative relationships among variables. Nevertheless, many studies combine quantitative-descriptions with qualitative-descriptions in seeking to describe a phenomenon, and our sub-type of *combined exploratory-descriptive studies* was created to include those studies. The sub-type, therefore, includes aspects of both exploratory and quantitative-descriptive studies.

A second requisite for exploratory studies is that *relatively systematic procedures for obtaining empirical observations and/or for the analyses of data should be used.* However, the data may not be systematically analyzed in the form of quantitative-descriptions. For example, Lewis' exploratory study of a poor family in Mexico City involved systematic tape-recorded interviews of each member in a Mexican family (1961); the descriptions, however, were in narrative form.

A third requisite for exploratory studies is that *the investigator should go beyond the qualitative and/or quantitative-descriptions by attempting to conceptualize the interrelations among the phenomena observed.* This means that the investigator should attempt to construe his observations into some theoretical or hypothetical framework.

We offer the following definition of exploratory studies.

Exploratory studies are empirical research investigations which have as their purpose the formulation of a problem or questions, developing hypotheses, or increasing an investigator's familiarity of a phenomenon or setting for more precise future research. The intent to clarify or modify concepts may also be predominant. Relatively systematic procedures for obtaining empirical observations and/or for the analyses of data may be used. Both quantitative- and qualitative-descriptions of the phenomenon are often provided, and the investigator typically conceptualizes the interrelations among properties of the phenomenon being observed. A variety of data collection procedures may be employed in the relatively intensive study of a small number of behavioral units. Methods which are employed include such procedures as interviewing, participant observation, and content analysis. Representative sampling procedures are typically not used. In some studies, there is a manipulation of an independent variable in order to locate its potential effects.

We have identified three sub-types of exploratory studies. These are (1) studies which combine features of exploration and description; (2) studies which use specific data collection devices in searching for ideas; and (3) studies which involve the manipulation of independent variables in demonstrating the feasibility of practical techniques or programs. Combined exploratory-descriptive studies employ both quantitative- and qualitative-descriptions of a particular phenomenon. Studies which use specific data collection procedures do not necessarily contain quantitative-descriptions. They attempt to summarize qualitative data through abstractions in the form of categories in order to consider possible relationships for more accurate description in further research. The distinguishing feature of an exploratory study which manipulates independent variables is its experimental character. This type of study is different from experiments in that procedures to control for extraneous variables are usually not included. In addition, there may be only one unit for study as opposed to experiments which must include many units for proper analyses.

Definitions and examples for each of the three sub-types of exploratory studies are presented below.

Combined Exploratory-Descriptive Studies

Combined exploratory-descriptive studies are those exploratory studies which seek to thoroughly describe a particular phenomenon. The concern may be with one behavioral unit, as in a case study, for which both empirical and theoretical analyses are made. The purpose of these studies is to develop ideas and theoretical generalizations. Descriptions are in both quantitative and qualitative form, and the accumulation of detailed information by such means as participant observation may be found. Sampling procedures are flexible, and little concern is usually given to systematic representativeness.

"Solidarity and Delinquency in a Street Corner Group" by Leon Jansyn, Jr. (1966) is an example of *a combined exploratory-descriptive study*. In his review of the literature on gang delinquency, Jansyn concluded that existing theories did not sufficiently explain the internal dynamics of gangs. Accordingly, he wished to "illuminate some of the ways in which variations in group activity are related to internal processes of the group and variations in group structure over time" (p. 600). His investigation involved the observation of one delinquent group for approximately two years. The group consisted predominantly of adolescent boys, and it was identified by community residents as the Dons. The neighborhood in which the Dons resided was a working class neighborhood with a high rate of official delinquency.

The investigator used the method of participant observation to gather the data for his study. He lived in the Dons' neighborhood, and he associated with the group in his official capacity as a "detached worker." After he had associated with the group for three months, he began to systematically record data. The data consisted of attendance records for each member of the group and written daily accounts of the group's activities. Observations and attendance data were systematically recorded for approximately 150 days during a year, and the locations for observations were gathering-places for the group members: a particular street corner, two restaurants, and a recreational agency.

Having defined attendance as the appearance of any member of the group during a daily three-hour period of observation, the investigator computed average attendance figures for the group members for a period of one year. In addition to attendance records for the entire group, which was comprised of 28 to 60 members during the year, Jansyn provided records for sub-types within the group. Based on his daily observations of group activity, he identified nine boys as core members; the remaining members were regarded as fringe members. A core member was defined as a group member who influenced other group members in their activities. Quantitative data on attendance indicated that core members attended meetings more often than the fringe members.

Jansyn observed that the group went through different phases of organization during the year. The two predominant activities of the group were fighting other gangs and club-type activities. Two identified leaders were influential with respect to each of these activities, and conflict emerged when there was dissension over the priority of delinquent or club activities. Conflict among the two leaders and their respective followers led to relative disorganization in the group. Concomitant with this reduction in group solidarity was an increased influence of lower status members on the group. Jansyn noted that attendance records paralleled his observations of group organization; attendance was less when the group appeared to be relatively disorganized, and attendance increased as organization increased. After disorganization occurred, there was a change of meeting places and increased activity among the group members. The gang became involved in restructuring itself and in forming a closer network of interrelationships among the members, which resulted in increased group solidarity. As a result of the investigator's conceptual analysis of his data, he formulated a tentative hypothesis: "In corner groups, deterioration of group solidarity is followed by an increase of group activity and a revival of solidarity" (p. 601).

Studies Using Specific Data Collection Procedures

Studies which use specific data collection procedures for developing ideas are those exploratory studies which exclusively use one specific procedure for extracting generalizations. Such procedures may include content analysis and the critical incident technique. The purpose of these studies is to produce conceptual categories which can be operationalized for subsequent research; it is not to report accurate quantitative-descriptions among variables.

"Some Concepts about Therapeutic Interventions with Hyperaggressive Children: Parts I and II" by Goodrich and Boomer (1958) is an example of *an exploratory study which uses specific data collection procedures for developing ideas.* The setting in which the research took place was at the Child Research Branch of the National Institute of Mental Health. Residential treatment of hyperaggressive children was the focus of interest for the investigators. A therapeutic program which included 24 staff persons was devised to treat chronically disturbed boys who were nine or ten years old. Staff persons were comprised of psychiatrists, teachers, social workers, and child-care workers.

The investigators assumed that long term residential treatment by skilled staff members would produce behavioral changes in the disturbed children; yet they observed that there was no useful system of concepts which could be used for testing hypotheses relevant to residential treatment. They wished to derive concepts which could be useful for clinicians: principles of effective therapeutic intervention with hyperaggressive children. In order to develop such principles they decided to use Flanagan's critical incident technique (1954), which is a method devised to derive generalizations by inductively abstracting them from specific events.

The procedure involved the definition of a critical incident and the specification of a series of critical incidents by observers. Staff members of the residential treatment program were regarded as observers, and each staff member was interviewed periodically by the researchers over a time span of three months. In the interview each person was asked to describe "an actual incident involving a child and an adult (himself or another) in which the adult *did* something which the respondent felt was either good or bad for the child, in terms of the over-all goals of residential treatment" (p. 210). Thus, the critical incident was the respondent's recall of a specific attempt by an adult to deal with the child's behavior. The observers were asked to describe the behaviors of both the child and the adult for each critical incident. In addition, each respondent was asked to generalize a principle of intervention which he believed was illustrated by the critical incident. In this way, 240 critical incidents were collected from 130 interviews with the 24 staff members.

Having obtained the "critical incidents," the investigators then set out to classify them. They first discussed similarities and differences among the incidents; then they tentatively assigned sets of incidents with common themes to categories which they created. The incidents were sorted and reclassified into three levels of abstraction: specific behaviors of adults, concepts about therapeutic intervention, and concepts about "effective therapeutic intervention." Their final classification contained 31 principles of therapeutic intervention, which were grouped under four categories: *promoting personality change by helping child to learn to view his own behavior evaluatively, promoting ego growth, supporting existing ego controls, and managing one's own conduct as a staff person* (pp. 211, 212, 286, and 289). Two illustrative principles are as follows (p. 212):

1. Therapist welcomes and encourages instances of positive or affectionate relatedness.
2. Therapist fosters rapport with the child by responding to his manifest interests.

The investigators concluded their research by pointing out that they did not know whether the 31 principles they derived were actually effective. In essence, the "principles" formed a basis for the delineation of researchable hypotheses pertaining to therapeutic interventions with hyperaggressive children.

Experimental Manipulation Studies

Experimental manipulation studies are those exploratory studies which manipulate an independent variable in order to locate dependent variables which are potentially associated with the independent variable. Typically, one behavioral unit is studied in its natural environment.

Often the purpose of these studies is to demonstrate the feasibility of a particular technique or program as a potential solution to practical problems. A variety of data collection procedures may be employed, and observational techniques may be developed during the course of the research.

"Intensive Treatment of Psychotic Behavior by Stimulus Satiation and Food Reinforcement" by T. Ayllon (1963) is an example of *an exploratory study which includes the manipulation of an independent variable.* The investigator was interested in demonstrating that behaviors of patients could be modified by using techniques derived from theories of learning. The study took place in a female ward in a mental hospital. The subject for research was a 47 year-old female patient who was diagnosed as a chronic schizophrenic. The patient stole food, hoarded towels in her room, and wore an excessive amount of clothing. Her behavior was regarded as undesirable, and attempts by the staff to change her behavior were unsuccessful.

The researcher attempted to demonstrate that the patient's behavior could be modified by the experimental control of relevant variables. To control the patient's stealing of food the investigator employed several procedures. First, the extent of food stealing was determined by having the ward personnel observe and record the patient's behavior on the ward for one month. It was determined that the patient ate all of her regular meals, and in addition stole food from other patients and from a food counter during two-thirds of her meals. She weighed over 250 pounds, and the medical staff indicated that her excessive weight was detrimental to her health. Attempts to persuade or coerce the patient to eat less food were unsuccessful. Ayllon employed a principle derived from learning theory: "the strength of a response may be weakened by the removal of positive reinforcement following the response" (p. 55). The response was considered to be food stealing, and the reinforcer was regarded as the patient's access to meals. Ayllon used a procedure which resulted in the withdrawal of a meal whenever the patient picked up unauthorized food or approached a dining room table different from her own. The patient was allowed only to eat alone at one dining room table. This procedure was applied systematically, and her food stealing was eliminated in two weeks. The patient's new response of not stealing food was virtually maintained for one year after the treatment, and her weight was reduced to 180 pounds.

Ayllon also used the withdrawal of food as a reinforcer to eliminate the patient's behavior of wearing excessive clothing. To change her behavior of hoarding towels the researcher used "stimulus satiation," which involved giving the patient an overabundant supply of towels. After the patient accumulated 625 towels over approximately a three-month period of time, she began to discard the towels until she virtually had none. She reduced the number of towels she kept in her room from the 19 to 29 towels per week prior to the experimental manipulation to approximately two towels per week after the experimental manipulation.

Ayllon recorded data on the frequency of occurrence of the patient's behaviors, and he carefully maintained control over the patient's environment. The patient's undesirable behavior was reduced, and the researcher attempted to determine whether other pathological behavior patterns would develop. The patient was observed by staff members every 30 minutes during a 16 hour time span for each observation day. A selected number of observation days were specified for a period of one year. When the patient's environment was first manipulated, emotional responses of crying and shouting were observed. The researcher reported that these responses were quickly eliminated when the staff members ignored them. The observations were analyzed in gross behavioral categories which were developed for the study: violent, seclusive, socially accessible, etc. The investigator concluded that the patient did not become less well adjusted on the ward, and that the behavioral techniques which he employed were potentially useful.

Summary of Classification System

In the preceding portions of this chapter we have presented our classification scheme for categorizing research studies. The categories for classification were defined and described in detail in an attempt to familiarize the student with each of the major categories and sub-types of research. In order to summarize the types and sub-types which have been defined, an outline of the classification system along with page references to definitions is presented below.

How to Use the Classification System

SOME GENERAL ISSUES. A research study may have many objectives, and it may include a variety of methods to accomplish those objectives. Such a study may not be categorized easily by our classification system, or by any classification scheme, because it may be classifiable into more than one sub-type of research. In fact, every research study may not be amenable to a unique classification within our system. For example, a survey of a particular population may include features of both population description and searching for variable relationships; a field experiment may also include a description of the characteristics of a specific population. In our review of the literature we devised two procedures in an attempt to overcome this basic problem. One procedure was to create a sub-type—combined exploratory-descriptive studies—to accommodate the appearance of studies in the literature which included overlapping categories of exploration and description. A second device was to view a research investigation with respect to its major purpose, which is identified as that purpose to which more than.50 percent of the content of the published research is devoted. In the event that an investigation has two distinct but equal purposes, our solution would be to categorize the study into more than one sub-type. However, in our use of the classification system we found that all of the studies we reviewed could be uniquely assigned to one of the nine sub-types.

A potential problem for users of the classification system is that if they see labels similar to the sub-types in a particular study, they might assume that such labels have the same meaning as intended in this chapter. In our own experience we have found that labels are used inconsistently by different investigators; thus, for classification purposes it is more efficient to ignore the labels presented in research studies. An investigator, for example, might say his study is experimental; but we would not classify the study on that statement alone. Essentially, we would determine whether or not the study had the requisites for an experimental study before classifying it as one.

Before using this classification scheme, the research reader should become thoroughly familiar with the typology by following these steps:

1. Read the chapter carefully. Pay particular attention to the definitions of the categories and sub-types.

2. Study the examples included in the chapter for each sub-type. Most of these studies are reproduced in their entirety in the reader, *Exemplars of Social Research* (Fellin, Tripodi, and Meyer, 1969).

3. The research reader should attempt to define each sub-type in his own words; if necessary, he should elaborate the definitions to suit his own purposes for classification.

Having followed these steps, the research reader should be prepared to classify published research studies.

GENERAL GUIDELINES. To facilitate efforts at classification, the following general guidelines are suggested for classifying any particular research study:

1. First read the article quickly in order to obtain an overview of the research study. Then read the study carefully, paying particular attention to the objectives of the study and the methods employed to accomplish such objectives. It is important to note that objectives may be included throughout the presentation of the study, as well as in sections devoted to problem formulation and to the conclusions of the research.

2. List the explicit and implicit objectives of the study, and arrange the objectives into a hierarchy of importance for the investigation. Hierarchy of importance refers to a rank ordering of objectives in terms of what was done in the research. If most of the study is devoted to describing a particular population, then that may be the most "important" objective.

3. List the specific research methods and procedures which were used in the study, and determine which procedures were used to accomplish each objective listed above.

4. Determine the major purpose(s) and the minor objectives of the study.

5. If the author classifies his study, ignore it. Look for the necessary ingredients for classification as discussed in this chapter.

6. In order to classify the study it is recommended that the research reader begin with the most explicitly defined category, experimental studies. Determine whether or not the study can be classified as experimental. If the study is experimental, then decide whether it should be categorized as a field experiment or as a laboratory experiment.

7. If the study is not experimental, then the research reader

should determine whether it can be categorized as a quantitative-descriptive study. If the study is quantitative-descriptive, decide to which one of the four sub-types the study could be assigned. The study would be categorized by that sub-type which is most representative of the research.

8. If the study is not quantitative-descriptive, determine whether or not it can be regarded as an exploratory study. If the study is exploratory, decide on its appropriate sub-type.

9. After the study is classified, review the specific classification to determine if it is in accordance with criteria outlined in this chapter.

10. Have another research reader classify the same study. If classifications are different, discuss the reasons for classification in an attempt to achieve consensus.

An example is provided by the classification of the study by Northcutt *et al.* (1965), which was abstracted and presented as a program evaluation study in the section in this chapter devoted to quantitative-descriptive studies. The major purpose of that study is to evaluate the effects of a specific program. Minor purposes which are interrelated with but subordinate to the major purpose are the testing of a hypothesis, a demonstration of the feasibility of the program, and a description of selected characteristics of patients who have been released from mental hospitals. The research methods employed are the use of an experimental county and its comparison with a county to which it was matched, and the use of structured interviews to obtain information about the patients. These research methods were employed in an effort to achieve the major purpose of the study.

The study is not classifiable as an experimental study because it does not use randomization procedures in assigning patients to either an experimental or a control county. It is classifiable as a quantitative-descriptive study since it includes variables which are amenable to measurement and has a purpose of testing a hypothesis. It is further sub-typed as a program evaluation study because the major purpose of the study is to evaluate the effectiveness of a specific program.

An Application of the Classification System

This classification system was initially utilized in a study by Weinberger and Tripodi (1968), who attempted to describe trends in research by systematically reviewing empirical research studies included in four social work journals: *Child Welfare, Social Case-*

work, Social Service Review, and *Social Work.* In this concluding section of the chapter, we are presenting a brief analysis of some selected results from that study in order to illustrate the potential utility of the classification system for describing trends in research for social work. Weinberger and Tripodi assumed that the social work journals selected for analysis included research literature which was representative of research in the profession of social work, and that comparisons of two adjacent five-year time periods would be sufficient to reflect relatively recent research trends. Therefore, they decided to review all of the articles in the four journals from 1956 through 1965, and to compare the numbers and types of research articles for the two time spans of 1956 through 1960 and 1961 through 1965. A total of 1,894 articles were reviewed systematically, but only those articles exemplary of empirical research were employed in the analysis. As previously indicated, consensus was attained by the authors in their classifications, and a reliability test indicated a high degree of agreement among two independent classifiers.

A total of 172 empirical research studies were located; 67 for the 1956–1960 time period, and 105 for 1961–1965. There were 941 total articles in the first time period and 953 total articles in the second time period. Thus, there was an increase in the percentage of research articles from seven percent in 1956–1960 to 11 percent in 1961–1965. Recognizing that shifts in research reporting may be due to other factors such as changes in editorial policy, one could infer that these results may be indicative of an increase in research. However, this information provides very little insight into the nature of increased research production, and a classification system for categorizing different types of research studies may be useful in this regard. Accordingly, all of the empirical research studies were classified further. Each study was assigned uniquely to one of the nine sub-types of research identified in the classification system. In addition, the percentages of the different types of research were computed for each time period. Comparisons could then be made with respect to shifts in the types of research.

Table I includes the percentages of empirical research articles classified by types of research. Our subsequent discussion is based on these data. It is evident that there is an increase in both the percentages of experimental studies and of exploratory studies from 1956–1960 to 1961–1965. Experimental studies increase from 1.5 percent to 10.5 percent, while exploratory studies increase from 12.0 percent to 15.2 percent. At the same time, the percentage of quantitative-descriptive studies decreases from 86.5 percent to 74.3 percent.

TABLE I

PERCENTAGES OF THE TOTAL NUMBER OF EMPIRICAL RESEARCH STUDIES FOR SUB-TYPES OF RESEARCH IN FOUR SELECTED SOCIAL WORK JOURNALS BY TWO FIVE-YEAR PERIODS

	Experimental			Quantitative-Descriptive				Exploratory		
	Field	Lab	Hypothesis Testing	Program Evaluation	Population Description	Variable Relation- ship Seeking	Combined Exploration- Descrip- tion	Use of Specific Data Collection Procedures	Experi- mental Manipu- lations
Time Period									
1956–1960 (N = 67)	0	1.5	10.4	8.9	19.4	47.8	6.0	3.0	3.0
1961–1965 (N = 105)	5.7	4.8	18.1	15.2	12.4	28.6	10.5	2.8	1.9

From this information, it appears that greater emphasis was placed on experimentation and exploration with less concern devoted to description. However, several observations can be made. There is an increase in all of the studies which include attempts to verify hypotheses: field experiments, laboratory experiments, hypothesis testing studies, and program evaluation studies. Combining the percentages for these sub-types in each time period, it is observed that there is an increase from 20.8 percent in 1956–1960 to 43.8 percent in 1961–1965. In addition, those quantitative-descriptive studies which do not attempt to test hypotheses decrease from 73.2 percent in the first time period to 51.5 percent in 1961–1965. Although exploratory studies increase slightly, it is evident that the increase is due to one of the sub-types, combined exploratory-descriptive studies. *Both* exploratory studies which use specific data collection procedures *and* exploratory studies which use experimental manipulations decrease slightly from 1956–1960 to 1961–1965. These observations suggest that there appears to be a trend towards the seeking of higher forms of knowledge in research for social work. There are relatively more studies devoted to the verification of hypotheses, and there are fewer studies entirely concerned with developing concepts and describing specific situations.

Chapter 3

Evaluation of Research: Principles and Guidelines

In this chapter we develop principles and guidelines for evaluating experimental, quantitative-descriptive, and exploratory research studies. The work in Chapter 2 on classification of research studies provides a foundation for the specification of evaluation guidelines for different levels of scientific inquiry. In the development of guidelines, we emphasize the fruitfulness of evaluating research studies in terms of the research methods employed and the form of knowledge sought. Accordingly, attention is directed to the procedures used in securing knowledge, and to factors which influence the degree of relative certainty of the knowledge produced.

In developing guidelines, evaluation is defined as a systematic assessment of the methodological qualities of each aspect of an empirical research investigation, i.e., problem formulation, research design and data collection, and data analysis and conclusions. Evaluation of research studies is to be distinguished from evaluative research, a term which usually refers to studies concerned with understanding the effects of a specific program or method of helping (French, 1952). Different types of evaluations of research studies can be found in the literature: essay reviews of single studies, journal articles that review a series of research studies concerned with the same substantive area, and monographic reviews of research. The first type is illustrated by Macdonald's (1966) essay review of the Meyer et al., study of *Girls at Vocational High;* the second type is illustrated by Tripodi and Miller's (1967) review of studies of clinical judgment; the third type is illustrated by Maas' (1966) monograph, *Five Fields of Social Service: Reviews of Research.*

While published evaluations of these types are invaluable to the student and the social practitioner who want to benefit from research, the actual evaluation of particular research studies constitutes an important activity for understanding given phenomena, for assimilating new knowledge into frameworks of previously obtained knowledge, and for utilizing research procedures and knowledge in further research. For the social practitioner, an additional purpose of evaluation is likely to be the utilization of knowledge for change purposes, i.e., interpersonal change, organizational change, community change, and societal change.

For all these purposes, an important concern of the research reader is with ascertaining the degree to which an investigator has reduced uncertainty in regard to the phenomenon studied. Because of the difficulty of obtaining knowledge of all the variables operating in relation to a given phenomenon, it is never possible to accumulate sufficient evidence to attain absolute certainty, i.e., truth. However, for hypothesis-testing studies, the relative degree of certainty of knowledge is estimated within the frameworks of internal and external validity and predictions are expressed in terms of probabilities. As Eaton (1960) notes in his excellent discussion, "Science, Art, and Uncertainty in Social Work," hypotheses in science are accepted or rejected in terms of approximate certainty, and the concept of relative validity is utilized rather than the concept of absolute truth. As we have pointed out in Chapter 2, the experimental study is the principal approach for improving prediction through reduction of threats to validity. Quantitative-descriptive studies which seek to test hypotheses may also be assessed in terms of the relative certainty of the knowledge produced, e.g., by examining ways such as randomization procedures in which an investigator attempts to increase validity of his results. In quantitative-descriptive studies designed to describe quantitative relations among variables, such as surveys describing facts about selected populations, the concepts of validity and reliability may be employed to assess the accuracy of the knowledge produced. For exploratory studies the focus of evaluation is also on the potential of such studies for reducing uncertainty. The major contribution to knowledge from exploratory studies is, however, in providing ideas and sharpening insights useful for developing hypotheses which can be investigated in future research studies. As a result, the modification, clarification, and development of concepts, hypotheses, and measurement procedures all serve as a foundation for improving the certainty of knowledge to be produced by further research endeavors.

By engaging in the differential assessment of different types of research studies, the research reader can increase the potential forms and content of knowledge considered useful for social work practice. Knowledge gained from exploratory studies will not be evaluated in terms of criteria appropriate only to studies which test hypotheses, and the unique contributions of such studies will become highlighted for the social practitioner. Increased recognition is thus given to the entire range of knowledge which can be produced through scientific inquiry, and to the range of methods which can be employed to clarify and measure concepts, develop hypotheses, produce descriptive findings, test hypotheses, produce empirical generalizations, and to develop and test theoretical frameworks and scientific theory.

GUIDELINES FOR EVALUATION: AN OVERVIEW

In our review of the literature we found no work that provides a set of guidelines focused on major aspects of the research process differentiated by both purposes and methods of research. We have undertaken the task of developing such guidelines, since our construction of a typology for classifying research indicates significant differences as well as similarities in the nature of experimental, quantitative-descriptive, and exploratory research studies. Differential assessment is necessary to achieve maximum utilization of research knowledge, particularly in the case of the social practitioner who must act on the basis of knowledge available at a given point in time.

The literature we reviewed is rich with materials directly and indirectly bearing on evaluation frameworks, and we have utilized a range of sources in the development of evaluation guidelines. Such sources include general frameworks for evaluation, such as one provided in *Social Casework* by Goldstein (1962), in which general criteria are presented as a guide for practitioners in evaluating research studies for the purpose of understanding and using research findings. Another example of a general framework comes from the work of Knop (1967) in the *American Sociologist*. Knop identifies key conceptual and procedural questions which can be used by the student to evaluate sociological journal articles which present empirical research. These frameworks, as well as others by Caplow (1958), Anderson (1954), Macdonald (1959), and Finestone (1959), have in common an emphasis on the research process. The guidelines begin with the conceptualization and formulation of the problem of research, followed by the research design appropriate to the problem and the types of data collected and analyzed in accordance with the goals of the study. They conclude with an assessment of the conclusions and implications of the findings.

For the most part, general frameworks appear to be skeletal, to assume considerable knowledge of research terminology, and to assume a sequential nature of the research process from conceptualization to conclusion. These frameworks also assume that the research reader can adapt the general guidelines to specific studies. They are limited from our viewpoint because they tend to assume an ideal model of research and explicitly or implicitly deal with the evaluation only of research concerned with hypothesis testing (Knop, 1967). They imply a hierarchy of research from the pre-scientific phase to the scientific phase of experimentation (Lundberg, 1942). Accordingly, the tendency might be for the reader to attribute greater significance to an experimental study than to a survey study or an exploratory study, without assessing the strengths and weaknesses of each type of study in the context of its purposes. While general frameworks can be used to some extent for evaluating all types of research strategies, it is a major defect that they do not specifically deal with questions concerning the evaluation of exploratory studies or quantitative-descriptive studies other than those whose purpose is to test hypotheses. No recognition is given to the fact that standards vary according to research purposes and methods, and that compromises occur in most research endeavors. Nevertheless, these general evaluation frameworks have been useful to the development of our guidelines because they focus on the evaluation of a study as a whole piece of research, and they are presented in the form of questions for the evaluation of research studies.

In addition, by stressing phases of the research process, the frameworks are closely related to the materials presented in most standard research texts on methodology. Such texts provide a handy reference to the evaluator of research studies, as they typically cover a range of relevant information on such topics as: formulating the research problem, hypotheses, concepts, operational definitions, problems of measurement, sampling, observational methods, scaling, statistical inference, and inferring causal relations (Selltiz *et al.,* 1959).

We have drawn on these general frameworks and on selected research texts in formulating our major categories of questions for evaluation of research studies. The organization of our guidelines differs from more general frameworks in our reduction of categories of questions to three: Problem Formulation, Research Design and Data Collection, and Data Analysis and Conclusions. An understanding of the essential elements of the research process can be grasped within these three categories and a limited number of major areas facilitates evaluation. But these categories are applied differentially to the types of research distinguished by purpose and method.

The major differences between the three major research approaches are detailed in Chapter 2. The literature used to develop the classification system was helpful as well in the construction of questions for evaluation. From this source, a few selected books contained the most pertinent concepts and information regarding the designated research approaches. Thus, for the evaluation of experimental research studies we relied heavily on the work of Campbell and Stanley (1963), which is concerned with the basic concepts of external validity and internal validity and sources of variation which should be controlled in experimentation (*see* Chapter 2). Ideally, experiments attempt to maximize both internal and external validity, but because of practical, ethical, or other constraints, such an ideal is usually not attainable. For example, in order to increase internal validity an investigator may restrict the range of the population to which he wishes to generalize, and consequently reduce external validity. On the other hand, in quasi-experimental designs, such as studies concerned with quantitative-descriptive hypothesis testing, the investigator may take means to insure representative sampling, with a broader population which increases external validity, perhaps at the expense of internal validity. He may use compromise, "after-the-fact," statistical manipulations in order to approximate control over other relevant variables thought to be responsible for the obtained relations between the independent and dependent variables. Campbell and Stanley review a number of factors which serve to jeopardize *internal validity,* such as history, maturation, and testing; and those affecting *external validity,* such as sample bias, interaction effects of testing, and reactive effects of experimental arrangements. These factors are used to view the validity of a number of experimental designs, and they provide a useful reference for the research reader in his evaluation of the findings produced through various experimental and quasi-experimental arrangements.

Another useful reference for the evaluator of experimental research is the work of Herzog (1959), *Some Guidelines for Evaluative Research.* Although Herzog's purpose is not to develop guidelines for research readers, her questions with regard to studies which attempt to evaluate change techniques in practice can be used as indirect guidelines for evaluating research studies of this type. By considering some "do's and don'ts" of research concerned with evaluating change, Herzog provides a good, general point of view for evaluating field experiments and quantitative-descriptive field studies. Her work is clearly written and particularly useful for individuals with limited sophistication in research, covering important research concepts such as reliability, validity, and sampling with particular reference to evaluative studies. Along these lines, the work of Suchman (1967) is also useful, as he considers strengths and weaknesses of various designs used in evaluative research. He rejects the notion that there is such a thing as one "correct" design for experimental research.

The works of Campbell and Stanley (1963), Herzog (1959), and Suchman (1967) are helpful in isolating areas of attention for evaluation of research studies devoted to hypothesis-testing, particularly through experimental designs but also for quantitative-descriptive studies devoted to hypothesis-testing or program evaluation. In regard to other studies designated as quantitative-descriptive, works such as those of Hirschi and Selvin (1967), Zetterberg (1954), and Blalock (1961) contribute to the development of evaluation guidelines. Hirschi and Selvin are concerned with making inferences from delinquency research based on survey data. Their work focuses mainly on the analysis phase of research studies, noting how investigators have presented and analyzed their data from a logical and statistical point of view. Hirschi and Selvin examine the findings of a number of studies in the delinquency area and discuss approximations to control through statistical manipulations of data and other problems of inference connected with quantitative-descriptive studies. In particular, they use schemes to try to uncover spurious relations and to refine or confirm relations among variables in cross-section studies in which variables are collected concurrently. Such considerations lead to significant questions to be asked by the evaluator as he attempts to find out what the research investigators are trying to do; to identify strengths and limitations of such procedures as sampling, measurement, and the manipulation of data; and to weigh the limitations in terms of the meaningfulness of the data and the probability that research will not be perfect. Of considerable merit is their view that critics of research must stress objectivity, vigilance, and sympathy in viewing the works of investigators in order to learn the most and benefit from the effort of evaluating research. The approach of Hirschi and Selvin is derivative from the tradition of The Columbia University Bureau of Applied Social Research. Other works in the same tradition are those of Lazarsfeld (1955), Kendall (1950), and Hyman (1955) which are also useful references for evaluating quantitative-descriptive studies.

For the third major category of research studies—that of exploratory studies—the work of Riley (1963) is especially useful. Riley is concerned with most types of research, but she makes exceptionally acute commentaries on descriptive case studies and field studies which our classification would label exploratory. A range of studies is offered to provide examples for specific topics of research, such as measurement, use of available data, collection of data, and seeking relationships between variables. The studies that are reproduced are not discussed in terms of all aspects of the research process, but commentaries concentrate on a single topic for each study. While this approach contrasts with ours, in that we are interested in evaluating total studies, the work of Riley is instructive for the development of guideline questions. Particularly helpful are her considerations of the advantages and disadvantages of studies not having the objective of testing hypotheses, but rather of developing conceptual systems and elaborating observations—studies we would regard as exploratory studies. Thus, Riley examines Malinowski's (1926) study of *Crime and Custom in a Savage Society,* and Whyte's (1943) *Street Corner Society,* both identified as case studies with exploratory objectives. These studies seek to locate and describe relevant variables and to suggest how they are related to each other. Concepts are not explicitly defined or measured in a systematic way, and the data are collected by means of participant observation.

Riley notes that this approach has the advantage of providing a wide range of detail, with the opportunity to uncover latent patterns of behavior, and to view behaviors in a whole rather than in a fragmented way. On the other hand, limitations to this type of study are likely to come from the researcher's taking a role in the group under investigation, from the lack of reliability connected with the collection of descriptive data, and from limits to generalizing from the use of a single case. Significant for the development of our evaluation guidelines is the clear distinction between exploratory studies and other types of research based on systematic measurement. The use of actual studies to indicate the benefits of knowledge produced through exploratory studies, and the discussion of ways in which the methods utilized can be strengthened to reduce study limitations, are also contributions. In sum, Riley's perceptive treatment suggests that in evaluating exploratory studies we should be concerned with efforts to minimize bias in the collection of data, to benefit from previous work and literature related to the problem of investigation (Selltiz, 1959), and to interpret findings within the context of the purpose and methods of the research.

GENERAL PERSPECTIVE ON EVALUATION

We have already noted our view that different standards should be used for different levels of scientific inquiry. In our general perspective, a central concept is the relative certainty of knowledge, and the confidence an evaluator of research can place in the generalizations derived from empirical research. Scientific knowledge is based on cumulative, replicative studies, and in the social sciences and social work, it is highly unlikely that any one study will resolve all pertinent questions about a single phenomenon. Based on the level and nature of knowledge which exists at any given time about a phenomenon, one research approach may be selected over another as the most appropriate method for investigating a research problem.

A number of general problems face the evaluator of studies presented in journal articles. In the first place, the article may not contain sufficient information and detail to allow for a meaningful evaluation. Several factors may influence the amount and kind of information available to the reader. In some cases, the author or the journal editor may exclude from the presentation certain kinds of information, such as key tables. In other cases, limits imposed by journals on the number of pages allowed per article may reduce the amount of information about research design necessary for evaluation. It is especially crucial for our evaluation system that sufficient information be presented to allow for classification of the research by purpose and method.

The information problem for evaluation concerns, in part, the type and extent of documentation given in a research report, i.e., the degree to which the reader is provided with appropriate sources and references for further information. In research studies based on data collected by questionnaire or interview schedule, examples of questions may be offered by the author, but generally all data collection instruments are not included. However, the author should indicate where the interested reader can obtain more detail about the instruments. Another example involves the documentation given to sampling procedures, with footnotes indicating where the reader can obtain full details. In all cases, sufficient information for understanding the major objectives of the study, the methods employed to reach the objectives, and the use of data in forming conclusions, should be included in the written report. The importance of accurate and adequate documentation comes from the emphasis in scientific inquiry on the accumulation of knowledge. The possibility of replication of research studies demands information or access to information necessary for such study. And the adequacy of a research report in this respect affects the adequacy of the report for evaluation by a research reader.

Not all research studies published in social work and social science journals will be clearly written. To the extent to which the written presentation is not systematic, clear, and internally consistent, it will be difficult for the reader to classify and evaluate the research study. For example, the purposes of the study are presented in a number of places throughout some articles, sometimes elaborating earlier statements and at other times contradicting them. The expectation of clarity in written materials does not imply that research terminology should be absent, but that it be used accurately, consistently, and clearly. The reader cannot expect to understand research studies without knowing the commonly accepted concepts pertaining to the research process as well as the terminology of the substantive area which the research investigates.

The classification and evaluation of research studies presumes a minimum level of sophistication in research methodology. In addition, the greater the degree of substantive knowledge of the area under investigation possessed by the research reader, the greater the potential for assessing the research study. In some substantive areas reviews of research are available, such as Levinger's (1960) review of findings concerning continuance in treatment. These reviews provide a foundation for the evaluator, but usually must be updated. In other cases, the evaluator will need to provide his own review of the literature. The reader who is familiar with previous works in a particular substantive area is in a position to evaluate a study on its own merits from a methodological point of view and place it in the context of currently available knowledge. Familiarity with previous studies also allows the reader to assess the appropriateness of the methodology employed by the investigator. For example, a combined exploratory-descriptive study of success in nursing home placements may be the only research approach feasible in the light of existing knowledge in the field of aging.

Exercise in evaluating research studies is extremely beneficial for understanding research and as a foundation for the utilization of research based knowledge in social practice. We have noted the different ways in which research has been evaluated by authors such as Riley (1963), Hirschi and Selvin (1963), and Glaser and Strauss (1967). These works have been helpful in the development of evaluation guidelines and can be a useful procedure for learning.

FIRST STEPS IN EVALUATION

The evaluator should read a research study through once quickly in order to get a picture of the substantive area under investigation. With this reading the evaluator gains some overall understanding of the research methods employed. The reader then should proceed to read the article carefully with the goal of locating the major purpose or purposes of the research, and of ascertaining whether or not the report has sufficient information upon which to base an evaluation. Minimal information required for evaluation would include some background regarding the study, the articulation of relevant hypotheses and/or questions of the study, the presentation of the research design employed, discussion of the types of empirical data collected and methods of collection, and the presentation of data analysis and conclusions of the study. The work of Marks (1960) on *Research Reporting* can be used as a guide in regard to the content and form of materials included in the research report. Selltiz *et al.* (1959), also provide such a guide. In addition, the Publication Manual of the American Psychological Association (1967) is a useful reference to the types of information generally included within journal research articles.

If the reader determines that the research report provides sufficient information for classification and evaluation and appears to have sufficient relevancy to his purposes (i. e., for utilization of the knowledge in practice), then the reader should type the study into its major research classification. Detailed guidelines for this purpose were presented in Chapter 2. Following classification by major research approach, the study should be subtyped. For example, a study classified as quantitative-descriptive should be further classified according to its purpose of testing hypotheses, seeking of relations among variables, and so forth. Experimental studies should be subtyped as laboratory experiments or field experiments. An exploratory study should be carefully reviewed in order to ascertain if it is exploratory in nature only, or if it includes a mixture of purposes and differential use of methods.

Early in the reading of the research report the reader should be sensitive to alternative strategies which might have been pursued with regard to the topic being studied. It is useful for the reader to consider the relative advantages and disadvantages of alternative designs vis-á-vis the purposes of a study. A basic reference for comparing the general advantages and disadvantages of research designs is provided by Campbell and Stanley, who report on a number of experimental designs, as well as quasi-experiments which we classify as quantitative-descriptive studies. With respect to experimental studies, the works of French (1953) on field experiments and Festinger (1953) on laboratory experiments are useful for the reader. These references provide background for the reader and help sensitize him both to alternative research designs and to different techniques for sampling and for data collection.

Having completed these first steps in evaluation, the reader should follow the guidelines appropriate to the classification of the research study. In general the reader should assume the role of the researcher and attempt to follow the research process in its entirety. This procedure will assist the reader to achieve perspective regarding "ideal" and "possible" research designs. Thus the reader should consider the formulation of the problem, the specific research design and types of data collected, the presentation and analysis of data, and the conclusions and interpretations made about the study. Guidelines for the evaluation of experimental, quantitative-descriptive, and exploratory studies are now presented.

GUIDELINES FOR EVALUATION OF EXPERIMENTAL STUDIES

Problem Formulation: Experimental Studies

The problem formulation of an experimental research study should contain the researcher's statement of study purposes, the identification of the hypotheses for study, the rationale for the selection of study variables, conceptual and operational definitions of the variables, and the identification of the assumptions made by the investigators (Ripple, 1960).

The formulation of a problem for study is likely to include a mixture of the researcher's ideas and ideas drawn from the substantive and methodological literature pertaining to the phenomenon under investigation. The researcher is expected to cite literature relevant to his investigation and to incorporate into his research the ideas and methods of other studies. The use of the literature is likely to appear in the author's explication of concepts, rationale for hypotheses, and statement of assumptions of the study.

The reader should list the major concepts discussed by the author, and note the extent to which the author's use of the concepts is consistent with the definitions cited in references to the literature. For example, in their laboratory experiment on effects of close and punitive styles of supervision, Day and Hamblin (1964) formulate a study to test hypotheses involving the relationship of four supervisory styles to aggressive feelings and actions of subordinates. They define the concept of close supervision as "one end of a continuum that describes the degree to which a supervisor specifies the roles of the subordinates and checks up to see that they comply with the specifications" (Day and Hamblin, 1964, p. 500). A "general" style of supervision is defined as being somewhere in the middle area of this continuum, i.e., moderate specification and checking on subordinates. Punitive and non-punitive styles of supervision are also conceptualized in the problem formulation. The authors cite references to studies which have employed these concepts, and also make use of this literature in identifying investigations which have shown support for a hypothesis which relates style of supervision to aggressive feelings and indirect aggression on the part of subordinates toward supervisors. In this example, the concepts of supervision and aggression constitute the major variables of the study, with supervision serving as the independent variable to be manipulated by the experimenters, and aggression identified as the dependent variable. Assumptions necessary to test the supervision-aggression hypothesis are considered, and Day and Hamblin make use of the literature to discuss self-esteem as a mediating or *contingent* variable. (A contingent variable is any variable which could potentially qualify, modify, or explain any obtained relations between an independent and a dependent variable.) Rather than making the assumption that the variable of self-esteem is unrelated to the hypothesis being tested, the authors make different predictions for subordinates with high self-esteem and those with low esteem. In this way the authors include in their conceptual framework a variable suggested by the literature as relevant to the hypothesis being tested.

Occasionally the reader will find limited use of the literature in the formulation of a problem for study. In such cases the reader should attempt to discern whether or not the study could have been improved by the incorporation of known available knowledge about the study problem. The reader may have knowledge of other similar studies which can be used to place the research being evaluated into a comparative context. Pollak's (1963) study of "Worker Assignment in Casework with Marriage Partners" is an example of an experimental study which appears to be related in a limited way to previous research and in which the study hypothesis was mainly generated from social work practice. The primary question from which a hypothesis was formulated concerned whether one or two workers should be assigned in cases in which both marital partners were involved in treatment. The number of workers assigned to marital problem cases was manipulated as the independent variable, with the hypothesis for study being that "Marriage partners whose relationships suffered from undue remoteness would benefit more from the experience of having one worker than from having two workers" (Pollak, 1963, p. 44). The dependent variable concerned the "benefit" derived by couples from treatment, conceptualized by Pollak in terms of family relationship improvement. The dimensions of improvement or deterioration of relationship were identified as communication and cooperation. However, the author cites no studies dealing with the substantive area of marital counseling or with the concepts of communication and cooperation.

The literature may be used not only in the formulation of a conceptual framework for an experimental study, but also in regard to relevant methodology. In the example of Pollak's study of casework with marital partners, the author makes use of judgments for the measurement of the concepts of communication and cooperation by drawing on the work of Hunt and his classic study of "movement." Pollak indicates how these concepts were operationalized for his study in a methodological appendix which describes criteria for measuring communication. The reader should examine such materials as these to determine if sufficient methodological detail is included or available to allow for a replication of the study. In addition, the reader should assess whether or not the indices of the concepts appear to correspond with the conceptual definitions of the variables, and whether or not the author has included any evidence regarding the reliability and validity of the concepts being measured. In Pollak's study every case was subjected to three judgments, but the measurement of reliability was not reported. In regard to the identification of relevant contingent variables, Pollak took into account two major kinds of treatment needs thought to be related to the relationship between number of workers and improvement in treatment. These treatment needs are derived from practice in terms of members of a family requiring a unifying experience or a separating experience. The author was not willing to assume that the variable was of no consequence. Since he could not include families of both types in his experiment, he confined the families studied to a single type of treatment need. However, decisions about families to be included in the study were not reviewed, no reliability check was made, and the loss of eligible cases occurred. This suggests that while an author may take into account relevant factors which need to be controlled in the experiment, there may be limitations in the ways in which control is provided.

A field experiment on "Insight versus Desensitization in Psychotherapy" by Paul (1967) illustrates the extensive use of the literature pertaining to methodological issues in experimentation, particularly with reference to problems of follow-up assessment of effects of treatment. Paul is concerned with selected methodological problems of follow-up studies of psychotherapy, such as the uncontrolled nature of client experiences during the post treatment period and "the practical difficulty of sample maintenance and attrition" (Paul, 1967, p. 333). His work illustrates the use of extensive references related to these problems, and his attempts to overcome the major problems with a well-controlled outcome study. In short, the reader focuses his attention on the way in which the researcher incorporates his ideas and those of other investigators into a statement of the rationale for the study, its purposes, explication of what is to be investigated, and major substantive and methodological issues confronting the investigator (Ripple, 1960).

In evaluating experimental studies, the reader should identify and examine carefully the hypotheses proposed for study. A hypothesis may have originated from one of several sources, such as a theoretical framework, prior research, practice experience, systematic organization of facts, or unsystematic observations and hunches. Understanding of the origin of a study hypothesis provides a context for evaluating the appropriateness of the specific design features and procedures employed in the experimental study. If the author is testing more than one hypothesis the reader should ascertain whether or not the hypotheses are linked in any theoretical or substantive way. As Thomas (1960) has pointed out, the hypothesis for study in experiments may be implicit, and can usually be made explicit by the reader by identification of the variables being manipulated and the dependent variables being measured in the experiment. For example, Thomas and McLeod (1960) studied the influence of in-service training for ADC workers on worker behavior and client change. The training of the workers was manipulated as the independent variable, and the implicit hypothesis involved the relationship of training to the provisions of effective service to ADC recipients.

In all experimental studies, the reader should locate the independent and dependent variables and determine whether or not the author is in a position to manipulate the independent variable. Contingent variables which may link the independent and dependent variables should be identified and the reader should examine the way in which the author proposes to account for such variables. The reader should determine if the study variables are defined conceptually, and the extent to which alternative definitions have been considered from previous research and/or from theory. Since actual testing of the hypothesis demands operational definitions of the concepts (Blalock, 1960) the reader determines how the major concepts are operationalized by examining the actual measurements proposed for the variables. The reader should then consider the extent to which the conceptual definitions correspond to the operational definitions, i.e., the extent to which evidence is provided in regard to the validity of the measures, such as face validity or construct validity (Kogan, 1960b). The reader also considers any evidence stated in regard to the reliability of the measures of the independent and dependent variables.

Assumptions made in experimental studies must be identified, both in regard to the conceptual framework and to measurement. Assumptions are defined as propositions which have not been verified, but which are taken as given for the purposes of investigation. Since the investigator cannot study all variables, nor control for all variables, he frequently must make assumptions about relevant variables, based on previous research, on theory, or on the collective wisdom of colleagues.

Review of the researcher's formulation of the problem for study allows an initial judgment in regard to the appropriateness of the experimental design for the study. If the problem formulation suggests that the independent variable cannot be manipulated, e.g., for practical, ethical, or other reasons, or if the concepts in the hypotheses do not have empirical referents, or are inadequately conceived, then the reader is alerted to the fact that the study does not meet the requirements of an experimental study. The reader should be aware that some of the aspects we have included under problem formulation may not be presented in the initial problem statement of a study, but may be interspersed throughout the journal article. When the reader's review of the problem reveals that the requirements of an experimental study are met, the reader proceeds to an evaluation of the research design and data collection aspects of the study.

Research Design and Data Collection: Experimental Studies

In classifying the study, the reader has determined that an experimental design is employed. The sub-type classification of the study, i.e., field experiment or laboratory experiment, should now be considered in terms of the relative advantages and disadvantages of these experimental approaches vis-á-vis the particular problem of study. While the field experiment takes place in the natural environment and presents obstacles to experimental control, this design may offer the greatest potential for testing hypotheses pertinent to practical situations. For example, the study by Paul (1966, 1967) referred to in Chapter 1 was concerned with assessing the outcome for individuals undergoing different types of psychotherapy. A field experiment was designed for the purpose of determining the overall comparative effects of the different treatments from pre-treatment to two-year follow-up and to assess the stability of improvement during the post-treatment period. A laboratory experiment would have been impractical in relation to the problem under investigation, as the subjects could not be isolated under laboratory conditions during the period of time necessary for the experiment. The field experiment was selected in the light of previous efforts of an experimental nature, but with the additional effort of the author to approximate in the field the controls inherent in laboratory study.

The work of Day and Hamblin (1964) on the effects of close and punitive styles of supervision utilized the laboratory experimental approach. While previous studies had been carried out through field experiments, the authors decided that the hypothesis involving relationships of supervisory styles to feelings and actions of subordinates could appropriately be carried out under laboratory conditions. The subjects could be engaged in the experimental tasks in an experimental room designed to "simulate" an industrial work station. In this case, testing of the hypotheses did not demand that the independent variable be manipulated in the natural environment, e.g. an industry setting, and the laboratory offered more rigorous control features than were possible with a field experiment. Thus, supervisors were trained to give uniform responses and to present uniform stimuli, and the tasks for the subjects were uniform. These conditions would have been difficult to achieve in the field setting. The Day and Hamblin study also illustrates ways in which the laboratory situation can be structured to approximate the natural setting, e.g., words such as "supervisor," "work efficiency," and "production line" were used to convey the atmosphere of the industrial setting.

These studies by Paul and by Day and Hamblin illustrate the need to consider sub-types in relation to the problems for study, as they point to specific design features employed in experimental studies. In evaluating experimental studies the reader should consider whether or not alternative design features could have improved the study, within the same constraints of cost, organizational factors, obstacles to control of variables, and the potential manipulation of the independent variable. The reader should focus on the extent to which an experimental study approximates maximal internal and external validity through the introduction of design features which promote validity.

In addition to considering the research experiment in terms of field and laboratory setting, the reader should examine the specific experimental design utilized in the study. Campbell and Stanley (1963) discuss three true experimental designs: the Pretest-Posttest control group design, the Solomon Four-Group Design, and the Post-test Only control group design. Each of these designs varies to some extent in the degree to which controls for internal and external validity are possible.

Several variables relevant to internal validity are history, maturation, testing, instrumentation, regression, selection, mortality, interaction of selection and maturation. Campbell and Stanley (1963) and Sussman (1964) include discussion of these variables and the ways in which experimental designs attempt to control for them. For example, the effects of history are minimized when the time between observations is very short. Maturation, i.e., growth of the individual in selected ways during the period of the experiment, can be handled by a control group in the design and by the randomization of subjects. Instrumentation involves the effects of the administration of instruments, the instruments themselves, and how they operate to produce change. Several methods can be used to control for these effects, such as having the same researcher for both experimental and control groups, or using a "blind" approach where the observer does not know which respondents are in the control or in the experimental groups.

In regard to external validity, the reader should consider ways in which the authors have attempted to control such factors as reactive or interaction effects of testing. These factors are controlled in the Solomon Four-Group Design and the Post-test Only control group design. Other factors influencing external validity concern selection biases and interaction with the experimental variable. The reader should consider the author's definition of the population with which the study is concerned, and the extent to which the author is able to generalize results to the population. Attention here is directed toward the external validity problem, which may be handled by various sampling techniques and the inclusion of evidence that a random sample is representative of the population.

One of the requisites for an experimental study is that randomization procedures be employed in the assignment of subjects to experimental and control groups. The reader should examine the process the experimenter uses to assign subjects, objects, and so forth to study groups, and what evidence is presented to verify that his goals of assignment have been reached, e.g., the extent to which equivalencies among groups are checked. The reader must also be alert in regard to the mortality, or loss of cases, which may occur during the experiment, and the extent to which such loss threatens the validity of the study.

Once the researcher has set up experimental and control groups, he must manipulate the independent variable, with such manipulation occurring prior in time to the anticipated changes in the dependent variable. The reader should identify the way in which the experimenter manipulated the independent variable. An example of variable manipulation is provided in the Day and Hamblin (1964) study, in which 24 groups were assigned systematically to four different experimental conditions of supervision: close supervision with high and low punitive styles; and general supervision, also with high and low punitive styles. In the case of the Paul (1967) study, different treatment modes were used with the experimental and control groups. The reader should consider the strength of the independent variable, e.g., number of treatment sessions, length of time in treatment, and instructions used in styles of supervision, in order to assess alternatives to manipulation procedures. Particularly, the reader should be alert to weak independent variables, and to ways in which they could have been strengthened (Thomas, 1960, p. 288), such as increasing the intensity and length of time over which the variable is manipulated. The independent variable must be potent enough to give a fair test of the hypothesis.

In regard to the manipulation of the independent variable, the reader should be alert to manipulation with respect to conditions of measurement. What is involved in the actual measurement process? Who does it? Is the researcher aware of which subjects are in the experimental and control groups? In essence, the reader attempts to locate potential sources of bias which could have influenced the dependent variables during the course of the experiment. Having located potential sources of bias, the reader assesses the extent to which the experimenter has introduced checks or procedures to deal with these problems. The reader should evaluate the efforts made to control the effects of the measurement process, e.g., the subjects' reactivity to manipulation of independent variables. This should be done in the context of the type of data collected by the experimenter, which should be identified by the reader and viewed in relation to the measurement process.

Ideal conditions are rarely possible in experimental studies due to lack of knowledge, lack of capacity to anticipate problems which occur once the research is undertaken, constraints of organizations, ethical considerations, voluntary nature of participation in experiments, and time available for the research. Any one or more of these items may be used by the researcher to justify compromises in ideal conditions for the experiment, and the reader must consider the impact of these constraints on the study, as well as possible alternative designs and procedures.

Data Analysis and Conclusions:
Experimental Studies

At this point the reader is interested in the results of the experiment, which are presented through statistical analysis of the data collected, interpretation of the findings, and conclusions inferred from the findings. The first task of the reader is to ascertain the appropriateness of the use of statistical controls which have been used in the analysis of the data, i.e., the way relevant variables which could not be controlled in the experimental situation are introduced as control variables in the testing of a hypothesis. Secondly, the reader should attempt to determine whether there is contamination in the process of data collection which leads to non-independent observations and built-in correlations. These factors are considered because they are relevant to the claims the researcher makes in regard to support for his research hypotheses. The reader then considers whether or not the statistical tests are appropriate for the data, i.e., whether assumptions of the statistical model are tenable (Blalock, 1960). The reader considers the way in which the author deals with findings in relation to his hypotheses, determining whether or not they support the hypotheses, and any qualifications which must be made in relation to the nature of the support. For example, the hypothesis may not have the same amount of support when potentially contingent variables are introduced as controls. The reader should be alert to the way in which the researcher deals with "negative" findings, i.e., those which do not support his hypothesis, to make sure they are not ignored or misinterpreted. In addition, the reader should note how the results are related to time factors, particularly in regard to whether the author has considered the persistence of effects over time. The reader should compare the data reported in tables to the claims made by the author in the text of the study report to determine the degree of consistency between these two locations of information. For example, the author may generalize beyond or without data, and the reader can check against this by examination of the data presented by the author.

As the reader views the author's conclusions, he should assess their internal consistency with respect to all phases of the research. The researcher should have achieved a test of his hypotheses, and the reader must distinguish between conclusions drawn from such a test and the implications of the findings. When the findings are not consistent, or straightforward, the reader must assess the plausibility of the inferences made by the researcher. In consideration of his findings and conclusions, the researcher may relate his study to other knowledge from the literature about the problem under investigation. He may also use his findings as a foundation for the development of new hypotheses regarding the study phenomenon, and for new ways of researching the problem.

At this point the reader should determine if the researcher has learned anything from the study that he didn't know previously. Does the study contribute to knowledge or ways of producing knowledge? More specifically, the reader asks to what extent the research has achieved the goals and purposes of the study stated in the problem formulation, and how the findings relate to previous research.

In following these guidelines for the evaluation of experimental research studies, the reader assesses a study in the context of its purposes and methods. Additional areas for evaluation may occur to the reader as he explores research methods texts, and as he gains experience in evaluating research studies. While use of the guidelines will likely reveal limitations and gaps in studies being evaluated, the reader should concentrate on the contributions made by the study through the development of knowledge and ways of producing knowledge.

To assist the reader in evaluating experimental studies, evaluation guidelines are now stated in the form of key questions.

Evaluation Questions: Experimental Studies

I. *Problem Formulation*

1. How does the author utilize the literature in conceptualizing the problem for study?

2. What major concepts are formulated for the study and how well are they defined conceptually and operationally?

3. What hypotheses are proposed for test in the experiment? What is the rationale for the inclusion of concepts in the hypotheses, and the predictions made in the hypotheses?

4. What assumptions are made by the author in regard to the selection of variables for study?

5. What are the independent and dependent variables proposed within the hypotheses, how are they operationalized, and are they conceptually and operationally independent?

6. What potentially influential variables are recognized by the author, and how are they handled, i.e., through assumptions or controls?

7. What methodological issues are raised by the author which are believed to be relevant to the testing of the hypothesis, and how does the author propose to handle the issues?

8. Are there conditions which prevent the manipulation of the independent variable, or of measurement of the effects on the dependent variable?

9. To what extent is the experimental design appropriate for investigating the problem of the study?

II. *Research Design and Data Collection*

1. In what ways does the experimental design include provisions for maximizing the internal validity of the experiment?

2. What assumptions are made in the design?

3. What variables are not controlled, but considered relevant to the study?

4. What alternative experimental designs might have been employed?

5. What sampling procedures were employed in the study? How were assignments made to experimental and control groups?

6. How were the data collected? To what degree were the data reliable and valid?

7. To what extent does the experimental design maximize external validity?

8. Was the independent variable manipulated successfully, and to what extent were the effects of measurement controlled or handled?

III. *Data Analysis and Conclusions*

1. Do the data provide evidence for testing of the study hypotheses?

2. Are the statistical tests employed appropriate to the design of the study and the problem under investigation?

3. To what extent are the hypotheses supported by the data?

4. Are the author's claims for the findings consistent with the data?

5. What are the author's principal conclusions, and are they consistent with the findings?

6. What are the implications of the study as defined by the author?

7. To what extent did the researcher accomplish the purposes set forth for the study?

GUIDELINES FOR EVALUATION OF
QUANTITATIVE-DESCRIPTIVE STUDIES

Problem Formulation: Quantitative-Descriptive Studies

Formulation of the problem for a quantitative-descriptive study will vary somewhat according to the sub-type in which the study is classified. If the study is concerned with hypothesis-testing, the reader should identify the study hypothesis, and consider the origin of the hypothesis. The problem formulation of a quantitative-descriptive hypothesis-testing study is illustrated in Gamson's (1966) study of reputation and resources in community politics. Gamson was concerned with the role individuals with reputation for influence play in relation to the outcome of community issues. One of his hypotheses states that it takes more effort to change the status quo than to maintain it, and he discusses the "natural advantage" thought to obtain in community groups who would maintain a present arrangement as against groups who would change facilities or services. In his problem formulation Gamson takes into account prior studies from the literature which deal with community power, leadership, bases of social power, influence, and persuasion, as well as ways of identifying reputational leaders. As with the experimental study, the reader should review the author's use of the literature and practical experiences in the identification and formulation of problems in quantitative-descriptive studies.

For studies which seek to discover relationships among variables or to locate facts, the reader should identify the major questions which guide the research and attempt to understand why particular variables are selected for study. In a study by Ripple and Alexander (1956) of motivation, capacity, and opportunity as related to the use of casework services, the major question for research concerned how a client's ability to use help was related to his continuance with a social agency. This research focus led the investigators to develop a problem classification scheme which permitted grouping clients with similar problems together. Their study formulation describes the rationale for the selection of variables, such as economic dislocation, intrafamilial conflict, and so forth, for inclusion in their problem classification scheme.

In all types of quantitative-descriptive studies, the reader should determine how well the variables for study are defined conceptually and whether the author has considered alternative definitions from previous research or theory. For example, in Ripple and Alexander's study, conceptual distinctions are made for situations characterized by external problems, and these distinctions are illustrated by case examples. The reader also determines how well the variables are defined operationally, i.e., in terms of measurements of the variables, so that they can be identified with indicators for the concepts. This clarifies the meanings of the concepts used in formulating the problem and also allows for replication by independent investigators. The reader must also consider whether or not the author offers sufficient evidence in regard to the reliability and validity of the measures being used.

For quantitative-descriptive studies with the purpose of hypothesis-testing, the reader should discern whether the author is trying to validate a hypothesis with implied cause-effect relations or to establish the existence of a relationship between selected variables. In regard to cause-effect relationships, the reader should identify the independent and dependent variables and consider evidence necessary to show support for a hypothesis. The reader should consider whether or not the author has conceptualized potentially contingent variables which may influence the relationship between the independent and dependent variables. To show cause-effect relations the independent variable must precede the dependent variable in time, and relevant "contingent" variables must be controlled.

In evaluating hypothesis-testing studies which include a series of hypotheses, the reader should determine what, if any, relationship exists among the hypotheses. They may be connected according to a theoretical scheme, according to a substantive area, or by some other accounting model. The reader should be alert to the possibility that a general hypothesis may be presented on an abstract level in the problem formulation, with hypotheses for testing presented elsewhere at a lower level of abstraction. The reader should ascertain the relationship among the hypotheses tested and the more general hypotheses which may have been introduced into the problem formulation statement. Hypotheses proposed for study should be considered in relation to the author's statement of the study problem to determine the degree of their correspondence.

Included in the researcher's formulation of the study problem should be a statement of major assumptions in regard to selection of variables, definitions of concepts, and measurement procedures. The reader should identify the explicit and implicit assumptions stated by the author. For example, Zander and Newcomb (1967) in their study of group levels of aspiration in United Fund Campaigns explicitly state the assumption that when a community fails to achieve its goal in a United Fund Campaign, the need of the community increases. The reader evaluates the reasonableness of such assumptions in terms of knowledge known about the study problem, and with respect to the purposes and methods of the research study. The reader then continues his evaluation by examining the research design and data collection aspects of the study.

Research Design and Data Collection:
Quantitative-Descriptive Studies

In classifying the study the reader has identified the particular subtype of quantitative-descriptive study being evaluated. In this context, he considers specific features of the research design of the study. Major consideration is given to problems of internal and external validity. Threats to validity for experimental studies are also relevant to studies which approximate experimentation. The reader should review these problems, as previously discussed in the section of guidelines for evaluating experiments, and ascertain the extent to which the author has attempted to handle them in the quantitative-descriptive study. However, the reader should recognize that the researcher using quasi-experimental designs will not be in a position to overcome some of the validity problems to the extent that it is possible with true experimental designs.

Since the author of a quantitative-descriptive study wishes to describe accurately relations among variables, provide accurate facts, and/or test hypotheses, rigorous sampling procedures are called for. The reader should determine the target population to which the author wishes to generalize and the units of analysis or behavior being studied, e.g., welfare recipients in Michigan. The procedures for sample selection should be identified, and the reader should look for evidence which indicates the representativeness of the sample obtained by the researcher. The essential task of the reader is to assess the generalizability of the results of the research from the actual sample studied. He does this by identifying the sampling procedures, by considering the author's stated problems in sampling, and by considering alternative procedures which could have been employed in the study.

Procedures for the collection of data, the kinds of data collected, and the nature of the data collected are now evaluated by the reader. Important factors to be taken into account are the extent to which the data are non-biased, systematic, and correspond to the major concepts of the study. In short, the researcher's efforts to establish the reliability and validity of the data collected should be evaluated. For example, Ripple and Alexander (1956) report on the agreement of research judges with caseworkers on 85 percent of the cases in which client problems are defined. Specific procedures for data collection should be identified, such as questionnaires, interview schedules, and participant observations. The reader should consider general problems connected with types of data collection, such as bias of the interviewer, wording and order of questions, effects of social desirability in responses, acquiescence response set, halo effects, and so forth. Matters such as these are discussed by Webb et al. (1966), and Campbell and Stanley (1963). The reader should seek to discover specific sources of bias, unreliability, and non-validity, and consider whether improvements in these areas could have been made, especially at minimal costs.

Data Analysis and Conclusions: Quantitative-Descriptive Studies

With respect to the author's analysis of his findings, it is important in evaluating quantitative-descriptive studies to ascertain whether the author is using statistical inference or descriptive statistics (Blalock, 1960). In studies using statistical inference, the reader determines if the author has specified desired levels of significance in advance of his data analysis, so that the development of hypotheses can be distinguished from the testing of *a priori* hypotheses. Of particular importance in quantitative-descriptive studies is the analysis of data by the provision of statistical controls regarding contingent variables, i.e., cross tabulations of the findings under conditions of control variables. The reader should consider to what extent the findings are potentially spurious. Spurious relations are discussed in Chapter 2, with a spurious association identified as one which can be explained by another variable introduced into the statistical analysis of data (Blalock, 1961, p. 84).

Depending on the sub-type of quantitative-descriptive study, the researcher's conclusions may be statements regarding the status of the stated hypothesis, descriptions of relationship between variables, or specification of variable characteristics. In each instance, these statements should be based on the data provided in the research. The reader should be alert to conclusions based on peripheral data, or inferences from the connection between the data and opinions, as they are likely to have the status of assumptions rather than hypotheses to be tested. For all studies the reader should distinguish between conclusions and implications, and he should determine if the author has been internally consistent in his use of concepts in the study. In addition, the reader should ascertain whether the author has answered the questions or tested the hypotheses he set out to examine in his study.

The researcher's presentation of data and conclusions should be characterized by impartial reporting, rather than an expression of his biases. This may be a particular problem when the findings are not straight-forward and the interpretation of findings is a matter of inferences made by the researcher. Finally, the researcher should relate his findings to current knowledge about the phenomenon under investigation. In this way the reader can assess the contribution the researcher makes to the understanding of the problem posed, and the meaning of the study for the utilization of knowledge for practice, theory, and research.

To assist the reader in evaluating quantitative-descriptive studies, evaluation guidelines can be stated in the form of key questions.

EVALUATION QUESTIONS:
QUANTITATIVE-DESCRIPTIVE STUDIES

I. *Problem Formulation*

1. How does the author utilize the literature in conceptualizing the problem for study?

2. What major concepts are formulated for the study and how well are they defined conceptually and operationally?

3. If the study has as its purpose the testing of hypotheses, what are the hypotheses, and what are the independent and dependent variables proposed by the author?

4. What assumptions are made by the author in regard to the selection of variables for study?

5. What potentially influential variables are recognized by the author, and how are they handled, i.e., through assumptions or controls?

6. To what extent is the quantitative-descriptive approach appropriate for investigating the problem for study?

II. *Research Design and Data Collection*

1. Could other alternative designs have been used more appropriately to carry out the purposes of the study?

2. If the study sought to test hypotheses, what efforts were made to approximate experimentation, and to maximize internal and external validity?

3. What sampling procedures were employed in the study?

4. How were the data specifically collected, and how were potential sources of bias taken into account?

5. To what extent did the author attempt to increase the reliability and validity of the measurements in the study?

III. *Data Analysis and Conclusions*

1. Does the author use descriptive statistics or statistics for inference in his analysis of the data, and is the choice of statistics appropriate to the data and the assumptions of the study?

2. If hypotheses are tested in the study, are they supported by the data?

3. Were cross tabulations introduced in analyzing the data in order to take account of potentially influential variables?

4. What are the author's principal conclusions? Are they consistent with the data?

5. What are the implications of the findings as defined by the author? Are they logically related to the data and to the conclusions stated by the author?

6. To what extent did the researcher accomplish the purposes set forth for the study?

GUIDELINES FOR EVALUATION OF EXPLORATORY STUDIES

Problem Formulation: Exploratory Studies

The problem formulation of an exploratory study varies in terms of the particular sub-type of exploratory research. For the combined exploratory-descriptive study, concentration is placed on the statement of the purposes of the study, the selection of variables to be studied, and some indication of the systematic procedures required to describe quantitatively the phenomenon under study. In studies which use specific data collection procedures for developing ideas, the focus of the problem formulation will be both on the problem of study and on data procedures proposed for the development of conceptual categories. In experimental manipulation studies which have exploratory purposes, researchers state the problem for study in terms of the variable to be manipulated, and the controls deemed necessary to ascertain the potential effects of the experimental variable on the presumed dependent variable.

For all the exploratory sub-types, the reader should be alert to the rationale given for conducting the exploratory study. Is the study being launched within some theoretical framework regarding the phenomenon under study? Is the investigator concerned with a practical problem for which he seeks to develop ideas, hypotheses, or measurements, for further and more systematic study? In either case, the reader should identify the major variables dealt with by the investigator, and consider the goals the researcher has in regard to these variables, such as conceptual modification, elaboration, and operational definitions. The reader should keep in mind that the requirements for conceptualization and operationalization of variables required for experimental and quantitative-descriptive studies do not hold for the exploratory study. However, since the exploratory study anticipates further research, efforts to quantify concepts and control relevant factors add to its value.

The reader notes the ways in which the relevant literature is employed in the researcher's problem formulation for exploratory studies. The reader is concerned with the extent to which relevant studies are cited, the ways in which the major concepts are defined, and the ways in which variables are measured. While the use of the literature is sometimes limited in exploratory studies, it is important that the reader identify whether or not the authors have searched the literature, and the extent to which they follow up on the relevant aspects of the literature cited in the study. The reader should consider any leads which the researcher gains in regard to sources of data, types of data, and uses of data relevant to the problem under investigation. For example, in a study by Faunce and Clelland (1967) of "Professionalization and Stratification Patterns in an Industrial Community," the authors extend a conceptual framework regarding community processes in order to take into account data from a number of community studies which deal with the division of labor within a community. They consider the implications of differences in patterns of division of labor for class, status, and power structures of the community. These concepts provide the framework for a community study utilizing a variety of sources of data.

The Faunce-Clelland study illustrates a combined exploratory-descriptive study, in which relatively systematic data collection procedures are proposed in the problem formulation. The study includes the measurement of a number of concepts suggested by the literature as relevant to an examination of the impact of professionalization on community processes. The goal of the researchers was to draw from a number of sources of data to explain changes over time in one community. This was expected both to increase the researcher's familiarity with the nature of community change and to refine propositions for further study beyond the confines of a single community.

As long as the purpose of a study is exploratory, any one of a number of methods may be employed, and the data proposed for collection may be both qualitative and quantitative in nature. In a study by Ayllon (1963) of "Intensive Treatment of Psychotic Behavior by Stimulus Satiation and Food Reinforcement," the patient's environment is manipulated in a mental hospital ward to demonstrate the effectiveness of behavioral modification treatment on the patient's behavior. The independent variables manipulated included towels and food, and the data collected were quantitative, e.g., records of frequency of behaviors such as stealing of food and the measurement of loss of weight. Selected laboratory principles regarding reinforcement were demonstrated in "successive experiments" with a single patient over time.

Our examples of exploratory studies thus far have been based on theoretical frameworks. Yet, in some cases the investigator has a concrete question in need of answer, or a problem for which there has been limited theoretical development. For example, in their study of hyperaggressive children, Goodrich and Boomer (1958) sought to explore the natural therapeutic situation by studying interactions between staff and patients. Their decision to proceed in this manner was based on a view that theoretical and technical issues were not sufficiently clear to undertake other study approaches, such as field or laboratory experiments. Goodrich and Boomer employed the critical incident technique with data gathered through interviews with staff members, and developed a system of concepts dealing with therapeutic intervention. An exploratory study may be carried out with the purpose of formulating a problem for future research. In such cases, the investigator may focus on the requisites for problem formulation, such as identification of concepts, ideas, and facts which are relevant to the development of a problem statement as the foundation for further research.

By its very nature an exploratory study is likely to depend heavily on assumptions. The reader should identify the assumptions the researchers make in regard to their definitions of concepts, their measurements proposed, and the selection of variables to be investigated. In the Goodrich and Boomer (1958, p. 208) study referred to above, the authors made the assumption that treatment of children by skilled staff results in behavior changes in the children. They also assumed that "one important class of 'change agents' is the observable transactions between staff and children." Assumptions may also be introduced in the conclusions and implications of the findings.

Research Design and Data Collection: Exploratory Studies

The problem formulation of the exploratory study provides a context for evaluating the specific design features proposed for the study. The reader should consider the advantages and disadvantages of the sub-types of exploratory studies for reaching exploratory goals in general, as well as in relation to the particular study under evaluation. In evaluating the exploratory study the reader should examine the kinds and sources of the data obtained, and the extent to which the variables selected by the researcher are consistent with the purposes of the study. For example, in the Faunce-Clelland (1967) community study, the authors do not rely entirely on census data, but extend their sources to structured interviews with selected samples of occupational groups, as well as including loosely structured interviews with community leaders.

In regard to sampling design, the reader recognizes that the sampling plan need not be rigorous, as required in other major types of research. However, the reader should determine if the sample selection is pertinent to the purpose of the study. The reader should be aware of the relationship of sampling to the development of ideas for future research. Thus, the reader may find that sampling appears to be related more to groups or units of analysis which will support the author's previously held ideas, rather than to his development of new ideas. This is likely to occur in instances where the sample is purposive or highly selective. The study cited by Faunce and Clelland illustrates a range of sampling techniques, including selection of occupations for study, selection of samples of professionals, technicians, and hourly workers, and selection of community leaders. The first three samples were drawn randomly from lists of employees of a chemical processing firm, and only city residents were included. The latter group included 29 community leaders representative of major appointive and elective positions in the community. This study illustrates the inclusion of non-rigorous and rigorous (occupational samples) sampling, with the latter providing more empirical support for the author's ideas than the former. In the combined exploratory-descriptive study, some rigorous sampling is required.

The reader should consider how alternative modes of sampling could have served to minimize potential bias in the study, although it is recognized that bias cannot entirely be eliminated in such a study. To illustrate, the Faunce and Clelland study presents data for which they recognize bias in responses, as their samples were not drawn from the whole community but only from selected occupational groups.

The reader should consider the kinds of data collected, both qualitative and quantitative, and the ways in which the data were collected, e.g. participant observation, interviewing, questionnaire, or from available records. The reader should consider any reliability and validity checks the researcher makes in relation to the kinds of data collected. The reader should keep in mind the limitations of the study in regard to checking these aspects of the data collected, and consider ways in which reliability and validity could be introduced into the current or future studies of the phenomenon.

Data Analysis and Conclusions: Exploratory Studies

The reader should first determine the extent to which the findings of the study are sufficient in terms of the purposes of the study. In the development of hypotheses, did the author already have hypotheses and seek evidence for their support, or did he develop hypotheses from the study? Are the findings sufficient to warrant future study based on a hypothesis developed from ideas of the study? The reader should consider the initial biases of the researcher, and the extent to which the presentation of the findings is related to such biases.

In studies which seek further understanding of concepts, the reader should determine if the concepts have been modified, clarified, and to what extent they can be operationalized. When hypotheses are developed, the reader examines them in terms of their researchability. Are the independent and dependent variables identifiable, independent of each other, and amenable to operationalization?

The reader considers if the researcher's conclusions and inferences are consistent with data in the study. If the author draws implications, it should be determined if the researcher distinguishes potential implications from conclusions. When authors introduce findings and discussions from the literature, the reader should be alert to the ways in which the researcher makes use of such literature in relation to his own findings.

The reader should not only examine the ways in which the authors use their data, but the ways in which they could have made additional analyses within the purposes of the study. Since in some cases exploratory studies will also have purposes which are non-exploratory in nature, such as a description of accurate relations among variables, the reader should be concerned with the degree to which sufficient information is available to allow for replication.

Finally, the reader examines the extent to which the author goes beyond his data to conceptualize the phenomenon under study, to formulate hypotheses, and to clarify and extend the meaning of concepts, so as to contribute to current understanding and to future research endeavors. Thus, in Parnicky and Brown's (1964) study of institutionalized retardates, the authors indicate the possibility suggested by their study of developing an index of readiness for placement of patients into the community. This would enable testing of hypotheses developed in their exploratory study, e.g., "Success in community placement is facilitated as positive attitudes toward community living are relatively stronger than those toward residential living" (Parnicky and Brown, 1964, p. 83).

In the light of the foregoing considerations for evaluating exploratory studies, the following summary of guideline questions are presented to assist the reader.

Evaluation Questions: Exploratory Studies

I. *Problem Formulation*

1. What rationale is given by the authors for conducting the study? Is the study concerned with a theoretical or practical problem, or with both?

2. How does the author utilize the literature, and previous experience, in conceptualizing the problem for study?

3. What major concepts are formulated for the study and how well are they defined conceptually and operationally?

4. What assumptions are made by the author in regard to the selection of variables for study?

5. What sources of data are considered by the authors, and what types of data are sought for the study?

6. To what extent is the exploratory approach appropriate for the investigation of the problem posed for study?

II. *Research Design and Data Collection*

1. Could other alternative designs have been used more appropriately to carry out the purposes of the study?

2. What sampling procedures were employed in the study? What alternative plans would have been appropriate?

3. What specific kinds of data were collected?

4. To what extent were potential biases minimized in the collection of data?

5. To what extent did the author attempt to increase the reliability and validity of the measurements in the study?

III. *Data Analysis and Conclusions*

1. What are the findings of the study? Are they derived from qualitative, quantitative, or both kinds of data?

2. If statistics are employed in the study, are they appropriate to the data analyzed, and to the purposes of the study?

3. What concepts, hypotheses, and ideas for future research are developed from the findings of the study?

4. Are concepts developed consistent with the findings, and to what extent are new concepts developed, and old concepts modified or expanded?

5. Are the hypotheses developed researchable, i.e., stated in testable form?

6. In what ways could the authors have used their available data for additional analyses, and for development of other ideas consistent with their purposes?

7. Do the concepts and hypotheses developed in the study stem from the findings, from other literature, or from the initial biases of the authors?

8. To what extent have the authors achieved the purposes of the study?

Chapter 4

Utilization of Research:
Principles and Guidelines

As a consumer of research, the social work practitioner is particularly interested in how to make use of the findings of a study in his own practice, or to get new ideas that he or others in the profession can translate into practice. The previous chapters have dealt with issues to which the sophisticated reader of research must be alert so that he can usefully classify a study and evaluate how well it was carried out in reference to its objectives. The purpose of this chapter is to consider issues that bear on utilization of reported research. By "utilization," we mean the application of knowledge gained from the research to the professional objectives of the social worker or of the social work profession. Unlike questions about classification and evaluation, questions about utility for social work require the reader to consider *relevance* of the research to goals of social work practice. The context of the reader as a social worker as well as the qualities of the research itself are important for this chapter.

We will briefly review some of the literature dealing with frameworks for utilization of research in order to present a general perspective on utilization. Then, we will develop in some detail the guidelines for the reader to follow when considering utility of published research. Finally, we present special considerations for using the guidelines for each type of research study previously distinguished—experimental, quantitative-descriptive, and exploratory.

UTILIZATION FRAMEWORKS: AN OVERVIEW

There are many general discussions of the application of scientific knowledge to practical problems (Gouldner and Miller, 1965; Likert and Lippitt, 1953), and some discussions of issues presented when practitioners seek to use scientific knowledge (Bartlett *et al.*, 1964). There are, however, few explicit analyses of ways to judge the usefulness of research knowledge. A number of papers deal with utilization of knowledge in social work and we draw on them in developing the perspective of this chapter.

In *Behavioral Science for Social Workers* (1967a), Thomas discusses the types of contributions behavioral science makes to social work and he considers, also, the components of social work to which aspects of behavioral science may be applicable. In addition to a scientific stance, behavioral science contributes, Thomas notes, (a) conceptual tools, (b) substantive findings, and (c) methods of research. These components are all evident in the research process and hence constitute points of attention for the reader of research. *Conceptualization*—the mode of reasoning as distinguished from results of research or methods of doing research—contributes to clarification of concepts, their operationalization, and their use in hypotheses and theories. Thomas notes the need to conceptualize the "very process of utilizing behavioral science knowledge." He says:

. . . Both the increasing knowledge of behavioral science and its selective applicability to social work necessarily compel a conceptualization of what contributes to social work and what does not. . . . Behavioral science knowledge must be selected for use, assimilated by educators and practitioners, amalgamated into the larger fabric of social work knowledge, introduced into educational and agency contexts, and subsequently evaluated and tested. This process, which begins with selection from the heartlands of the academic disciplines of behavioral science and terminates in the front lines of practice in the social work profession, is a complex intellectual, practical, and institutional transition in the engineering of behavioral science knowledge . . . (Thomas, 1967a, p. 7).

Substantive knowledge—including the insights and sharpened observations from exploratory studies as well as empirical generalizations aimed for by experimental studies—constitutes, of course, what research is all about. Reduced uncertainty about aspects of the world with which social workers must deal is the basis for taking the next steps in assessing in what ways the increased knowledge may be useful. A further contribution—*research methods*—is important not only because the methods of behavioral science research are applicable to most problems of social work knowledge, but also because research design and techniques of data gathering and analysis sometimes suggest procedures directly applicable to practice. For example, the experimental manipulation of the single case, systematically pursued, may increase both the deliberate provision of a service and its knowledge-producing consequences. Or, for another example, the technique of sociometric analysis can, and has, become an instrument by which to structure groups.

Just as such general features of behavioral science can be differentiated, so Thomas suggests component features of social work as objects of analysis for which the contributions of behavioral science are applicable. He lists the following points of attention when applying social science: (Thomas, 1967a, pp. 10–11)

1. the clientele of social welfare services
2. the social workers and related professionals
3. the programs of welfare
4. the services provided, including direct practice
5. the agencies and organizations through which services are offered and programs are implemented
6. the education and training of welfare workers
7. the research in social work
8. the knowledge of the profession of social work
9. the institution of social welfare

Such categories describe topics of interest in the literature of social work and social work research. Their listing calls attention to the need to identify what it is about social work we wish to apply knowledge to.

Thomas contributes further to a general framework for utilizing knowledge by proposing criteria for selecting useful knowledge from behavioral science (Thomas, 1964). Distinguishing the levels of social practice as concerned with the individual, the group, the organization, the community, and the society, he notes that scientific knowledge is useful to the extent that it has *content relevance* to the subject matter of social work. That subject matter is divided by Thomas into: normal behavior; abnormality and deviancy; growth, maturation, and change; and the helping process. In addition, knowledge is useful, Thomas says, to the extent that it has *power* (i.e., represents valid empirical generalizations) , and to the extent that the variables used have *referent features* (i.e. accessibility, manipulability, cost and ethical suitability) that link them meaningfully to the world of social work. The framework Thomas has sketched is a basis for our perspective on utilization in this chapter. Thomas has applied his analysis to points of potential contribution from social-psychological literature as it bears on the inter-personal helping relationship (in Lazarsfeld *et al.*, 1967, pp. 162–70) . In this same paper on "Social Work and Social Welfare" there are further examples of application of knowledge from sociology to the organizational and the community level that also illustrate aspects of a framework for utilization (Meyer *et al.*, in Lazarsfeld, 1967) . Among other pertinent sources, Kadushin (1964) presents a system which accepts the three areas of the typical social work curriculum as objects to which knowledge is pointed: social policy and administration, growth and behavior, and social work methods (casework, group work, community organization) ; and he illustrates how this facilitates the orderly assessment of useful knowledge about one area of social work concern: homemaker services. He does not, however, develop specific criteria, as Thomas does, for selecting knowledge. A conference sponsored by the National Association of Social Workers looked at possible contributions of social science theory and research to social work, considering role and reference group theory, organizational theory, and small group theory (Kogan, 1960a) . The thrust of the considerations was, however, the location of applicable concepts. Beyond illustrating that some concepts generated in social science theory and research have utility, the discussions do not go far toward clarifying criteria for utilizing knowledge.

A growing literature of reviews of research pertinent to particular areas of social work is suggestive of issues of utilization although it provides little in the way of specific criteria. Notable among these is *Five Fields of Social Service: Reviews of Research* (Maas, 1966) which attempts to present the knowledge from research that can be drawn on for use in the following areas: family services, public welfare, child welfare, neighborhood centers, and social planning. These reviews do not address problems of using knowledge directly, but they do identify substantive problems and bodies of research that are pertinent, suggesting limitations and gaps in research knowledge for social work. Other reviews of research deal with particular substantive areas of social work, or particular theoretical or methodological problems of research for social work. Among the areas so considered are child welfare (Fanshel, 1962a, and Norris and Wallace, 1965), social welfare administration (Fanshel, 1962b), manpower problems (Schwartz, 1966), and poverty (Herzog, 1967). There have been reviews and criticisms of research on special problems related to social work, such as the use of judgments in research (NASW: 1959), the clinical judgment process (Tripodi and Miller, 1966, and Bieri *et al.*, 1966), and behavior modification (Krasner and Ullman, 1965). Likewise, reviews of research on social work methods—for example, casework (Shyne, 1962) and group work (Silverman, 1966)—have been suggestive.

A sense of some problems of utilization of social science theory and research can be obtained from compilations of readings directed to social work readers, and also from counterpart compilations of papers directed to social scientists. Representative of the former are *Behavioral Science for Social Workers* (Thomas, 1967a), *Social Perspectives on Behavior* (Stein and Cloward, 1958), and *Social Welfare Institutions* (Zald, 1965). Representative of the latter are *Psychotherapy Research* (Stollak *et al.*, 1966), *Uses of Sociology* (Lazarsfeld *et al.*, 1967), *Applied Sociology* (Gouldner and Miller, 1965), and *The Planning of Change* (Bennis *et al.*, 1961). A general comment made by Gouldner and Miller characterizes much of these considerations of usefulness of social science for practice by noting that it is usually in the form of "concepts rather than the generalized propositions of pure social science" (Gouldner and Miller, 1965, p. 7).

Some more general discussions of the relationships of social science and social practice have pointed up issues relevant to criteria for utilization. Of particular pertinence are papers by Greenwood (1955, 1961) on social work and social science, and by Gouldner (1956, 1957). The latter's paper, "Theoretical Requirements of the Applied Social Sciences," in particular points out that criteria of manipulability, accessibility, economy, and ethical suitability are crucial. This point was further developed by Thomas and it was suggested earlier by Hyman (1955) when he noted that " . . . a non-manipulable determinant demonstrated to have a high correlation with a phenomenon is generally of less significance than a manipulable determinant demonstrated to have only a moderate correlation" (Hyman, 1955, p. 354). Zetterberg provides a suggestive lead by noting "three fallacies" in most discussions of how academic social science can help practitioners: the fallacy that social science is put to use simply by popularizing its content, the fallacy that the content of the knowledge must match exactly the content of the problem faced by the practitioner, and the fallacy that the number of social problems with which the practitioner is concerned is so very large that social science cannot address them all (Zetterberg, 1962, pp. 39–43).

Discussions of how social scientists can engage in the application of their knowledge sometimes contain other suggestions that contribute to the development of criteria for assessing the usefulness of research. A selection of papers dealing with aspects of deliberate efforts to produce change in social situations (Bennis et al., 1961) include considerations of training, consulting, and research as mechanisms of application. Zetterberg devotes two chapters of his short book to consultation by scholars and social scientists to practitioners. Likert and Lippitt (in Festinger and Katz, 1953), discuss various mechanisms for introducing knowledge to practitioners in a number of professions. Assuming three sources of motivation for the consumer of knowledge—problem sensitivity, a sense of potentiality for change, and willingness to innovate—they suggest the following mechanisms: use of the scientist as consultant in conferences on research application or research review; publication of scientific literature expressly in form for application; and in-service seminars of practitioners with social scientists. In the sort of literature here discussed, the scope of useful knowledge is recognized as broader than the empirical generalizations and findings of research, and this reminds us that useful knowledge from research may come from types of studies intended to explore and describe as well as to test hypotheses. This viewpoint is basic in the perspective on utilization developed for this book.

We have made extensive reference to literature as an introduction to this chapter in order to supply the reader with sources he may pursue in further interest in the problems of relating social science and social work, and also to indicate the foundations of our own criteria of utilization of reported research. By noting some points by others, we suggest the direction we take in developing our perspective.

Utilization: General Perspective

We are interested in developing practical guidelines to help the social worker decide how useful a piece of research is. Therefore, we are less concerned with the ideal characteristics of useful research than with providing a perspective that encourages the research reader to maximize the potential usefulness of the research by judging what it may contribute as well as where its limits are. In general terms, we view different kinds of research as differentially useful, and we view usefulness as a judgment arising from the research reader's recognition of the broadest range of social work interests. Two questions frame the problem of utilization: "What knowledge does the research offer" and "What activity of social work practice does it concern?"

With respect to the kinds of knowledge research may offer, we do not limit our interest to the empirical generalizations of tested validity for which science strives. These can be, of course, of the greatest importance and usefulness in some instances, but they may be less valuable for the practitioner in other instances than research intended to clarify concepts, establish or measure relationships between concepts, or develop hypotheses for subsequent research on some phenomenon. All the following kinds of knowledge have potential usefulness: (1) "Facts," i.e., verified observations about some phenomenon identified by a concept. For example, the number of families in a community willing to accept a foster child may be a "fact" of considerable relevance to an agency that provides placements for children, and to welfare planning bodies trying to assess the need for residential facilities. Like other research knowledge, a study that provides "facts" must be evaluated for its validity, as we have indicated in Chapter 3. (2) *Concepts* point us to the phenomena we call "facts." We have defined concepts as verbal symbols, or ideas, abstracted from experience (Chapter 1), and in this sense concepts themselves may be useful even before we have valid information about the phenomena to which they refer. They may sensitize the practitioner to variables that could affect his practice, e.g., social class, as in studies of mental illness (Hollingshead and Redlich, 1958), or role performance, as in studies of client continuance in treatment (Ripple, 1955). (3) *Hypotheses* that relate two or more concepts to one another and make predictions about the relationship may also be useful. For example, the hypothesis that role satisfaction of social workers will be related to the discrepancy between their ideal definition of what their role activities should be and their actual role performance gives us a way of approaching some problems of supervision of social workers and of agency structure and management (Billingsley, 1964). (4) When hypotheses have stood the test of empirical examination and acquired relatively high degrees of confidence that they represent what can be observed, we may view them as *empirical generalizations* within the context they describe. Such knowledge has great potential usefulness because it provides the most valid understanding available of phenomena of interest. We do not assume that such scientific knowledge is eternally "true" but only that it has relatively a higher degree of certainty than other knowledge.

Since different kinds of research offer different kinds of potentially useful knowledge, it is helpful for the research reader to identify the purpose of the research and the strategy it employs. Our classification of research as exploratory, quantitative-descriptive, and experimental facilitates this identification. In general, exploratory studies are more relevant to the generation, application, and modification of concepts and hypotheses and less relevant to the establishment of empirical generalizations. We should not ignore, however, the concepts and hypotheses in research that is quantitative-descriptive or experimental; such concepts and hypotheses may constitute useful knowledge with respect to some aspect of practice along with the specific findings themselves. The "facts" and established relationships of quantitative-descriptive studies allow other potential uses. Likewise, experimental research offers still other possible uses. We are unwilling to exclude any kind of scientific research from consideration for its usefulness because of the methods it uses or its purpose.

We also take a broad view of social work practice for which we seek useful knowledge in research studies. We believe that the same kind of knowledge—e.g., a clear concept, or an empirical generalization—may find use across the range of social work practice interests. Therefore, the user of research should not narrow his definition of potential value by assuming that the research is applicable only to one practice method (e.g., community organization, or casework), or to one field of social welfare (e.g., public assistance, or mental health). Assessing the usefulness of research is a creative activity in which the user actively looks for the implications of the research in those areas of his practice which he seeks to inform with new knowledge. As Zetterberg points out, it is a fallacy to assume that the only useful research is that which studies the particular, concrete question the practitioner faces at a given moment.

Two examples may underline the point. An exploratory study that extends and clarifies the concept of community power structure (Bonjean, 1963), may be useful to the caseworker and group worker in understanding factors affecting availability of resources for clients; it may be useful to agency administrators seeking to introduce new services; it may be useful to social welfare

planners who want to alter the balance of services in the community. The fact that the exploratory study might be made only in
one community, that some of the observations are qualitative judgments, that historical events are noted as important in establishing
the pattern actually found—all these may caution the user against
expecting his own community to be accurately represented in the
study. But insofar as the reader is made more perceptive about
factors he might himself become aware of in his own situation, the
research can be said to have usefulness.

A second example may be an experimental study (Poser,
1966) testing the efficacy of group therapy when it is provided for
schizophrenic patients by professional and lay therapists. If the
findings favor lay therapists and the research has a high degree of
internal validity, this empirically tested generalization may be useful and suggestive to practitioners in various locations within social
work. It may alert the caseworker or group worker to qualities in
treatment efforts associated with characteristics other than their
training; the agency administrator may have reason to ask himself
whether he can increase his agency's effectiveness by adding lay staff
members; the social work educator may look more carefully at what
is trained in and trained out of social work students; the welfare
planner concerned with manpower will have his own obvious interests in the research. The same practitioners should not, of course,
ignore the limitations that reduce the applicability of the findings
to their particular interests, for example, that this is only a single
study, made with schizophrenic patients and not with their types of
clients, that particular kinds of persons were used as lay therapists
and so forth. The point is that practitioners with varied concerns can
take something from the research that may be useful to them.

Although knowledge from a given piece of research may have
relevance to all levels of social work practice, it may be more relevant to one level. Thus the concept of community power is more
salient to the community organizer than to the caseworker; and
evidence of the effects of tokens as rewards for changing behavior of
children is more salient to the caseworker or group worker. The
practitioner's target of intervention, and his tools of intervention,
will affect the use he can make of knowledge from a particular
research study. But irrelevance and nonusefulness are not to be
assumed about a piece of research for any practice area because it is
more relevant to another area.

A perspective on utilization requires a brief statement of our
view of the nature of social work. Social work includes a range of
functions, and its practitioners work in a variety of jobs. Social work

draws the knowledge it needs from many sources: academic disciplines of the social and behavioral sciences such as psychology, sociology, economics, and others; other helping professions such as medicine, psychiatry, law, public health, education, and others; accumulated experience and systematic study by social workers themselves of their clientele, programs and processes of intervention to effect changes in keeping with a system of values. For our purposes, it is not necessary to delimit what social work is so much as to indicate the scope of its interest in knowledge derived from research under a wide range of auspices. We may quote from the bulletin of the School of Social Work at The University of Michigan, to provide a description of social work:

"Social Work Objectives, Settings and Methods

"Modern society has established a wide variety of social welfare programs and services directed toward enhancing the social functioning of individuals. Some of the programs promote well-being through providing needed resources, or seek to restore disturbed or disadvantaged individuals to normal functioning. Others are directed toward planning and improving social services or alleviating social problems.

"These services are sometimes classified according to types of social problems and/or client groups, commonly referred to as fields of practice. Thus, there are agencies which deal with mental health problems, medical problems, income maintenance problems, marital discord, disturbed parent-child relationships, and other services to children or the aged, services to juvenile delinquents or adult offenders (corrections). These agencies may be public or private, sectarian or non-sectarian. They provide institutional or non-institutional services, or through legislative or other action, work to improve standards or to modify conditions which promote problems.

"Social workers have been assigned heavy responsibilities in these programs through the practice of casework, group work, community organization, research, social welfare administration, and social welfare policy development. All of these methods are helping processes aimed at solving personal and social problems affecting individuals, groups, communities, and society. There is a common core of knowledge and values essential in all social work methods. Methods differ primarily in regard to the special skills needed according to whether the objective is to change the individual, the community, the organization, or public social policy.

"Workers in social treatment (casework and/or group work) provide service to people involved in stressful life situations for the purpose of helping them to achieve better social and emotional adjustments. The service is offered through interviews with individuals, with families, with others on behalf of clients, and through small groups to achieve desired changes in client behavior, attitudes, and social relations.

"Community organization workers help to improve services for people in trouble and facilitate planning and action to prevent social ills. They foster team work among groups, and gather information on social change efforts. Social work researchers engage in fact finding and experimentation which provide a basis for the development of practice methods and social policy.

"Social welfare administrators in both top executive and beginning administrative assistant and supervisory posts participate in operating and strengthening social welfare programs. In such positions as program or policy analyst or social legislation advisor, persons trained in this method also participate in shaping social policy relating to health and welfare concerns.

"All methods of practice are used with all age groups, in all types of settings, and all fields of practice. Both caseworkers and group workers practice as psychiatric social workers, as well as in welfare departments, settlements, hospitals, child guidance clinics, and institutions for emotionally disturbed or delinquent children. Community organization, research, and administration practitioners likewise may elect to work in mental health services, leisure-time activities, health facilities, child welfare, or any of the other programs or fields. In some positions social workers participate as members of a professional team with a doctor, psychologist, nurse, religious advisor, teacher, or other appropriate specialists."

With such a broad conception of functions and activities, it is not surprising that knowledge considered relevant to social work is diverse. No single social worker could hope to master all of it and hence specializations within social work focus on particular parts of the professional knowledge base, and on particular modes of intervention and helping. Research from within social work and from social science disciplines is a basic source of knowledge. Our efforts in this book are to guide evaluation and utilization of research that is appearing in social work journals, and in psychology and sociology journals. These are prime sources of knowledge for practitioners although we do not mean to exclude the research literature of the related professions and the other social sciences. We believe the same principles can be useful wherever scientific research is examined.

We particularly emphasize the view that competence of social workers must rest as much on sound knowledge from theory and research as on practice experience. This is a widely held view but few practitioners, as Rosenblatt reports in his study in New York (Rosenblatt, 1968), use knowledge from research or rate it as helpful. We believe this results partly from the fact that social work training has not included deliberate instruction in the use of research.

If the reader wishes to test the proposition that social science research and theory do, indeed, have pertinence to the practice of social workers in quite direct and concrete ways, he can examine as examples a recent publication of the Council on Social Work Education, *The Socio-Behavioral Approach and Applications to Social Work* (Thomas, 1967a). In that series of papers the reader can find illustrations of the direct application of some aspects of learning theory to inducing changes in clients, of the relevance of behavioral theory in administration, and of its implications in community practice as well as a consideration of the requisites in agency organization for its use. Thus a variety of uses of a research based scientific theory are exemplified, with differential uses at different levels and for different fields.

We have shown earlier (Chapter 2) that social work journals are increasingly reporting research. There is an evident increase as well in the interest of social work in social science research. In recognition of this trend and in the conviction that social workers need to make increasing use of a broad range of research literature reported in journals and monographs, the general guidelines in keeping with our perspective on utilization are inclusive.

UTILIZATION: SOME GENERAL PROBLEMS AND THE KEY QUESTIONS

The paradox for the practitioner who would utilize research knowledge is that the more he already knows about the subject of a study the more useful it will be for him. This is not surprising since it is only a re-affirmation of the observation that knowledge is cumulative for the learner and that the base from which he learns determines the level he can attain. A social worker who has a good grasp of the substantive and methodological problems and the previous work done in an area on which research is reported will be able to assess it more fully, to recognize what it adds and where it falls short of other studies. Therefore, to a very real degree the utilization of research is benefited by the reading of more and more research.

What does prior familiarity with research methods and the substantive area of a piece of research provide for the reader? First, a familiarity with methodological questions and a more ready skill in evaluating the research. Second, a familiarity with what has previously been found through research on the subject, including the ways the concepts have been defined and operationalized, the

results of various ways of formulating the problem, and the generalizations that are in the making on the subject or are awaiting more
rigorous test. Third, a sense of the unanswered questions about the
topic which allows a given piece of research to be recognized as a
replication of prior research or as a fresh attack on some aspect of
the problem. Familiarity helps the more learned research reader
decide how seriously to take the research report that is before him.

We do not mean to discourage the less informed reader by noting
the advantages of prior knowledge. Such knowledge can be
acquired by reading and the social worker who spends the energy
reading research articles regularly for a few months will soon find
himself locating research that fits the context of his growing knowledge. Furthermore, a little practice at reading, evaluating and utilizing research reports will show the practitioner—often to his sur-
prise—that his training and experience generate questions on which
published research often bears. Then, his reading of research ceases
to be casual, forced, and disconnected and begins to cumulate. This
is the direction of sophistication in the knowledge base for his
practice.

There are a number of handicaps that the social work practitioner may feel when he begins to use research. Unfamiliar vocabulary is one, and he may have to work at understanding the terms
used in formulating problems and stating hypotheses and theoretical contexts. An abstract, rather than a concrete, statement of the
problem may be another handicap since much scientific research is
put at theoretical levels in the attempt to see the general issue
whereas the practitioner often starts at the opposite pole, seeking
the unique and concrete as his primary question. These two
approaches are often not so far apart: the practitioner can readily
recognize, for example, that his client's distress about her husband's
"irresponsibility" may be visualized in the more abstract context of
"role relationships" used as a concept in a research study. Such a
conceptualization does not fully describe the concrete behaviors
that the practitioner observes; it can seldom do so. This is why the
prior knowledge and experience of the practitioner invariably form
the context for his assessment of what a research study will contribute to his handling of a problem. The question is whether, and
in what ways, visualizing the general problem of role relationships
contributes new and additional understandings that can be used in
his practice. It is in this sense that research utilization is a creative
endeavor, not passive absorption.

In our view, the practitioner should approach a research report
with an open sense of inquiry, just as the researcher should
approach the problem he studies. This does not call for the aban-

donment of the theoretical perspective that the practioner has been trained to bring to his work, or that he has developed through his experience. It calls only for accepting the research in its own terms so that it may be evaluated and utilized to expand the practitioner's knowledge for practice.

The practitioner should not expect, furthermore, that all research that he recognizes as useful can be immediately put to use even if he is satisfied that it would improve his work. The use of new knowledge is constrained by conditions other than its applicability. Among these conditions are the restrictions of agency or organizational setting in which the practitioner works, both in the formal or permissive sense and in the sense of providing the structural supports (resources, personnel arrangements, external linkages) to facilitate a change in practice (*see* Sarri and Vinter, 1967). Not all uses in practice of what is learned from research necessarily call for drastic changes in the practitioner's work. Indeed, some research will strengthen and confirm the basis of his current practice; some will call practices into question or stimulate ideas for limited changes mostly within the control of the practitioner. Nevertheless, innovations in practice that use research knowledge require the practitioner to be aware of their implications in the operating situation.

Luxurious detachment, necessary to allow concentration and imaginative reading of the research, should not represent isolation. The objective is utilization, not merely understanding. The practitioner should guard against several temptations. One is the temptation to lose sight of his own practice situation, as already mentioned. Another temptation is to confuse ideas stimulated by a piece of research with tested knowledge. Creative imagination is necessary to recognize implications of the research for use, but we warn against accepting with equal certainty all research, produced by any type of research strategy. Proper evaluation is an essential prerequisite to proper utilization. The dangers of these temptations will be progressively reduced as the social work practitioner becomes more skilled in reading research by reading more of it.

The guidelines that are presented in the following section are directed to the key questions the research reader should ask himself about any research he considers for utilization. These questions are applicable to all types of research we have classified as experimental, quantitative-descriptive, and exploratory. The key questions are:

1. Should the research report be read at all?
2. To what aspect of social work is the research relevant?

3. What knowledge content of the research may be useful?
4. How useful can the research knowledge be for practice?
5. What types of uses can be made of the research?

GENERAL GUIDELINES FOR UTILIZATION OF RESEARCH

1. *Should the Research Report Be Read At All?*

In Chapter 1 we considered this question in some detail. Its restatement here is only to remind the research utilizer that he must answer for himself. The temptation to answer in the negative may be strong for the less experienced research reader, because the effort involved in reading research requires considerable concentration. Furthermore, the sense of relevancy is cultivated by recognizing the more general theoretical context, the more abstract level at which a problem becomes pertinent beyond its immediate empirical referents. Such a sense comes with experience in reading research. What may be a labored effort and a troublesome question about relevance of a research report becomes in time a matter of discriminating judgment. The lingering sense that an unread research report might be just what the practitioner needs, or in contrast that the effort to read an article was wasted, soon dissipates with more reading.

The decision to read a research report is affected by the judgment that it is relevant and making this judgment involves all the other key questions that have been noted above.

2. *To What Aspect of Social Work Is the Research Relevant?*

The principle of "content relevance" of the research is the theme that runs through the answer to this question. We noted earlier the work of Thomas (1964, 1967) on the subject of selecting applicable knowledge from behavioral science. We adapt his analysis for guidelines to help the reader place a research study within the activities and interests that make up social work.

Any scheme for representing the various aspects of social work will be incomplete, or excessively complex, and its categories will be imprecise and overlapping. Therefore the scheme we propose should direct the research reader to sectors within which he should make more refined discriminations. His objective should be to locate to his own satisfaction the place in social work to which the research is relevant. As with other guidelines, only the leading questions are asked.

The framework of our scheme is indicated by the following questions:

a. What objects of social work interest or activity does the research pertain to?

b. Does the research pertain to current or potential objects of social work?

c. From what value perspective are the objects of social work viewed?

d. At what level are the objects of social work viewed?

e. To what purposes of social work does the research pertain?

a. THE OBJECTS OF SOCIAL WORK INTEREST OR ACTIVITY. The social work enterprise can be visualized as directed toward three inter-related classes of objects: *recipients,* the *process of serving,* and the *purveyance of services.* "Recipients" are not merely the individuals whom social workers try to help but may also be collectivities (e.g., groups, organizations) and aggregates (e.g., children, the mentally ill). The "processs of serving" as a social work activity includes what is often referred to as "the helping process," "treatment," or "therapy," but we use a more inclusive term to avoid clinical con-notations only. The agencies, institutions, programs, and other social organizations, as well as the professional and non-professional personnel involved in providing social welfare services, make up the system of "purveyance of services."

A research study will rarely be applicable only to one of these objects of social work. Studies of recipients are often studies of clients, i.e., of recipients of some helping process in some system of purveyance. For example, the decisions of unmarried mothers to keep their babies or place them for adoption may be studied in the caseload of an agency (as in Meyer *et al.,* 1956) ; the adjustment of young adults may be focussed on their wartime residential nursery experiences (as in Maas, 1963). Sometimes, the research is fairly clear in its location. For example, a study of correlates of crime (as in Bacon *et al.,* 1963) or a study of stratification of a community (as in Faunce and Clelland, 1967) —both study recipients but in neither case *individuals* as recipients. A study by laboratory experi-ment of the observational process in casework is an example of research on the helping process (as in Miller, 1958). Using this scheme, the research reader can usually determine the *primary* object to which the research is directed, noting as well the other objects to which it is secondarily directed.

Locating the content of a study by its applicability to an object of social work interest is different from deciding the purpose of the research so as to classify it as a type of research. The purpose and method may be exploratory, or quantitative-descriptive, or experimental when the object of social work studied is a category of recipients, a process of serving, or a system for purveyance of services. We shall see that classification by type of research is helpful at another stage of the utilization process, but not with respect to the objective of social work. All types of research are possible with reference to all objects of social work.

A study may sometimes be of use to the social worker even if it is not directed toward objects of social work we have identified. We do not include, for instance, the interest of social work in methods of research. Research to construct and validate diagnostic tests, for example, may be useful to social work researchers and to practitioners as well. A technique of research may itself be the object of interest. For example, the critical incident method (Flanagan, 1954) may be demonstrated in research whose object of study is quite apart from social work and yet it might find applicability in pertinent social work research (as in Goodrich and Boomer, 1958) and in practice methods such as the life-space interview or crisis-intervention. The omission of research methods as an object of social work interest, like the omission of historical and legal research—to mention two other categories—is in keeping with our focus in this book on empirical research. We believe, nevertheless, that the approach to classifying, evaluating, and utilizing research has general usefulness for reading all kinds of research.

Empirical research examines concrete objects, such as children, delinquents, youth courts, mental hospitals, casework interviewing, families of alcoholics, programs of job training, and so forth. The problems studied are viewed through specific concepts, hypotheses, and theories. The reader must always come back to the actual content of the research study after he has decided what category of social work interest or activity it addresses. Within the categories we suggest—recipients, serving processes, and the system of providing services—the research reader should differentiate the particular aspect of social work to which the content of a study may be relevant.

b. CURRENT OR POTENTIAL OBJECTS OF SOCIAL WORK. The content of a research report may be relevant to *current* or *potential* objects of social work interest. Recipients, serving processes, and service systems may be recognized as within social work today or they may be recognized as potentially within the social work domain. How the distinction is made will depend, of course, on how the reader defines the scope of social work and how familiar he is with current practice. In his own area, at any rate, he is likely to know the existing practice and be aware of emerging directions of practice.

Deciding whether research is *potentially relevant* in content is also a matter of judgment and imagination. In some instances, the subject matter is easily recognized as pertinent to social work even if it is primarily an object of other helping professions. Thus, studies of school children, mental hospital patients, residents of housing projects, race relations agencies, community planning commissions, and the like are readily recognized as potentially relevant to social work even if the research is not about anything social workers now do. Studies of helping methods that are new, even if not used by social workers, may have potential relevance. Content that may seem quite distant—for example, demographic studies, animal experiments, industrial relations research, and the like—may have potential relevance. Sensitivity to potential relevance will depend on breadth of perspective. Not all research content is potentially relevant, but the reader is alerted here not to confine his perspective too narrowly to existing social work activities and interests. Most practitioners will be aware that recipients, helping processes, and social services that were considered outside the interests of social work a few years ago are now prominent in professional attention.

c. The Value Perspective Toward the Objects of Social Work. It will help the research reader locate a study's relevance to social work if he keeps in mind the continuum suggested by such terms as: *normality-abnormality, socially approved-socially deviant,* and *organized-disorganized.* The research reader does not need to make this sort of judgment about the objects that are studied. That is, his question is not whether the recipients (e.g., families with female heads) are "normal" or "abnormal," or the purveyance of services, (e.g., a correctional institution or court system) is "functional" or "dysfunctional." His question is *whether the research has been conceived as a study of behavior or conditions that fall toward one or the other side of this continuum.*

The concern of social work with serving always implies values about the condition of some object of service. Therefore, a social worker will necessarily be alert to studies of problematic situations, e.g., the disturbed child, the family in stress or crisis, the inadequacy of welfare benefits, and the like. Implicit in such an interest is the assumption of "normal" or "healthy" states. Research on these states may be relevant because it supplies baselines for understanding "abnormality" and because it is assumed that some principles will be found to operate across the entire continuum from "normal" to "abnormal."

The research reader need not expect studies to fall at the

extremes of the normal-abnormal continuum. He will be able to judge the use he can make of the research better, however, if he recognizes the extent to which the research views recipients as normal or abnormal, or looks at the serving process and service system from the viewpoint of its strengths or its weaknesses.

d. THE LEVEL ON WHICH THE OBJECTS OF SOCIAL WORK ARE VIEWED. The content relevance of research is also assessed by identifying the level of the social work interest or activity that is studied. By level, we mean to suggest broad distinctions that may be made in the targets of social work practice—from helping the individual to changing features of the social system—as well as distinctions in the methods of achieving these objectives—from the use of interpersonal interaction to social legislation (Meyer *et al.*, 1967). Although they are interrelated, the levels mark distinctions that are generally recognized in social work and in the social sciences between the *individual,* the *group,* the *social organization,* the *community,* and the *society* (Thomas, 1964).

One need not struggle with the philosophical issues of emergent reality (i.e., whether each successive level constitutes more than aggregations of lower levels) or the associated issue of reductionism (i.e., whether each level can be understood in terms of the levels below it). We may simply accept the levels as familiar conceptualizations of the phenomena that social work and social science are concerned with.

The distinctions between individual, group, organization, community, and society are expressed in somewhat different ways when applied to different objects of social work. The vocabulary of social work reflects different levels of recipients when "clients" are defined as individuals, or groups, or agencies, or communities. When research is about actual or potential *recipients* it will not often be difficult to locate the level on which the research is conceived. Sometimes the researcher may collect data at more than one level and sometimes in analysis of data he may shift from one to another level. For example, his data may be about social conditions in various census tracts (e.g., family income, marital status of household heads, housing, etc.) which he correlates with rates of delinquency, or mental illness. It is the "ecological fallacy" to interpret such correlations of variables about geographical areas (community level) as applicable to the behavior of persons (individual level) (Robinson, 1950) except under special conditions (*see* Goodman, 1955). A study of members of families on welfare is different from a study of welfare families. Although the research may provide knowledge about several levels, its questions, concepts, and hypotheses will usually be formulated in terms of one level. The reader can often determine that level by asking what phenomena are sampled. Did the researcher, in fact, study individuals or groups or some other collectivity?

When the *process of serving* is the aspect of social work that is studied, the vocabulary of social work usually differentiates the various levels in forms of social work methods, i.e., casework and group work (sometimes called "direct" methods), community organization and social welfare administration (sometimes called "indirect" methods). The following scheme may aid in identifying the level on which the process of serving is located:

RECIPIENT LEVEL	RELATED SOCIAL WORK METHOD	CHANGE OBJECTIVE OF SERVICE	TYPICAL MEANS OF INTERVENTION
Individual	Casework	Internal states of persons; relations between persons	Interpersonal influence (usually one-to-one)
Group	Group work	Internal states of persons; relations between persons	Interpersonal influence (usually in small groups)
Organization	Administration	Structure and process of organizations, e.g., agencies, treatment institutions, etc.	Manipulation of organizational patterns and external relations
Community	Community organization practice	Relations between groups and organizations	Inter-group and inter-organizational manipulation by social action, planning, etc.
Society	Social welfare policy	Some aspect of the social welfare institution, e.g., programs of service	Policy proposals and development, legislation, reform movements, etc.

The overlap of levels, particularly contiguous ones, is evident. The levels are sufficiently distinguishable, however, to allow the research reader to locate the aspect of social work to which a study is primarily pointed. Using such a scheme as the above, the reader may note the level of the serving process within the interests of social work whether or not it is explicitly identified by the researcher as concerned with one of the usual social work methods.

The idea of levels requires some adaptation when applied to the location of research on *purveyance of services*. Three kinds of distinctions may be useful:

1. Individuals, groups, and communities may be viewed as involved in some *field of practice* (e.g., mental health, child welfare, corrections) or some *problematic area* in which services are provided (e.g., race relations, job training and employment, income maintenance). Fields of

practice and problematic areas can be classified in various ways. One way is to identify them as concerned with: (1) socialization, e.g., educa-cation, corrections, marital and family adjustment, child care, recreation, etc., (2) physical and mental health, e.g., medical and psychiatric patients, public health and community mental health programs, etc., (3) economic provision, e.g., income maintenance, housing, employment, etc., (4) par-ticipation in citizen roles, e.g., racial discrimination, political influence on public decisions, the political process, etc. Obviously these are not discrete categories; some services (e.g., for the aged or for children) fall into several or all categories. It is not necessary that a way of looking at social services be definitive; the changing social services of the "welfare state" make a definitive classification impossible. The research reader need only be alerted to the value of locating a study of purveyance of service in some such scheme so as to recognize the aspect of social work to which it may be applicable.

2. *The targets of various social services* may be conceived usefully for some purposes as recipients at the different levels, e.g., individuals (the mentally ill), or groups (delinquent gangs), or organizations (correctional agencies), or community relations (between races, between agencies), or the societal level (income maintenance policies).

3. A useful distinction for locating research studies of the purveyance of services can be made between *professional* arrangements and *organiza-tional* arrangements in their provision. Professional arrangements have to do with the numbers, sources, training levels, and deployment of man-power in social welfare. Research may be reported on all these aspects of providing services, and also on the characteristics of the social work profession itself (e.g., social work education, associations in the profession, and so forth). Studies of the use of non-professionals and clients as work-ers (indigenous workers) also come to mind. Organizational arrange-ments have to do with the complex of agencies (public and private; local, state, and national), their interrelations, their operations, and their changes. Studies of social welfare policies and their implementation through programs and agencies are also included. Both professional and organizational arrangements may be studied as they bear on all levels of recipients in various fields of practice or problematic areas.

e. THE SOCIAL WORK PURPOSE OF THE RESEARCH. A final ques-tion to ask about the content relevance of a research study is its bearing on the different purposes of the social work enterprise. The reader may examine a study in terms of its social work purposes even if the research was produced with no awareness or interest in such purposes. The reader's intent is to assess utility for social work; the intent of the researcher is usually quite different.

Of the many attempts to summarize the mission, responsibilities, and domain of social work, the following is representative: (Meyer, 1968, p. 495)

The objectives of social work are to help individuals, families, communities, and groups of persons who are socially disadvantaged and to contribute to the creation of conditions that will enhance social functioning and prevent breakdown. These objectives commit the social work profession both to helping persons adapt socially in keeping with their capacities and the norms and values of the society, and to modifying or reforming features of the social system. The term 'social worker' refers to a special group among those employed in rendering social welfare services or conducting programs of agencies and institutions that make up the social welfare system. The professional social worker is expected, because of his specialized training and experience, to bring a high degree of skill to the process of helping, and modifying the social conditions of, individuals, groups of persons, and communities. The special competence of the professional social worker is exercised in such tasks as providing material assistance for the needy and dependent; assisting those of whatever means who have difficulties in adjusting to their economic and social environment because of poverty, illness, deprivation, conflict, or personal, family, or social disorganization; and participating in the formulation of social welfare policies and preventive programs.

In view of such objectives, the reader may ask if knowledge from a research study contributes to his understanding of how to *alleviate* undesirable conditions, to *enhance* desirable conditons, or to *prevent* undesirable conditions from occurring. Knowledge from a research study may serve all three purposes or be more pertinent to one than another. All these purposes involve the exercise of some control over an aspect of the social world. As he reads the research, the practitioner can ask how the increased control that knowledge from the research may give will be useful for the treatment, facilitative, or preventive aspect of his practice. As we shall discuss later, he must also ask what kind of use, if any, the knowledge can be put to. But our emphasis here is on the ends to which knowledge may be put in social work practice.

3. *What Knowledge Content of the Research May Be Useful?*

The preceding section has dealt with aspects of social work the research reader should think about when he reads a research report. Equally important is the content of the research study itself. What kinds of knowledge can the reader get from the research? By "knowledge" we mean all that is cognitively contained in the study. Three kinds of knowledge may be distinguished: (1) empirical knowledge, (2) conceptual knowledge, and (3) methodological knowledge. Considerations of each of these kinds of content will help the reader assess the utility of the research.

Empirical research investigates some aspect of the observable world. What is investigated is the empirical referent of the research and what is reported about the empirical referent is the *empirical content* of the research. The study may be about mental retardates, or about race riots, or about groups of boys at a settlement house. It may be about what social workers do or about rates of mental illness or about families where marriage partners are in conflict. Some kind of behavior, some social condition, some set of events will be looked at through the concepts and methods of the research. Knowledge about that empirical content may have focal, or immediate, interest to the social worker because his own practice is concerned with the same empirical area. For example, a study of aftercare of institutionalized mental retardates has focal empirical relevance to a social worker whose caseload contains retardates, or one who works with families of retardates. A study of group work with street gangs of delinquents will have focal empirical relevance to social workers engaged in such practice. Often the research will not fall squarely in the empirical area of the reader's practice. Its empirical content may, nevertheless, be of adjunctive relevance. The phenomena of after-care may be relevant to the practitioner whose clients include the mentally ill, delinquents, or persons whose chronic illness involves periodic institutionalization. Those who work with delinquents in community centers may gain useful knowledge from a study of delinquents in street gangs, and social workers working with groups of adolescents in any setting may learn more about the phenomena of group work from a study of group work in the streets. The reader should consider the classes of phenomena examined by the research and ask if these phenomena also are directly or adjunctively involved in his practice.

Empirical research studies also provide *conceptual knowledge*. The empirical phenomena are always viewed through concepts; concepts are often related to one another in hypotheses which may be explicitly or implicitly linked in theories; generalizations about the empirical phenomena may be established or suggested. The level of conceptual content that the reader can make use of from the study is dependent on the purpose and methods of the research (and hence its type) and also on the success with which the research achieves its purpose (and hence on an evaluation of it). Experimental research may allow the reader to consider applicability to his practice of the empirical generalizations it demonstrates (with due regard to limitations of generalizability) ; it may allow him also to consider applicability of hypotheses tested and the concepts that have been used. The conceptual content of an exploratory study, on the other hand, will not include empirical generalizations; the knowledge it offers may be limited to hypotheses and concepts. All levels of knowledge may be useful to the practitioner, each in different ways allowing him to deal with problems in his practice with increased awareness of the nature of the phenomena he works with and his own ways of working. The reader should determine not only what level of knowledge the research provides, but also what level is most useful to him in relation to particular interests he brings from his practice.

The research reader may gain useful *methodological knowledge* from a research study. We refer here not to knowledge about how to use methods to carry on research but to the possible uses of the research methods in social work practice. For instance, the test or questionnaire developed to collect data for a study of role conflict in marriage may be useful, or adaptable for use, in diagnosis of cases involving marital conflict. The method used to manipulate the independent variable in an experiment, e.g., creation of group cohesion, may be adaptable to use in a practice situation where a similar manipulation is desired. Sometimes the research design of a study will suggest ways the practitioner can think of his own practice. For example, research based on the comparison of continuing and discontinuing clients may suggest that looking at one's caseload in similar terms is useful. A method of identifying community leaders for study of community power may be useful for identifying community leaders for the board of an agency.

4. *How Useful Can the Research Knowledge Be for Practice?*

If the research reader finds that the content of a study has relevance to social work, he will want to ask how useful the knowledge it offers can be. We follow the analyses of Thomas (1963) and Meyer *et al.* (1967) and Gouldner (1956, 1957) to approach this question.

The usefulness of a research study will depend both on the *soundness,* or validity, of its contribution to the reader's knowledge and on the extent to which the knowledge is *engineerable,* or capable of being put into practice.

The *soundness* of the study is related, as we have indicated earlier, to the purpose of the research and the methods employed. Classification of the research (Chapter 2) and its evaluation (Chapter 3) help the reader to judge soundness and hence to determine how much confidence he should place in the results. He will look for soundness not only in terms of generalizability of the findings (i.e., what they can say beyond the particular study), but also in terms of what specific addition the study has made to the limited questions the research set out to answer. One should not expect, for instance, an exploratory study to produce empirical generalizations but one may ask if the exploratory study has been well done and if its findings were derived on the basis of appropriate methods. In general the sounder a piece of research is found to be the more useful it can be. It is tempting to dismiss less sound research as useless, but, as we have stressed throughout this book, the research should be evaluated for its contributions as well as its limitations. Judging its limitations and strengths is prerequisite to making judgments about other aspects of its utility for the practitioner.

When judging soundness, the research reader may find it helpful to think of the guidelines for evaluating research (presented in Chapter 3) as testing the *power* of the knowledge. Thomas points out three features of knowledge that affect its power in application: (1) Validity of the propositions, i.e., the extent to which conclusions are corroborated by evidence. "If," Thomas notes, "the studies of a given domain are not well done, if the findings are inconsistent with what is otherwise known, or if there are precious few adequate investigations of a problem, empirically valid generalizations cannot be formulated and application would therefore be hazardous" (Thomas, 1964, p. 42); (2) predictive potency of the knowledge, i.e., the extent to which the conclusions of research allow propositions to be stated that link with more inclusive and coherent theory, thus providing additional derivations to be made that are logical consequences of the theory; (3) potency of the variables, i.e., the extent to which the independent variables of a research study account for the results. For a hypothetical example, if a study showed that both the degree of a client's anxiety and his ability to communicate verbally were related to continuance in treatment (Levinger, 1960), but the former variable (anxiety) was more weakly related, the latter variable (verbal communication) would be considered more potent. Variables that account for more of the variance in the dependent variable are likely to be more useful for the practitioner, if other things are equal.

The criteria of validity, predictive potency, and variable potency are most clearly applicable to judgments about studies seeking to establish empirical generalizations, such as hypothesis-testing studies. This does not imply that such research is always more useful than research producing limited results. Research in social work and the social sciences ideally strives toward production of knowledge with more power, but most of the research does not achieve this. Quantitative-descriptive and exploratory studies, like experimental research, reach toward the same objective and results may be assessed as more promising if they lead to new studies with increasingly powerful variables. The criteria of validity, predictive potency, and variable potency can be used for different types of research to help the reader achieve a better basis for judging the soundness of the research.

Usefulness of research results will depend, as we have noted, on *engineerability* as well as on soundness. This quality in research knowledge has also been called its "referent features" (Thomas, 1964). Engineerability is concerned with three sorts of questions: (1) To what extent are the variables of the research available for control by the practitioner? (2) Will manipulation of the variables have much or little effect in achieving the practitioner's objectives? (3) Is the manipulation of the variables feasible? These are questions about the real world of the practitioner and he must ask them if he is to utilize the knowledge no matter how sound the research is. As Thomas notes: "With few exceptions, the empirical indicators, or referents, of the variables of potentially useful knowledge have simply been ignored in the applied behavioral sciences" (Meyer *et al.*, 1967, p. 167). Users, too, have tended to apply only the criteria of researchers (i.e., criteria of soundness) without asking what other requirements the research knowledge must have if it is to be used in practice. We consider each question in turn.

(1) To determine if the research uses *variables available for control by the practitioner,* the research reader must determine to what extent the variables are identifiable, accessible, and manipulable. Variables are *identifiable* to the extent that they have clearly specified referents that are observable in the empirical world. This usually means that the operational definitions of the concepts which the variables define are made explicit, clear, and capable of systematic observation. Concepts such as the "unconscious," "libido," and "id," for example, seem to have no discernible empirical referents, whatever sense of clinical insight they stimulate. Other concepts—for example "ego strength," "sympathetic support," "group cohesion," and the like—gain in identifiability as they become operationalized by researchers through specific tests, and the specification of concrete behaviors and conditions. Still other concepts have referents that are clearly established, such as

group size, some indices of social class, and reinforcement of responses. *Accessible variables* are those that are, or can be, within the field of activity of the practitioner. For example, research might show that labeling a delinquent as such at school contributes to his delinquency, but the practitioner may not have access to the school teachers and peers who apply the label. This does not mean that the variable is necessarily of no use if, for example, it is linked by theory and other research to variables that connect it and the dependent variable of interest. To use the same example, if labeling is shown to be related to self-image and self-image to delinquent behavior, the practitioner may through his relationship with a client affect the delinquent's self-image and thus counter the effects of labeling. Without accessibility, a variable cannot be *manipulable.* That is, it may not be within the power of the practitioner to affect it. A variable with a high degree of manipulability, for example, is group size; another is the conduct of the caseworker in the interview with a client; another, an administrator's control over the budget of his agency. Like identifiability and accessibility, manipulability is usually a matter of degree since there are always limits to the practitioner's capacity and opportunity to effect changes. In general, he is better able to use the results of research if the variables of the research have high degrees of these attributes.

To find a research study useful, the reader need not conclude that the particular variables involved are duplicated in his own concrete situation. If the research shows, for example, that consistent and regular rewards to school children increase their studying, the practitioner can consider whether or not the class of variables involved (rewards) might be identifiable, accessible, and manipulable by him for purposes of his practice with his own clients.

(2) The second question to be asked about research to assess its engineerability is the degree to which the variables that can be manipulated *have an effect on the condition or situation* the practitioner wants to affect. Even if the research reader is satisfied with the validity of a study and concludes that the variables it uses are manipulable, he may find that the relationships are relatively weak ones, and hence their use promises little effect. For example, although it is related to continuance, the referral source for a client to a family service agency may be less strongly related than the client's sense of making progress in his first interview with the caseworker. The research that provides evidence of stronger relationships is likely to be more useful. In any event the strength of the relationship needs to be considered when assessing utilization.

(3) Similarly, the *feasibility* for the practitioner of using the

variables of the research should be assessed. Both the specific situation of the practitioner and the general situation of the profession must be taken into account. Among the factors affecting feasibility for manipulation of particular variables are the economic costs involved, the ethical suitability of the manipulations, and the organizational constraints imposed. An example of the former is seen in the difference between the cost of full field investigations of welfare applicants and the cost of having them file affidavits of need, with spot checks of accuracy. In general, on the principle of economy, the affidavit is to be preferred if research shows both practices equally satisfactory for getting information necessary for determining eligibility. Some variables that are manipulable may be prohibitively expensive on existing or realistically contemplated budgets as, for example, the reduction of class size to 10 per teacher in slum schools, or the complete resettlement of an entire population. Conditions affecting costs change, however, and the research reader needs to consider possible sources of economic support so as to follow the lead of a promising variable. Utilization is also affected by the ethical suitability of manipulating the variables involved. Massive deprivation may be demonstrably effective in changing some attitudes, as studies of concentration camps have shown, but such deprivation would violate professional ethics as well as humanitarian values. Sometimes what is effective in a laboratory research study, e.g., withholding of information, is unethical in the practice situation. There are no fixed rules to decide such questions, but they must nevertheless be asked of the research when considering its utilization. The reader will have to weigh them against his own standards of professional conduct and the standards that the profession generally accepts, expressed sometimes in codes of ethics of social workers and sometimes in agency rules. The organizational constraints under which the social worker practices may extend beyond questions of costs and ethics to include limitations and possibilities of the particular agency, as in the example of supplying contraceptive devices when agency policy forbids it. Such constraints may subject the practitioner to conflicting commitments between professional and agency values and the user of research needs to be aware of such conflicts in judging the utility of the research.

5. What Types of Use Can Be Made of the Research?

The most obvious type of use for a research study is in *direct application*. It may be useful *indirectly*, even if not directly. If limited in both these ways, the research may still be useful because it *clarifies understanding, sharpens insights,* or *provokes new ways of thinking* about an aspect of social work.

Direct application is possible when the conditions previously discussed about the research—its relevance to social work, its soundness and feasibility—are favorable. Much research will not meet these criteria, but some will. It may be sufficiently established, for instance, that non-professional workers can be of service to clients of a neighborhood center and that this is a feasible addition to personnel. This type of research knowledge can be directly applied by an agency director in making a decision. Even in such a case the practitioner cannot apply the knowledge automatically but must weigh the actual situation in all aspects when making his decision. From the viewpoint of utilization, however, the research has maximum usability.

Indirect applicability of research results may be of several sorts and the research reader should be alert to them. The study may provide knowledge of effective variables that are not manipulable (as previously illustrated) but which may lead to variables that are manipulable. It may allow the practitioner to take complementary action (Thomas, 1964, p. 46), such as the adaptation of his treatment method to the circumstances of the client that are known to affect the desired outcome. Knowing, for example, that lower class clients at psychiatric clinics discontinue more often than middle class clients when the help offered depends on verbal interaction, the practitioner may deliberately apply that knowledge to change his own style of service. There are many adaptations of practice that research knowledge will suggest to the creative and imaginative practitioner. Research studies should be read with such possibilities in mind.

We repeat here our reminder that the methods used in a research study, as well as its results, may find direct or indirect applicability. What the researcher has done that produces a predicted effect in a dependent variable may possibly be done by the practitioner. This is most clearly the case when an experiment has been performed using different forms of treatment (Paul, 1967), or different kinds of personnel (Poser, 1966). The techniques used in a study to define community leadership may be adaptable by the practitioner to affect decisions he seeks to influence (Bonjean, 1963). A study of conditions that affect clinical judgment (Orcutt, 1964) may supply the social worker with further understanding of his own diagnostic process which in turn is related to his choice of treatment techniques. Perhaps the best known example of research technique yielding a practice technique was the discovery of clinical uses for non-directive interviewing in the Western Electric studies in the 1920's (Roethlisberger & Dickson, 1939) .

Finally, research that does not offer direct or indirect application may nevertheless be stimulating, clarifying, and provocative. Research reading is not the only source of these effects, to be sure. Many other kinds of literature and many experiences of living produce such stimulations and they are not to be minimized for the practitioner. Our concern is that he be particularly alert to benefits to his practice that may come from the ideas stimulated by the research he reads. Creative responsiveness is quite different from casual speculation, and ideas stimulated from reading research are not to be mistaken for conclusions based on the research. If the research reader has carefully assessed utilization of the research through all the steps of the guidelines, he is in a position to think creatively about issues of his practice in the light of the research, and in this sense he can make use of it for the stimulation of new ideas. One sign that this is a useful result of reading a research study is the recognition and formulation of new problems for research. The research reader has not finished his study of the research until he asks what new or different research might be done that will be more useful.

Summary of Major Questions as General Guidelines to Utilization of Empirical Research Studies

For convenience of the reader, the major headings for the general guidelines discussed in the previous section of this chapter are reproduced below, as a set of related questions. The reader is reminded when using this summary that it is meant only to highlight the chief issues already discussed in more detail. The guidelines are not, we repeat, to be thought of as fixed and mechanical; they are supposed to suggest types of issues, orientations toward questions, and directions of analysis so that the research reader will develop his own guidelines and his own habits of critical and creative reading.

When looking over the summary of guidelines, the reader should also remember that there is no necessary sequence in which they are to be used. The research reader does not necessarily answer questions about relevance apart from questions about potential usefulness to practice. He will usually make judgments on many or most of the features bearing on utilization simultaneously, just as he will have done with respect to evaluation of the research. The guidelines to utilization should stimulate differentiated and discriminative reading. In short, they should heighten sophistication of the social worker as a research reader.

GENERAL GUIDELINES TO UTILIZATION:
SUMMARY OF MAJOR QUESTIONS

I. Should the research report be read at all?
  A. Does reader have a particular practice problem?
  B. Is the research likely to bear on reader's practice area?
  C. Is the research important for social work generally?
II. To what aspect of social work is the research relevant?
  A. What objects of social work interest and activity are addressed?
    1. Recipients?
    2. Process of service?
    3. Purveyance of service?
  B. Does the research pertain to current or potential objects of social work?
  C. From what value perspective are the objects of study viewed?
  D. On what levels does the research visualize the objects of interest?
    1. Recipients:
        a. Individual
        b. Group
        c. Organization
        d. Community
        e. Society
    2. Process of serving:
        a. Interpersonal intervention
        b. Manipulation of organizational patterns
        c. Inter-organizational and inter-group manipulation
        d. Policy proposals and development
    3. Purveyance of service:
        a. Professional arrangements
        b. Organizational arrangements
  E. What social work purpose does the research serve?
    1. Treatment?
    2. Enhancement?
    3. Prevention?
III. What knowledge content of the research may be useful?
  A. Empirical knowledge?
  B. Conceptual knowledge?
  C. Methodological knowledge?

IV. How useful can the research be for practice?
   A. How sound is the research?
   B. How engineerable are the variables?
      1. How available are variables for control by practitioner?
      2. How much difference in the practice situation will it make if the variables are manipulated?
      3. How feasible is it to manipulate variables of the research in the practice situation?
         a. Economic feasibility?
         b. Ethical suitability?
         c. Organizational constraints?
V. What types of use can be made of the research?
   A. Direct application?
   B. Indirect or complementary application?
   C. General stimulation?

First Steps in Utilization

As the reader makes his first quick examination of a research study or article, he will be able to make tentative assessments about utilization. As he becomes familiar with the research, the general guidelines for utilization presented in this chapter should be brought more consciously to the forefront. After the reader has classified and evaluated the research, he can apply the utilization guidelines more specifically, with attention to the special considerations for experimental, quantitative-descriptive, and exploratory studies.

We would re-emphasize the importance for the reader of considering what other knowledge is available that pertains to the area of inquiry of the research. An early step toward assessing the research for utilization should be a determination of the extent of ignorance and knowledgeability of the subject the reader has. It will usually be advantageous for the reader to check the summary of previous research often referred to in introductory sections of the report, including references to review articles and other means of gaining a secure sense of how the present research can be placed in the history of the problem. He should recall or look for prior work on application of knowledge about the subject to social work and related helping professions. A broad and informed perspective will enhance assessment of the utilizability of the research.

If the reader is not thoroughly familiar with the general guidelines of this chapter, or with the literature cited in its earlier sections, he may find it helpful to write his own summary answers to the major questions, leaving space on his work pages to fill in further details as he becomes more familiar with the research.

The reader should follow the guidelines, or his own rendition of them, in some detail, particularly noting the special questions pertinent to the type of research he is studying.

UTILIZATION OF DIFFERENT TYPES OF STUDIES:
SOME SPECIAL CONSIDERATIONS

Experimental Studies

Because they lead toward empirical generalizations, the findings of sound experimental studies may have much utility if the dependent variable has content relevance for the research reader and the independent variables are engineerable. The reader should judge these features of the research in the light of what he knows also about other independent variables that may be related to the effects examined in the experiment. The conditions controlled in the experiment may be stronger in the situation the practitioner actually faces than the variables that are manipulated in the experiment. In laboratory experiments particularly, situations may be contrived in ways that do not have analogues in practice. For example, the extreme cases presented in an experiment on "anchoring effects" on clinical judgment, (Orcutt, 1964), may not occur very often in actual practice. Nevertheless, such an experiment may sensitize the practitioner to the effects of "anchoring" and alert him to some of the determinants of his own diagnostic conclusions. The reader should judge how "unreal," i.e., unlikely to be found outside the experiment, the experimental situation is and what features of it are approximated in the practice situation. Sometimes the conditions of an experiment can readily be created by the practitioner. For instance, candy or other rewards shown effective by experiments in changing behavior of children might easily be introduced into practice. Not infrequently, the reader will find opportunities in his practice to approximate experimental situations. In some instances the experiment may be applied directly in practice, as when, for example, the independent variable is a form of group management (Lewin, Lippitt, and White, 1939). Subsequent field experiments may be necessary to establish empirical generalizations of the results of a series of laboratory experiments, but the reader can apply the implications to his own practice if he keeps in mind that he is using them only as hypotheses.

Field experiments face the risk of producing "negative" results, that is, results that fail to show that a practice technique, a program of service, or a special effort to help has succeeded. In fact, it is sometimes cynically said that the demonstration of successful treatment is inversely related to the rigor of the experiment testing it! A natural first reaction of a practitioner who reads the results of such an experiment is often defensive, as though the research was defective because it failed to substantiate the practitioner's hopes. Indeed, the research may be defective, and almost surely it will not be entirely satisfactory. The research reader should subject the research to severe criticism so that he can judge its soundness. He should not fail also to consider that the evidence may cast doubt on practice effectiveness, and hence stimulate him to think about alternative practice methods. Researchers often conclude reports of experiments that show disappointing effectiveness of practice with speculations about alternative approaches. These may be suggestive, but they should not be confused with the findings of the research, and the research reader should himself ask what implications negative findings have for his practice. Negative results cannot "prove" anything conclusively, but they are very valuable for correcting illusions, for creating, as it were, realistic doubts. These, in turn, can be a stimulus for creative thinking about new practice approaches.

Field experiments directly pertaining to practice may provide the reader with more than knowledge bearing on effectiveness of practice. They often call attention to variables that need consideration in conceptualizing practice and building practice theory. For example, attention to the specific behavior of the helping person may result from recognition in a field experiment that "service" or "casework" is only vaguely conceived (Meyer et al., 1965). Sometimes the actual arrangements made to conduct the field experiment are themselves applicable to practice, as when ways of reducing clerical tasks are developed to make more time available for training (Thomas and McLeod, 1960). When the vicissitudes of conducting the field experiment are described, the practitioner may often learn much about problems of resistance to change by social workers and agencies.

The types of side-products of experimental studies are numerous and we have suggested only a few examples to encourage the reader to be sensitive to many more.

Quantitative-Descriptive Studies

Many quantitative-descriptive studies, such as those assessing community needs, produce directly applicable knowledge when they have content relevance. The reader should be careful in using findings from these studies not to generalize improperly to other populations (e.g., other communities, other classes of clients, etc.), without taking into account differences that may affect the validity of the generalization. It is not necessary to read a survey study as though it could be applied only to the respondents, or even to the universe from which the respondents are drawn, provided the application is clearly recognized as uncertain and tentative and only as an approximation. It is better to err on the side of caution in making generalizations, but to be over-cautious is to deny the advantage of thinking of a population in the light of what is known about different populations.

Hypothesis-testing descriptive studies, and those showing the relationships between variables, can often provide a realistic sense of how a theory can be applied. They may reflect actual conditions and hence be more useful than experiments where controls are more rigorous. The reader may get information about multiple factors that bear on a relationship from analyses of descriptive data. When relationships between variables are translated into predictions, the contingent conditions may be more evident than in experimental studies. On the other hand, the less rigorous control of independent variables may weaken the relationships found and lead the reader to underestimate the validity of the theory.

Studies showing relationships of variables to some behavior of relevance to the practitioner do not, of course, establish cause-effect relationships. To show that lack of exercise, or cigarette smoking is significantly correlated with heart attacks does not mean that these have been shown to "cause" heart attacks. To show that children who are poor readers come from homes where the parental educational level is low does not mean that the one causes the other. The research reader is alerted by such findings, however, to seek possible explanations (hypotheses and theories) for the relationships. This may lead him to increased sensitivity to the meanings of the variables. For example, what is the meaning to the child of living with parents of low educational level? Is there some characteristic of persons who have little exercise that might be found to be causally related to heart attack? As a superficial example, the point may be illustrated by considering the finding that the religion of wives is related to the number of children they bear. Knowing the historical attitude of the Catholic church toward contraception, religion is readily translatable as an indicator of attitudes which in turn may be more meaningfully put into a theory of family planning. Refining the meaning of variables known to be related to one another is a useful step in thinking of the significance of knowledge from variable-relationship studies in terms of possible hypotheses that might illuminate aspects of practice.

Program evaluation studies usually have direct meaning for practitioners, but they are not to be taken as conclusive any more than they are to be ignored. The information they supply is often limited by lack of rigor in design, e.g., the lack of control groups or sufficient statistical controls in the analysis of data. They may, however, lead the acute practitioner, e.g., an administrator of an agency, to make his own assessments more carefully. Often, the process of examining limitations of impact studies provides an antidote to the tendency to overestimate effects of service, a tendency perhaps natural enough when practitioners assess their own work. Well designed and executed descriptive studies of impact—good demonstration projects, for example—can be very useful, provided they are not mistaken for experiments.

One value of descriptive studies is that they may provide base lines for looking at trends and changes. Re-surveys are obviously useful for this purpose. Even without a second study, knowledge of the state of a population, a condition, or a service, if it is based on more than impressionistic information, provides the practitioner with a reference point for making his own judgments about what may have changed. Cross-sectional, one-shot surveys may also give information about changes when, for example, they provide breakdowns of the data in terms of time strata such as age of respondents, length of residence, or years of service in a given position. The assumptions made to conclude that change, rather than selective factors, may be responsible for differences need to be carefully examined. If the reader does so, he may reach reasonable judgments about trends that may help him in some practical decision he faces.

Most quantitative-descriptive studies are based on samples and, as indicated in Chapter 2, the character of the sample is crucial for generalizing from the study. There is another aspect of the sample that bears on utility of the results and that has to do with the relevance of the sample to some action, or policy, of interest to the practitioner. A study from a sample that permits generalization to a segment of the population, such as leaders or legislators or rioters for example, may lead to information especially relevant to the community organization worker or the planner of social policy. Of course, surveys that allow responses to be differentiated for several segments of a population have the added advantage of permitting comparisons to be made. Not all surveys present data in this form.

Exploratory Studies

By their nature, exploratory studies do not produce findings of generalizability. Therefore, the principal use of these studies is to further sensitivity to problems, to help clarify concepts, and to stimulate differential thinking about phenomena of interest. This order of usefulness is worthy of attention and, indeed, it may be said that most of the use made of social science research in social work has been of this sort. Concepts that have been elaborated or specified by exploratory research have often been applied to phenomena the practitioner deals with. For example, the concepts of role, culture, bureaucracy, and others have been found useful for thinking about client behavior and agency organization. Often concepts rather than findings have been used from quantitative-descriptive and experimental studies.

Concepts and hypotheses can be more useful if they are precisely defined. The reader should note how studies operationalize concepts and whether or not there are parallels in practice that allow similar operationalizations. Can the concept be referred to particular behaviors or measures? Sometimes pinning down a concept to its operational meaning will call attention to the need for other concepts to describe a phenomenon sufficiently.

When exploratory studies examine a given research technique—e.g., the use of the critical incident—the reader should ask himself what potential use such a technique has in his practice. He should think beyond the technique itself and try to imagine other ways of observing, measuring, or manipulating variables that might be adapted for practice purposes.

It is particularly useful for the reader to ask of exploratory studies what potential lines of practice are suggested by the research. This question is directed to the stimulation of practice questions rather than research questions. The latter, too, may be usefully considered by the reader because research questions may lead to fresh ideas for practice. What are the unanswered questions about practice that emerge in the light of the research? What research might lead into these questions, and how can the practice implications be put to test? Like the conduct of research, the utilization of research ends, as it begins, with a question.

PART II

The Assessment of Social Research: Practical Applications

In the first section of the book we developed guidelines for the classification, evaluation, and utilization of social research. Our basic assumption was that research should be assessed differentially in regard to the specific objectives for seeking knowledge and the methods employed to achieve such objectives. Accordingly, in Chapter 2 we described a classification system which is based on both the purposes and the methods of research investigation. This resulted in three major categories and nine sub-types of research. Furthermore, in Chapters 3 and 4 criteria were delineated for evaluating and utilizing research studies for each of three major research categories: experimental, quantitative-descriptive, and exploratory studies. In addition to formulating different questions as a function of different research classifications, we also included criteria which are common to all types of research studies. Thus, our basic goal was to formulate criteria for the differential assessment of social research.

We regard the assessment of research as being comprised of three interrelated functions: classification, evaluation, and utilization. One classifies research to place it within the context of the goals of research for seeking knowledge. The evaluation of research involves a determination of the extent to which a researcher is able to accomplish his objectives, as well as a consideration of alternative procedures that might have been used to approximate more closely the objectives of research. Finally, the utilization of research includes a determination of the level of knowledge achieved in the research, and then the consideration of potential applications of the research findings to specific areas of social work practice.

We apply our guidelines for the assessment of social research to specific research studies in this section of the book. In accordance with our notion of differential assessment, we include a chapter on each of the three major research categories. Thus, Chapter 5 is devoted to the assessment of experimental studies; Chapter 6, quantitative-descriptive studies; and Chapter 7, exploratory studies.

The format for each chapter is similar and includes the following divisions. First, a research study is reproduced in its entirety. For example, in Chapter 5, the study by Poser on "The Effect of Therapists' Training on Group Therapeutic Outcome" (1966) is included. Following the reproduced study, we present a series of questions on the classification, evaluation, and utilization of the specific study. Our questions are derived from our criteria presented in the first section of the book, and they, as much as possible, are geared to the specific content of the article which is being assessed. For example, one question on the evaluation of the Poser study is "What sampling procedures were used for selecting hospitals, patients, and therapists?" For each question, we provide a narrative answer, which is indicative of how we would assess the research. At the end of our narrative, we include several selected references which are intended to aid the reader with respect to the review of concepts necessary for understanding the study and to the consideration of other completed research which relates to the findings of the study. In particular, we regard the inclusion of references to other research as a device for helping the reader to assess a research study in the context of other available knowledge. It is presumed that this will increase the reader's perspective for constructive criticism.

Within each chapter, a second research study is included. Questions for assessment are presented, and selected references for the reader are provided. However, we do not include answers to the questions for the second study; thus, one study within each chapter is intended to be an exercise in assessing research.

The reader will observe that the majority of questions on assessment are on evaluation, and that there are relatively few questions on classification and utilization. There are several reasons for this. First, the studies were selected with respect to their major research classification. We included several questions on classification, primarily to place the research study in its proper context for differential assessment. Secondly, questions on evaluation overlap to some extent with considerations of classification and utilization. Moreover, the questions on evaluation can be geared more specifically to the substance in the research article being assessed. Finally, the questions on utilization are considerations of potential applications of knowledge, and we assume that a sampling of such questions is sufficient for the student. In addition, it is to be noted that our questions are not necessarily exhaustive, but we assume that they are extensive enough to illustrate the way in which our guidelines can be applied to the assessment of specific research studies.

Our choice of the research studies which we include for assessment in this portion of the book is based on several considerations. We included studies which are assumed to be representative of different research approaches for seeking knowledge. Further, we decided to assess one research study from each of the disciplines of psychology, sociology, and social work. However, we do not claim that these studies are representative of all of the research conducted in these disciplines. Our primary assumption is that these studies are illustrative of social research, and that they provide concrete examples for the application of our criteria for differential assessment.

We recommend that the reader follows these procedures for each chapter: review criteria for assessment in Chapters 2, 3, and 4; read the first reproduced study, and determine whether the questions appear to be appropriate for the study; read the references pertinent to the study, and attempt to determine the basis for the narrative answers which are provided. Following this, the reader should attempt to provide his own narrative answers for the second reproduced study in each chapter. In addition, we recommend that the reader use the book, *Exemplars of Social Research*, as a source of additional research studies for differential assessment.

Chapter 5

Assessment
of Experimental
Studies

The Effect of Therapists' Training
on Group Therapeutic Outcome

by ERNEST G. POSER

The present manpower shortage in the mental health professions has given new impetus to investigations concerned with therapist variables in studies of therapeutic outcome. Hence, it is not surprising that recent work in this field, notably by Anker and Walsh (1961), Beck, Kantor, and Gelineau (1963), Rioch, Elkes, Flint, Usdansky, Newman, and Silber (1963), and Schofield (1964) should have focused attention on what appear to be the active therapeutic ingredients of the patient-therapist interaction. All of these authors suggest that effective therapy can be carried out by personnel without professional training, and most of them provide objective evidence in support of this view.

Truax (1963) and his associates also drew attention to non-academic qualifications of therapists by their ingenious demonstration that those rated high with respect to certain human qualities, such as "accurate empathy," tend to improve the psychological functioning of schizophrenics, while therapists rated low in empathy actually impair the clinical status of their patients. The therapist's personality attributes with which Truax is concerned are essentially those previously elaborated by Rogers (1957), who does not feel that special intellectual professional knowledge—psychological, psychiatric, medical, or religious—is required of the therapist. In this context he observes that "intellectual training and the acquiring of information has, I believe, many valuable results—but becoming a therapist is not one of those results (p. 101)." This view is consistent with the speculation that non-professional workers, possibly selected in accordance with Truax's criteria, could do effective therapy, at least with certain types of patients.

There is urgent need for studies seeking to define those aspects of the treatment process which crucially affect therapeutic outcome.

From: Ernest G. Poser, "The Effect of Therapists' Training on Group Therapeutic Outcome," *Journal of Consulting Psychology*, Vol. 30, No. 4 (August 1966), pp. 283–89. Copyright 1966 by the American Psychological Association, and reproduced by permission.

This project was supported by Canadian Dominion-Provincial Mental Health Research Grant No. 604–5–73. Special thanks are due to C. A. Roberts and H. E. Lehmann of Douglas Hospital for their part in making this study possible.

Without such information, it is difficult to distinguish between the necessary and the superfluous conditions of therapeutic personality change. But it may be misleading to think of the variance accounting for therapeutic outcome only in terms of active versus inactive ingredients, if the term "active" is meant to imply the deliberate application of some theory or procedure to the conduct of psychotherapy. There may be a third source of therapeutic change related to the familiar placebo effect operative in most other forms of medical and psychiatric treatment. Because, strictly speaking, there is no such thing as "inert" psychotherapy in the sense that placebos are pharmacologically inert, the term "placeboid" might serve to describe this effect in psychotherapy.

Rosenthal and Frank (1956) have dealt with the placebo phenomenon in some detail and conclude that

... improvement under a special form of psychotherapy cannot be taken as evidence for: (a) correctness of the theory on which it is based; or (b) efficacy of the specific technique used, unless improvement can be shown to be greater than, or qualitatively different from that produced by the patients' faith in the efficacy of the therapist and his technique—"the placebo effect" [p. 300].

More recently, Frank, Nash, Stone, and Imber (1963) have shown that some psychiatric patients recover simply as a result of attending a clinic or receiving placebo, without psychotherapy or other treatment being given.

Such studies, however, do not bear on the crucial problem of placeboid effects in the psychotherapeutic interaction itself. They do not tell us whether some of the supposedly active ingredients of therapy, such as the theoretical training or experience of the therapist, for instance, are or are not relevant to therapeutic outcome. Could it be that such behavior change as does occur post-therapeutically is due to other factors not hitherto considered to be necessary antecedents of therapeutic change? Fiedler (1950) and others have already shown that adherents of widely disparate theoretical persuasions achieve much the same results in psychotherapy, and more recently similar findings have been reported by Gelder, Marks, Sakinofsky, and Wolff (1964) with respect to the comparative outcome of psychotherapy and behavior therapy. Though rich in implication, none of these studies were specifically designed to test for placeboid effects in therapeutic outcome. To do so, according to Rosenthal and Frank (1956), requires, in addition to the therapy under study, the application of

another form of therapy in which patients had equal faith, so that the placebo effect operated equally in both, but which would not be expected by the theory of therapy being studied to produce the same effects [p. 300].

The present study constitutes an attempt to provide a controlled experiment in line with the above suggestion.

The therapeutic technique under study was group therapy with chronic schizophrenics. The fact that such therapy is most often carried out by psychiatrists, social workers, occupational therapists, and psychologists (Poser, 1965) suggests that training in one of these professions is commonly regarded as an appropriate, if not essential, prerequisite for the successful group therapist. To test the validity of this assumption three treatment conditions were compared in this investigation.

In the first, group therapy was conducted by highly trained psychiatrists, social workers, and occupational therapists. In the second condition all therapists were undergraduate students without previous training or experience relevant to the care of mental patients. Because a comparison of two treatments in terms of their effectiveness would be meaningless without first demonstrating the validity of the outcome criterion to be applied, a control group of untreated patients was also included.

In terms of Rosenthal and Frank's statement cited above, the untrained therapists in the present investigation were thought to provide a form of treatment which, by virtue of their lacking professional sophistication, would prove to be less effective than that offered by trained personnel. This, at least, would be the prediction if it is true that training and experience are relevant to therapeutic outcome. At the same time, there was no reason to believe that the patients had more faith in the trained than the untrained therapists, since they were in the main unaware of this distinction. Hence placeboid effects, if any, could operate equally in both therapeutic situations. In fact, the untrained therapists are here conceptualized as contributing nothing but placeboid effect, much as the pharmacologically inert substance does in a placebo-controlled drug study. By corollary, the theoretical sophistication and past experience of a trained therapist is, for the purpose of this study, viewed as the active ingredient in the therapeutic process. In other words, it is proposed that such therapeutic effectiveness as untrained therapists do attain is attributable to nonspecific aspects of the helping relationship, such as activation, sympathy, opportunity for verbal ventilation, regularity of attendance, and the like. These would appear to be formally comparable to the nonspecific factors thought to underlie placebo responses as, for instance, attention giving, expectation inducing, pill ingestion, and many other situational variables familiar to the drug therapist. Many of these variables are highly effective in the treatment of certain physical disabilities, as placebo studies of patients with headaches (Jellinek, 1946) or the common cold (Diehl, Baker, and Cowan, 1940) have abundantly shown. A similar phenomenon may operate in psychotherapy, which would account for the near-ubiquitous two-thirds improvement rate consequent upon most forms of psychotherapy.

METHOD

SUBJECTS. A total of 343 male chronic schizophrenics was studied. They represent almost the entire male schizophrenic population of a 1500-bed hospital, only assaultive patients and those suffering from known organic brain damage having been excluded. Their median age was 47 years (range 20–73). All of them had been hospitalized uninterruptedly for at least 3 years. Their median length of hospitalization was 14 years, with a range from 3 to 44 years.

The vast majority of these patients were receiving phenothiazine medication at the time of the study. This was continued throughout, and only in emergencies was medication changed during the course of the project.

THERAPISTS. The untrained therapists consisted of 11 young women between the ages of 18 and 25. All were undergraduate students in one of Montreal's universities, and most had never had a course in psychology. None intended to enter a mental health profession, nor had any of them ever visited a mental hospital. No attempt was made to select a particular type of applicant. Anyone who expressed interest in the project and accepted the terms of employment was enrolled. They were paid at the standard rate for summer employment at that time and were asked to consent to the taking of numerous psychological tests which were to be used for a subsequent investigation. As an additional control, two inpatients— one an alcoholic and the other suffering from hysteria—were asked to act as untrained therapists.

The professional therapists were seven psychiatrists, six psychiatric social workers, and two occupational therapists. In addition to their formal professional qualifications, that is, certification in psychiatry, all the psychiatrists had had from 5 to 17 years of professional experience. All but one had previously done group psychotherapy, and three were specialized in this area. Their ages ranged from 35 to 50, and all were male.

All social workers had had postgraduate professional training leading to a degree and at least 5 years' professional experience. Two were specialized in group work, and all but two had had previous experience doing case or group work with psychotic patients. Their ages ranged from 36 to 43, and two out of the six were male.

The two occupational therapists had professional experience of 5 and 7 years' duration, respectively, and this included some mental hospital work. Both were female, one aged 27 and the other 30.

None of the therapists taking part in this project were on the staff of the hospital where this work was done, nor were any of the patients known to the therapists prior to the start of the project. All were paid at the rate appropriate to their profession.

TESTS. Selection of these was guided by three considerations. First, the performance required had to be within the behavioral repertoire of chronic schizophrenic patients. Second, preference was given to tests which had previously been demonstrated to differentiate normals from psychotics. Since a large number of patients were involved, the third criterion was purely practical—those tests were chosen which could be administered in a relatively short space of time.

The final test battery consisted of two psychomotor, two perceptual, and two verbal tests, in addition to the Palo Alto Hospital Adjustment Scale (McReynolds and Ferguson, 1946), intended to provide a quantitative estimate of the patients' adjustment in the hospital. The tests were:

1. Speed of tapping (TAP). (The number of taps on a reaction key in 10 seconds.)

2. A test of visual reaction-time (RT) involving choice.

3. The Digit-Symbol test (DS) of the Wechsler-Bellevue Scale I.

4. A color-word conflict test (Stroop), in which the score reflects the time taken by the patient to read 100 color names under three conditions of increasing difficulty (Thurstone and Mellinger, 1953).

5. Verbal fluency (VF). (The number of different animals named in 1 minute.)

6. The Verdun Association List (VAL), a 20-item word-association test devised by Sigal (1956) to discriminate between working and nonworking mental hospital patients.

All of these tests were individually administered immediately before or after therapy. Occasionally a patient was found untestable before or after therapy. Such patients were seen by another examiner, so that no patient was given a zero score on any test unless he had been given two opportunities to take it from a different examiner on each occasion.

PROCEDURE. The 343 patients were selected for this project by the psychiatric staff of the hospital. Each patient was assigned to a group in such a way that every unit of 10 patients would be matched as closely as possible with every other unit in terms of the patients' age, severity of illness, and length of hospitalization. Following this, the groups were compared with respect to their mean test performance prior to therapy. Where major disparities between groups were noted, individual patients were exchanged, so that all groups were roughly comparable with respect to age, clinical status, length of hospitalization, and test performance prior to therapy.

At this stage six groups (one of them composed of 13 patients) were picked at random to serve as untreated controls. Patients in these groups received the usual hospital care, but were excluded from all forms of group treatment other than routine occupational therapy. The remaining 28 groups were each assigned to a therapist picked at random from among the project staff available at the time. The project extended over three periods of 5 months. In the first of these, 11 untrained therapists took part; in the second, seven professional and one untrained therapist; and in the final period, eight professional and one untrained therapist.

Each therapist met his or her group during 1 hour daily 5 days a week for a period of 5 months. A special attendant saw to it that patients would join their groups at the appropriate time and place. Even so, one or two patients in almost every group refused to attend regularly. Their absences were recorded, and only those patients who attended at least two-thirds of all available sessions were reevaluated at the end of the 5-month period. This reduced the total number of patients included in the study from 343 to 295. At the time of the post-therapy retest no group had less than six members who met the attendance criterion.

Both the trained and untrained therapists were quite free to conduct their therapy sessions in any way they wished. Wherever possible, the materials or facilities they required were provided by the hospital, but at no time did the project director offer suggestions for procedure or in any way facilitate communication among therapists while the project was under way. To get some idea of each therapist's approach, a few sessions of every group were attended by an observer. Also, each therapist was asked to keep a daily record of his group's activities. Some therapists used only verbal communication during therapy; others arranged activities ranging from party games and dancing to "communal" painting and public speaking. All stressed interaction among members of their group.

RESULTS

The pre- and post-therapy test scores of all patients were subjected to covariance analysis. The covariance adjusted post-therapy scores of the untreated control group were then compared to those of the patients treated by lay therapists (Table 1) and those of the professional therapists (Table 2), respectively. This was done for each of the six tests separately. On all tests, with the exception of the Stroop, a high score indicates better performance than a low score.[1]

TABLE 1
COVARIANCE ADJUSTED POST-THERAPY SCORES OF UNTREATED PATIENTS AND THOSE TREATED BY LAY THERAPISTS

Treatment		TAP	VF	VAL	DS	RT	Stroop
Untreated controls	Mean	45.763	11.699	26.218	20.428	.169	2.508
(N = 63)	SD	9.772	4.449	6.580	7.204	.054	.768
Treated by lay therapists	Mean	49.735	12.600	28.786	24.135	.197	1.025
(N = 87)	SD	10.222	4.370	8.264	6.812	.063	.698
	t	2.308†	1.295	1.801*	2.922§	2.613	2.336‡

† $p < .05$.
* $p < .10$.
§ $p < .01$.
‡ $p < .02$.

TABLE 2
COVARIANCE ADJUSTED POST-THERAPY SCORES OF UNTREATED PATIENTS AND THOSE TREATED BY PROFESSIONAL THERAPISTS

Treatment		TAP	VF	VAL	DS	RT	Stroop
Untreated controls	Mean	45.763	11.699	26.218	20.428	.169	2.508
(N = 63)	SD	9.772	4.449	6.580	7.204	.054	.768
Treated by professional therapists	Mean	46.372	10.948	28.104	23.187	.154	.835
(N = 145)	SD	9.894	3.061	6.950	5.612	.049	.579
	t	.387	1.148	1.427	2.313*	1.688	2.903†

* $p < .02$.
† $p < .01$.

Similar comparisons were made between the post-therapy scores of patients receiving lay therapy and those treated by professionals (Table 3). Finally, in Table 4, interprofessional comparisons are

---

[1] The reversal of direction in the Stroop test scores arises from the raw score's being expressed as a ratio.

made between the post-therapy test behavior of patients treated by social workers and psychiatrists.

TABLE 3
COVARIANCE ADJUSTED POST-THERAPY SCORES OF PATIENTS TREATED BY LAY AND PROFESSIONAL THERAPISTS

Treatment		TAP	VF	VAL	DS	RT	Stroop
Treated by lay therapists	Mean	49.735	12.600	28.786	24.135	.197	1.025
($N = 87$)	SD	10.222	4.370	8.264	6.812	.063	.698
Treated by professional therapists	Mean	46.372	10.948	28.104	23.187	.154	.835
($N = 145$)	SD	9.894	3.061	6.950	5.612	.049	.579
	t	2.331*	2.899†	.588	.930	4.998‡	.356

* $p < .05$.
† $p < .01$.
‡ $p < .001$.

TABLE 4
COVARIANCE ADJUSTED POST-THERAPY SCORES FOR PATIENTS TREATED BY SOCIAL WORKERS AND PSYCHIATRISTS

Treatment		TAP	VF	VAL	DS	RT	Stroop
Treated by social workers	Mean	47.332	10.613	27.687	22.324	.154	1.025
($N = 53$)	SD	10.222	3.05	6.618	6.603	.063	.656
Treated by psychiatrists	Mean	46.252	11.212	28.011	23.307	.151	.755
($N = 60$)	SD	8.978	3.162	7.899	5.459	.040	.561
	t	.564	.743	.203	.688	.249	.321

It appears from these tables that the largest number of significant differences in test behavior occur between the untreated group and those groups treated by lay therapists. Four out of the six tests reflect significantly better performance by the patients of lay therapists. The VAL approaches significance in the expected direction.

On comparing the test behavior of the untreated with that of patients treated by professionals, only two out of the six tests show significant superiority of the latter group (Table 2).

A direct comparison of patients treated by lay and professional therapists reveals a significantly better performance on the part of those treated by the former on three of the six tests (Table 3). It is of interest to note that the standard deviation on every test is smaller for the group of patients treated by professional therapists.

Table 4 suggests that there is no significant difference between posttherapeutic test performance of patients treated by social workers and the performance of those treated by psychiatrists.

Because the study began with patients treated by lay therapists, it was possible before the end of the project to retest some of the patients and most of the untreated controls who took part in that first phase of the investigation. These scores, obtainable from 61 patients, constitute a 3-year follow-up and are presented in Table 5. To save time, only four of the original six tests were given in this part of the study, and a t test for correlated means was used to evaluate the difference between the two test sessions, separated by 3 years. Table 5 shows that test performance after 3 years was still significantly better than it was before treatment on all of the tests used. That this result was not a function of greater familiarity with the tests at follow-up—by which time each patient had taken them twice before—is indicated by the result of retesting 23 untreated controls after 3 years. Only on the tapping test did they show significantly better performance on follow-up, much as they had done on the first retest after 5 months.

TABLE 5

THREE-YEAR FOLLOW-UP OF SCHIZOPHRENICS TREATED BY LAY THERAPISTS
$(N = 61)$

Stage		TAP	VF	RT	VAL
Before treatment	Mean	38.84	9.02	326.24	19.08
	SD	19.63	5.50	405.09	14.07
Three years later	Mean	48.15	10.52	183.07	24.20
	SD	17.50	6.43	320.04	14.53
	t	4.22‡	2.58*	3.61‡	3.32†

* $p < .02$.
† $p < .01$.
‡ $p < .001$.

In an effort to get some measure of change in the patients' ward behavior, the Hospital Adjustment Scale was administered to 80 patients, all of whom had been treated by lay therapists. The scale was administered before treatment, and again after 5 months. On each occasion it was completed both by the nursing supervisor and an attendant familiar with the patients. The supervisor's ratings showed significant improvement between test and retest, but the attendants' ratings did not. It was felt that this equivocal result reflected little more than the greater-ego involvement of the supervisors, whose wish to see the project succeed might well have influenced their ratings.

Unfortunately it was not possible to have the scale completed by personnel sufficiently familiar with the patients to assess their behavior and yet unaware of their participation in the project. For this reason and also because of the ward staff's strong resistance to the time consuming task of filling out the scale it was not administered to subsequent therapy groups.

DISCUSSION

The objection may be made that changes in psychological test performance, as employed in this study, do not constitute a relevant criterion of therapeutic outcome. The usual alternatives are rating scales, questionnaires, or the comparison of discharge rates before and after therapy. None of these seemed appropriate for the present patient population, consisting as it did of schizophrenics with many years of hospitalization. The behavioral repertoire of such patients is so limited that rating scales are difficult to complete, as our own attempt at using the Hospital Adjustment Scale clearly showed. For the same reason, questionnaires completed by the patients would be hard to interpret. Discharge rates during and after therapy were compared, but showed no significant difference between treated and untreated groups. Nor would this be expected in the light of previous findings, such as those of Beck *et al.* (1963). Their study showed that in a sample of 120 psychotics, those who were discharged during the Harvard undergraduate volunteer program had, on the average, been hospitalized for 4.7 years, whereas the undischarged patients had been hospitalized for 12.4 years. This is consistent with earlier studies, suggesting that after 4 years of hospitalization only 3 percent of patients are likely to be discharged.

With one exception (Stroop) the verbal and performance tests employed in the present investigation were known from earlier work to discriminate effectively between psychotics and normals. It therefore seems justified to interpret significant incremental change in the treated groups' test behavior as reflecting therapeutic gain. This conclusion is validated by the absence of such change in the untreated control group on five out of the six tests. That the TAP did show significant improvement on retest of the control group may reflect the greater emphasis placed on activity programs for mental patients in recent years. On the other hand, since tapping was the first test to be administered to each patient, initial performance on it may have been impaired by apparatus stress or the novelty effect of the test situation.

Why lay therapists should have done somewhat better than professional therapists in facilitating the test behavior of their patients remains a matter of conjecture. It seems likely that the naïve enthusiasm they brought to the therapeutic enterprise, as well as their lack of "professional stance" permitted them to respond more freely to their patients' mood swings from day to day. Certainly, the activities in which they engaged their patients had a less stereotyped character than that offered by their professional counterparts. On the other hand, the greater standard deviation in the test behavior of those treated by lay therapists suggests that they may have helped some of their patients at the expense of others. Professional therapy, by contrast, seems to have had a more even effect on all participants.

The 3-year follow-up data for the untrained group are highly encouraging and support the conclusion that the therapy given achieved more than transient activation. It is planned to carry out similar follow-up studies on the patients treated by professional therapists.

The groups treated by fellow patients were too small to make quantitative assessment very meaningful. Their results were, however, treated separately in the covariance analysis and showed no significant difference from patients treated by lay or professional therapists. They received excellent cooperation from their fellows, as evidenced by their group attendance record, which showed full attendance in one group and 8 out of 10 in the other. Those who knew the patient-therapists clinically agreed that participation in the project had enhanced their mental health. Both are now discharged after prolonged hospitalization.

To extend the conclusions from this study beyond its present context, that is, the outcome of group therapy with chronic schizophrenics, would clearly be premature. When viewed in relation to the literature reviewed at the outset of this paper, the present findings do, however, support the conclusion that traditional training in the mental health professions may be neither optimal nor even necessary for the promotion of therapeutic behavior change in mental hospital patients.

REFERENCES

ANKER, J. M., & WALSH, R. P. Group psychotherapy, a special activity program, and group structure in the treatment of chronic schizophrenics. *Journal of Consulting Psychology,* 1961, **25,** 476–81.

BECK, J. C., KANTOR, D., & GELINEAU, V. A. Follow-up study of chronic psychotic patients "treated" by college case-aide volunteers. *American Journal of Psychiatry,* 1963, **120,** 269–71.

DIEHL, H. S., BAKER, A. B., & COWAN, D. W. Cold vaccines, further evaluation. *Journal of the American Medical Association,* 1940, **115,** 593–94.

FIEDLER, F. E. A comparison of therapeutic relationships in psychoanalytic, nondirective and Adlerian therapy. *Journal of Consulting Psychology,* 1950, **14,** 436–45.

FRANK, J. D., NASH, E. H., STONE, A. R., & IMBER, S. D. Immediate and long-term symptomatic course of psychiatric outpatients. *American Journal of Psychiatry,* 1963, **120,** 429–39.

GELDER, M. C., MARKS, I. M., SAKINOFSKY, I., & WOLFF, H. H. Behavior therapy and psychotherapy for phobic disorders: Alternative or complementary procedures? Paper presented at the 6th International Congress of Psychotherapy, London, 1964.

JELLINEK, E. M. Clinical tests on comparative effectiveness of analgesic drugs. *Biometrics Bulletin,* 1946, **2,** 87.

McREYNOLDS, P., & FERGUSON, J. T. *Clinical manual for the Hospital Adjustment Scale.* Palo Alto: Consulting Psychologists Press, 1946.

Poser, E. G. Group therapy in Canada: A national survey. *Canadian Psychiatric Association Journal*, 1966, **11**, 20–25.

Rioch, M. J., Elkes, C., Flint, A. A., Usdansky, B. S., Newman, R. G., & Silber, E. National Institute of Mental Health pilot study in training mental health counselors. *American Journal of Orthopsychiatry*, 1963, **33**, 678–89.

Rogers, C. R. The necessary and sufficient conditions of therapeutic personality change. *Journal of Consulting Psychology*, 1957, **21**, 95–103.

Rosenthal, D., & Frank, J. D. Psychotherapy and the placebo effect. *Psychological Bulletin*, 1956, **53**, 294–302.

Schofield, W. *Psychotherapy: The purchase of friendship.* Englewood Cliffs, N. J.: Prentice-Hall, 1964.

Sigal, J. The Verdun Association List. Unpublished doctoral dissertation, University of Montreal, 1956.

Thurstone, L. L., & Mellinger, J. J. *The Stroop test.* University of North Carolina, The Psychometric Laboratory, 1953.

Truax, C. B. Effective ingredients in psychotherapy: An approach to unraveling the patient-therapist interactions. *Journal of Counseling Psychology*, 1963, **10**, 256–63.

An Assessment
of the Poser Study

CLASSIFICATION

1. What Are the Specific Purposes of the Study?

The author has two purposes in this study. His stated purpose pertains to assessing the relative efficacy of group therapy with chronic schizophrenics. Employing the notions of Rosenthal and Frank regarding the "placebo effect," Poser indicates that he is attempting to provide an experiment which controls both for "no treatment" and for "placeboid effects." However, he is also interested in comparing the relative efficacy of trained versus untrained group therapists. This is an implicit attempt to demonstrate that traditional training in the mental health professions is no more effective than is no training at all for therapists who conduct group treatment for chronic schizophrenics. In essence, the author's explicit purpose is to evaluate the efficacy of group therapy with chronic schizophrenics, while his implicit purpose is to compare the relative efficacy of trained versus untrained personnel in group therapy with chronic schizophrenics.

2. What Research Methods Does the Author Use to Accomplish His Purposes?

The researcher employed experimental methods in that 34 groups of male chronic schizophrenics were assigned randomly to three experimental conditions: group therapy by trained therapists; group therapy by untrained therapists; and no group therapy for a control group. Each group was comprised of approximately 10 patients, and prior to randomization the groups were matched with respect to age, severity of illness, length of hospitalization, and performance on six tests prior to therapy. The 343 patients included initially in the study were selected by the psychiatric staff of one 1500 bed hospital. The patients were reported to be comprised of practically all of the male schizophrenics hospitalized at the institution. All patients were hospitalized for at least three years, and only patients who were assaultive or were suffering from known organic brain damage were excluded from the study. Group therapy was conducted for a period of five months for each experimental group, and only those patients who attended two-thirds or more of the group sessions were retained in the study for statistical analysis. Data obtained for statistical comparisons consisted of six psychological tests which were individually administered to all patients prior to and subsequent to the introduction of group therapy. Differences of mean performances on the tests were compared for the three experimental conditions by using covariance analysis and t-tests of statistical significance.

3. Why Is the Study Classified as Experimental?

The study is classified as experimental because it involves the manipulation of an independent variable, group therapy, and the random assignment of groups of patients to one of three experimental conditions. In addition, the purpose of the study is to test a hypothesis regarding the efficacy of group therapy; and dependent variables of test performance are operationalized so that quantitative-descriptions can be provided. The study is sub-typed further as a *field experiment*. It takes place in a "natural setting," that of a mental hospital, and there is an attempt to manipulate an independent variable of group therapy for studying its effectiveness with actual schizophrenic patients in the hospital.

The research differs from other major research classifications in two basic ways. The study has the objective of testing a hypothesis, and the research procedures which are employed constitute an attempt of the researcher to achieve a relatively high degree of internal validity to provide evidence in support of the hypothesis.

EVALUATION: PROBLEM FORMULATION

1. How Does the Author Use the Literature in Conceptualizing the Research Problem?

Poser presents references from the literature to suggest that therapy can be conducted by personnel who have not had professional training. Having referred briefly to literature dealing with the interaction of patients and therapists in therapy, the author then presents a specific reference concerned with the personality attributes of therapists who attempted to treat schizophrenics. He cites Truax' finding that therapists rated high in "accurate empathy" tend to achieve improvement in schizophrenic patients, while therapists rated low in "accurate empathy" tend to impair the psychological functioning of schizophrenic patients. Poser regards "personality attributes" of therapists as "non-academic qualifications"; thus, he uses the Truax study in an attempt to strengthen his argument regarding the possibility of using persons without professional training as therapists. Poser does not refer to the Truax study in detail; however it appears to the reader that the equation of personality attributes of therapists to non-academic qualifications is based on an implicit assumption that personality attributes do not change as a function of academic training. If Truax studied therapists with academic training and found that some personality attributes were predictive of success with their schizophrenic patients, then it appears that Poser would assume that the personality attributes for the therapists were not changed as a function of training. Further, the finding that some patients are helped and some are hindered does not necessarily lead to the conclusion that therapists do not need training. Rather, it implies that therapists rated high in empathy are more effective than those who are rated low; hence, persons with a high degree of empathy may make better therapists.

Poser conceptualizes three ingredients of therapeutic outcome: active, inactive, and placeboid. His references indicate that improvement in therapy may be attributed to the patient's faith in the efficacy of the therapeutic intervention, which is regarded as a placeboid effect. Further, placeboid effects should be controlled in experimentation attempting to determine the efficacy of particular modes of therapy. Thus, Poser conceptualizes untrained therapists as analogous to an ingredient which could lead to a placeboid effect, and untrained therapists can be regarded as an additional *control* for assessing therapeutic outcomes. He further regards therapy by trained therapists as including both active ingredients of therapists' interventions plus the stimulus for placeboid effects. Poser uses the literature to lead to his research problem: an attempt to evaluate the efficacy of group therapy with chronic schizophrenics by employing both trained and non-trained therapists. He indicates that group therapy is most often carried out by psychiatrists, social workers, occupational therapists, and psychologists; and he believes training in these professions is appropriate for group therapy. In his conceptualization he does not consider differences among professions, nor does he consider different forms of group therapy. In view of this it would appear that the different therapists, irrespective of their professional affiliations, are assumed to be equivalent with respect to their functioning as group therapists.

2. *What Is the Hypothesis Being Investigated; What Are the Independent and Dependent Variables?*

Although the research hypotheses were not stated precisely, they appear to be as follows:

A. Chronic schizophrenics who receive group therapy are

more likely to exhibit increased performances on selected psychological tests than are chronic schizophrenics who do not receive group therapy.

B. There are no significant differences between chronic schizophrenics who receive group therapy from trained therapists and chronic schizophrenics who receive group therapy from untrained therapists with respect to their performance on selected psychological tests.

The independent variables are group therapy with trained therapists and group therapy with untrained therapists. The dependent variables are measurements on six psychological tests: speed of tapping, visual reaction time, Digit-Symbol test, color word conflict test, verbal fluency, and a word association test. In addition, there was an attempt to use the Palo Alto Hospital Adjustment Scale as a dependent variable.

3. How Are the Independent and Dependent Variables Defined Conceptually and Operationally?

Conceptions of group therapy *per se* are not considered by the author. The duration of group therapy and some information pertaining to the group therapists are discussed, but the content regarding what is done by therapists is not explicated. Six groups of patients who served as untreated controls did not receive any form of group treatment other than "routine occupational therapy." Twenty-eight groups of patients received "group therapy" from either trained or untrained therapists. Each therapist met with one group of patients for one hour daily five days per week for a period of five months. The therapists conducted their therapy sessions "in any way they wished"; thus, group therapy is assumed to be whatever is done by the therapists in their group meetings. The trained therapists were comprised of seven psychiatrists, six psychiatric social workers and two occupational therapists. None of them were employed by the hospital where the study was conducted, and all were paid their usual professional rates. All of the professionals had received appropriate educational training and at least five years experience in their fields. There appeared to be some variation in their experience with "group therapy": one psychiatrist had not previously conducted group therapy sessions; three psychiatrists were specialized in group therapy; two social workers specialized in group work; two social workers had no experience in working with psychotics; the occupational therapists had some experience doing mental hospital work. Eleven of the untrained therapists were young, female undergraduate students who did not intend to enter a mental health profession. Two untrained therapists were in-patients at the hospital.

Essentially, group therapy is operationalized as whatever therapists do with groups of patients over a specified period of time. Further, trained therapists have professional training in one of three disciplines with an apparent variation in their experiences in conducting group therapy and in treating schizophrenic patients. Untrained therapists are predominantly female undergraduate students, and they differ from trained therapists in that they are younger and do not have experience in group therapy or in dealing with schizophrenic patients.

The psychological tests were selected because the author believed that they were able to be completed by schizophrenics in a short period of time and they could differentiate normal subjects from psychotic persons. The author does not include evidence from previous studies which demonstrates that the selected psychological tests do, in fact, differentiate chronic schizophrenics from normal subjects. Nevertheless, he argues that change in test performance reflects therapeutic gain for schizophrenics. In this regard, it would be important to consider how much change is necessary to infer therapeutic gain. In particular, the reader would need to know to what extent "normals" differed from "psychotics" in the previous work alluded to by the author. The tests were defined operationally to include such things as the number of taps on a reaction key in 10 seconds; the number of different animals named in one minute; time required to read color names; and so forth.

4. To What Extent Are the Independent and Dependent Variables Conceptually and Operationally Independent?

To determine the independence of the independent and dependent variables one would need to have a clear conception as to what constitutes group therapy. Having articulated the content of group therapy, one could then compare it with what is involved in the process of testing. In this study it appears that group therapy involves something different from the psychological testing of individuals. However, it is possible that there could be some overlap between the independent and dependent variables. For example, in the author's discussion he considers the possibility that the TAP test may reflect an emphasis on activity programs for mental patients. If group therapy is comprised of activities which involve tapping, then there may be a degree of overlap between the independent and dependent variables. In particular, if untrained therapists engaged in activities related to tapping, while trained therapists did not, the possibility emerges that the results on the tapping test would be biased in favor of the groups conducted by untrained therapists. Nevertheless, this is speculation, and such an assessment could not be made with any degree of certainty unless the independent variable were specified more precisely.

> 5. *What Is the Author's Conception of Variables,*
> *other than the Independent Variables, which*
> *Could Affect the Dependent Variables?*

In experimental studies, procedures are employed in an attempt to rule out the influence of variables other than the independent variable. The researcher's conception of potentially influencing variables leads typically to those variables which are controlled in experimental design. Poser did not deal explicitly with potentially influential variables in his conceptualization. However, those variables which he considered to be important could be discerned from the matching procedures in his experiment. The groups of individual patients were matched on the basis of age, severity of illness, length of hospitalization, and mean test performance prior to therapy. Thus, it may be inferred that the author considered these to be variables that should be controlled in the experiment.

In Poser's experiment potential sources of influence which could confound the experimental results could be conceived as patient variables, therapist variables, situational variables which include hospital experiences and effects of the process of testing, and interactions among all of these classes of variables. In particular, several influential variables are suggested from Poser's discussion of the research problem. With respect to therapist variables, Poser employs literature which suggests that different degrees of "accurate empathy" may influence therapeutic outcome. Thus, "empathy" appears to be a variable which should be incorporated in his experimental design. Further, it is noted that trained and untrained therapists differ with respect to age as well as training. It is possible that patients may react differentially to youth rather than to the degree of training therapists have. In view of this, it would appear that the age of therapists needs to be controlled with regard to comparisons of trained and untrained therapists. In addition, the sex of therapists may be an important therapist variable to consider.

Little mention is made of who did the psychological testing and under what conditions, so it is difficult to specify the influences which differential testing could have. Considerations of such variables as the tester's knowledge of which patients were in which experimental groups are obviously important.

A potential source of influence on patients' reaction time and intellectual functioning may be the relative amounts of medication received by the patients. It was reported that most of the patients received phenothiazine, but the extent and duration of medication was not considered. One might be interested as to whether the author believes that differential amounts of medication might influence the patients' performance on the psychological tests, yet this aspect of conceptualization is not considered. If such medication could affect psychomotor functioning, then it is a variable which needs to be controlled during the course of experimentation.

EVALUATION: RESEARCH DESIGN AND DATA COLLECTION

1. *What Sampling Procedures Were Used for Selecting Hospitals, Patients, and Therapists?*

Sources of variation among hospitals, patients, and therapists are factors which could affect the extent to which one could generalize from this study. Specifically, are the therapists in the study representative of other therapists? Is the hospital in which the research took place representative of other hospitals? Are the chronic schizophrenics used in the research representative of chronic schizophrenics in other places and settings? In order to approximate answers to these questions the sampling procedures must be considered. No consideration was given to the sampling of other hospitals, and the untrained therapists consisted of undergraduate women who volunteered for the project and two in-patients. The chronic male schizophrenic population with the exception of assaultive and known organic brain damage patients was originally included in the study. Characteristics of trained therapists were presented, but it is not clear as to how they were selected for the study. Therefore, this is a study of selected trained and untrained therapists who attempted group therapy with male chronic schizophrenics at one hospital, possibly in Canada. The extent to which the patients are comparable to other male schizophrenics in other hospitals and settings is unknown. In addition, the comparability of "trained" therapists in this study to trained therapists at large is also unknown. In order to increase the generalizability of these findings the author could have employed one of at least two available procedures. First, he could have defined the populations of hospitals, patients, and therapists; then, he could have used such sampling procedures as are indicated in the monograph by Hess, Riedel, and Fitzpatrick on *Probability Sampling of Hospitals and Patients* (1961). Secondly, if sampling procedures were impractical, he could have attempted to demonstrate statistically that characteristics of the hospital, patients, and therapists were similar to hospitals, patients, and therapists in other settings with respect to *any known listing* of published characteristics.

2. *In What Way Does the Experimental Design Include Provisions for Maximizing the Internal Validity of the Experiment? What Assumptions Are Made in the Design; and What Variables Are Not Controlled?*

Three procedures were used for attempting to maximize internal validity: matching of characteristics of the 34 groups of patients on several variables; random assignment of the groups to three experimental conditions; and the use of two control groups, i.e., a "no treatment" group and a "placeboid" group. By using the randomization procedures, a mechanism was employed such that the assumption of the equivalence of relevant variables among the three experimental conditions is plausible.

In the experiment implicit assumptions are that the trained therapists are equivalent with respect to the way in which they conduct group therapy. Further, it is assumed that the trained therapists differ from untrained therapists only with respect to the variable of training. Since the untrained therapists are younger than the trained therapists, there is a confounding of age of therapists with training of therapists; hence, age of therapists is not controlled. In addition, the characteristic of sex of therapists is not controlled, i.e., there is a greater proportion of females among the untrained therapists than there is among the trained therapists. Since the variable of "accurate empathy" of therapists is regarded to be relevant for therapeutic outcomes, it is implicitly assumed that all therapists are equivalent in regard to "accurate empathy." The assumption does not appear to be tenable; thus, this variable should have been controlled in the experiment.

An important characteristic among the patients which may affect the dependent variables is the extent and duration of medication received during the course of the experiment. Evidence pertaining to the equivalence among groups assigned to the three experimental conditions with respect to relative dosages of medication could have been provided by the experimenter to demonstrate that the psychological test results were not confounded by medication.

The procedures for assigning groups of patients to experimental conditions with two control groups were appropriate. The use of the "placeboid" control group was an excellent feature of the experiment, especially since few studies of group therapy have employed such a control. Improvements might have been made by extending the design to control for characteristics of the therapists which might interact with characteristics of the patients. For example, a further randomization procedure of the patient groups to "empathic" or "non-empathic" therapists within both groups of trained and untrained therapists.

3. *What Evidence Is Provided that the Patients Assigned to the Experimental Groups Were Comparable Through the Course of the Experiment?*

The assumption was made that the initial assignment of groups of patients in the beginning phases of the experiment with respect to equivalence among those variables which were matched would be maintained throughout the course of the experiment. However, there were two events which reduced the effectiveness of those procedures. In the first place, groups of patients were assigned to the experimental groups at three points in time. The groups assigned to the "no control" group and to treatment by untrained therapists were selected at the beginning of the study. Then at two subsequent points in time the remaining groups of patients were assigned to the professional therapists and to two non-trained, in-patient therapists. Thus, the assumption involved is that the groups used at later stages in time were comparable to the groups used at earlier stages with respect to their own characteristics, as well as in regard to events taking place at the hospital. In essence, the matching and randomization procedures could have been strengthened if assignments of all groups to all experimental conditions were made at the same point in time, rather than over a 10 month time period. The second event which may have reduced the effectiveness of randomization is the fact that there was a shrinkage of the numbers of patients included in the study from 343 to 295. Only those patients who attended at least two-thirds of the sessions were included. Thus, the assumption of equivalence for unknown variables which could influence the dependent variables becomes less plausible. In addition, the use of probability testing becomes less tenable due to the *arbitrary* reduction of patients included for analysis. The experimenter could have done one of two things to justify his procedures. One possibility is to have included all 343 patients in the experiment and to have used "attendance" as another dependent variable. A second possibility is to have demonstrated that the groups of patients assigned to the three experimental conditions were equivalent with respect to those variables for which they were originally matched and with respect to other variables for which information was available, e.g., dosage of medication, activity in the hospital, prior test performance, and so forth. This could have been demonstrated by a *posteriori* statistical testing.

4. How Were the Data Collected, and to What Degree Were the Data Reliable and Valid?

Psychological tests were administered individually "immediately before or after therapy" by one or more examiners. Neither the conditions under which testing took place nor the extent to which the examiner (s) had knowledge concerning the experimental groups to which patients were assigned were included in the report. Therefore, it is impossible to determine whether there were biases involved in the testing process *per se* which could have affected the reliability and validity of the data.

The author did not present evidence from previous studies concerning the reliability of the tests, but he indicated that five of the six tests were valid in that they discriminated psychotics from normals. However, the extent to which the tests actually discriminated schizophrenics from normals was not included in the report. The author's choice of tests may have been appropriate in regard to his claim that the tests were within the behavioral repertoire of chronic schizophrenics. However, it appears that other kinds of variables could have been used as dependent variables: attendance, increased job performance within the hospitals, ratings of behavior by independent observers, etc. Essentially, the data may have been relevant for only a small domain of behavior, and the use of other dependent variables might have strengthened his overall conclusions.

The critical problem is concerned with the extent to which the data included as dependent variables in the study are relevant to group therapy for chronic schizophrenics. Since there was an insufficient conceptualization of group therapy, it is difficult to determine why the author expected such changes to occur in variables such as tapping speed and the naming of animals. If the author's

ASSESSMENT OF EXPERIMENTAL STUDIES

conception of group therapy would have been articulated more sufficiently, then the question of the relevance of the dependent variables might have been more easily answered. In conclusion, it appears that the dependent variables are relevant to a small domain or schizophrenic behavior. However, the relevance of the dependent variables to group therapy is not clear. It seems that these variables are more closely geared to groups which include recreational activities, but this is only speculation due to the insufficient amount of information included in the report.

5. What Alternate Research Designs Might Have Been Employed?

As implied previously, the experimental design was appropriate. However, a greater degree of internal and external validity might have been obtained by extending certain aspects of the design. A significant improvement might have occurred if a factorial design including selected therapist and patient characteristics had been employed. For example, stratified random sampling of patients located in more than one hospital might have been used to select the initial group of patients. Then, the patients could have been assigned randomly to one of five groups: a "no treatment group," a group of trained therapists with "accurate empathy," a group of trained therapists with "non-accurate empathy," a group of untrained therapists with "accurate empathy," and a group of untrained therapists with "non-accurate" empathy. Groups of patients could have been matched prior to randomization on variables listed by Poser, as well as on other variables such as dosage of medication. In addition, therapists could have been matched with respect to age and sex, with the only difference between trained and untrained therapists being that of professional training and experience. Random assignment could take place at one period of time, and what constitutes group therapy could be specified more completely. The experimenter could check his randomization procedures by a posteriori statistical tests regarding the equivalence of groups on those variables for which adequate information is available. Data other than psychological test results could be employed as dependent variables: attendance in groups, observed behaviors regarding symptoms of schizophrenics, changes in ward behavior, and so forth. In essence, the experimental design could have been more closely geared to the author's conceptualization of the problem for research.

EVALUATION: DATA ANALYSIS AND CONCLUSIONS

1. *To What Extent Do the Data Presented in Tables 1,
2, and 3 Provide Evidence for the Testing of the
Author's Hypotheses?*

It appears that covariance analysis was employed to adjust for the
effects of measurement prior to therapy on measurement subsequent to therapy. If this is the case, it is an appropriate procedure;
comparisons can then be made among the three experimental
groups on the six dependent variables of psychological tests. It is
noted that within Tables 1, 2 and 3, the variation due to groups
and therapists is ignored. The patients treated by the lay therapists
are combined into a number of 87 patients, and the patients treated
by professional therapists are combined into an aggregate of 145
patients. As previously indicated, this is reflective of the assumption of equivalence among patients, therapists, and interactions
among patients and therapists.

There are two conditions which lead to the possible distortion of
the probability estimates reported in the comparisons of means by
independent t-tests. One contingency is that the initial randomization procedure, which forms the basis of probability estimates, was
not maintained since there was shrinkage in the sample of schizophrenics. Another contingency is that statistical comparisons
between the three groups are non-independent. For example, once
"untreated controls" are compared against those patients "treated
by lay therapists," comparisons between "untreated controls" and
those patients "treated by professional therapists" are noninde-
pendent because some of the same sources of variation are included
in both computations of t-tests. This may result in an underestimate
of the probability level attained, which is biased in favor of the
hypotheses. The appropriate statistical procedures would have
included *a posteriori* comparisons as referred to in Edwards (1960)
at the end of this assessment of the Poser study. Nevertheless, the
directions of the test scores are in support of Poser's conclusions,
and more conservative statistical tests would probably continue to
be statistically significant, although possibly at different probability
levels than reported. Essentially the psychological test performance
of patients who were treated by either lay therapists or professional therapists was superior to that of patients who did not
receive group therapy. Interestingly, the test scores were in the
predicted direction on all scores for comparisons between patients
treated by lay therapists and patients who were not treated. For
comparisons between patients treated by professional therapists and
patients who were not treated, two of the tests were not in the

predicted direction: patients who were treated had lower reaction times and lower verbal fluency scores. This leads to the question as to whether the usual routine activities conducted for non-treated patients included recreational type activities. If so, then the non-treated control group could, in a sense, have had treatment, at least that kind of treatment related to superior performance on the reaction time test and verbal fluency test. However, this is unknown from the report, and only additional analyses by the investigator could have led to tentative answers regarding the question. What is clear in the study is that Poser considered this possibility when his retest of the control group indicated superior performance on the TAP test. Another possibility related to lower reaction time among the patients treated by the professional groups might have been that they were under greater dosages of medication. This possibility could be ruled out by additional statistical analyses utilizing the available information pertaining to drug dosage.

In general, the evidence appears to be in support of the hypotheses. However, additional analyses may have rendered more plausible the assumptions of equivalence among the experimental groups with respect to variables which could influence the dependent variables.

2. What Do the Data Presented in Tables 4 and 5 Contribute to the Testing of the Main Hypotheses?

The author provided comparisons between psychiatrists and social workers in Table 4. He did not indicate his rationale for doing so, but there are inferences that one could make from the data. First, the assumption of equivalence among professionals becomes more tenable, particularly with respect to the performance of their patients on psychological tests since there were no significant differences between patients treated by psychiatrists and patients treated by social workers. The second inference is more indirect. All of the psychiatrists were male, and two-thirds of the social workers were female. Since there were no differences among patients treated by these two groups of professionals, it might be inferred that sex differences among therapists are not crucial with respect to the dependent variables in this study. Thus, Table 4 provides indirect evidence which may increase one's confidence in the findings reported.

The data in Table 5 are follow-up data for 61 of the 87 patients treated by lay therapists. Comparisons were made for the same group on selected measurements prior to therapy and three years later. There is shrinkage in the original number of patients, and results from four of the six tests are presented. For those patients, it appears that the results are maintained over subsequent periods of time. Yet, it is obvious that the patients are still in the hospital, which leads to the fundamental question: what is the purpose of group therapy for chronic schizophrenics, and what does "therapeutic gain" mean? Poser also indicates that 23 of the untreated controls did not increase in their performance over a three year time span, with the exception of the tapping test.

These data add to overall considerations of the study, but they appear to be incomplete. Follow-up data for the majority of patients would be desirable. Moreover, the reader would be interested in what has transpired in the patients' lives, what their hospital status is, and to what extent the researcher attributes changes in patients' status to the independent variables of the study.

3. How Legitimate Are the Researcher's Notions about Therapeutic Gain as Reflected in the Selected Tests He Employed?

Poser indicated that selected kinds of data did not appear to be appropriate for the population of schizophrenics he studied. He attempted to use the Hospital Adjustment Scale, but found that ratings could not be made. In addition, there were no differences between treated and untreated patients regarding discharge rates. Thus, one reason for his choice of psychological testing was on grounds of practicality. This appears to be plausible, yet data from observations could probably have been included. His second argument for psychological tests pertains to the notion that they discriminated between psychotics and normals in previous circumstances. Further, there was no change on five of the six tests for the control group. This is plausible in that it appears that the testing is responsive to group therapy. However, one would be interested in knowing what do changes in test behavior relate to: are they predictive of discharge, better ward performance, or what? The notion of therapeutic gain is not validated until expectations from group therapy are conceptualized and predictions of test performance to actual patient behavior are provided. Essentially, the author's contention is plausible, but more validation is necessary.

4. To What Extent Is the Author's Conclusion Regarding Training in Mental Health Professions Appropriate?

Poser appropriately states that it would be premature to extend the conclusions from his study beyond the present context of group therapy with chronic schizophrenics. He then views his study in relation to the literature presented in the paper and argues that his findings support "the conclusion that traditional training in the mental health professions may be neither optimal nor even necessary for the promotion of therapeutic behavior change in mental hospital patients." Since Poser did not identify the kind of training the therapists actually received in relation to group therapy, it is difficult to determine whether such training is necessary. If therapeutic behavior changes refer to changes in psychological test performance, then the inference is plausible. However, since the majority of patients remained in the hospital, and since the notion of expected therapeutic gain in relation to group therapy was not clearly conceptualized, it may also be inferred that more appropriate training may be necessary. This training may be more in regard to such things as "accurate empathy." Hence, his study could be supportive of two opposing conclusions, and is not necessarily supportive of either one.

5. To What Extent Has the Author Accomplished His Purpose in This Study?

The author's main purpose was to assess the relative efficacy of group therapy with chronic schizophrenics by employing a controlled experiment using trained therapists, lay therapists, and a no treatment control group. His experimental design was appropriately geared to this purpose, and he attempted to include provisions for providing a degree of internal validity in the experiment. In general, we have suggested that the design could be extended in relation to a clearer conception of group therapy, so that a greater degree of internal control could have been provided.

By assuming that most relevant variables were controlled by his procedures of matching and randomization, the author made conclusions with respect to test performances that were appropriate. More detailed information regarding the reliability and validity of his tests would have strengthened the conclusions presented in Tables 1, 2, and 3. On the assumption that his data regarding therapeutic gain are valid, his findings do serve the purpose of leading to the question of training of therapists. In this regard, it appears that the author has accomplished the purpose of his study. Certainly, more detailed research of a replicated nature with more controls would lead to increased confidence pertaining to his results, for this would increase the extent to which his results could be generalized further. For the most part the author did not generalize beyond his data, i.e., his conclusions were consistent with the data presented. The primary problem in generalization would refer to the generalization of "group therapy," for it is well known that there are many forms and theoretical orientations pertinent to group therapy. With more specification of the independent variables, such generalizations might have been made on a more restrictive basis.

UTILIZATION

1. What Is the General Level of Knowledge of Conclusions from this Study?

The conclusions regarding the superior performance on psychological tests of patients receiving "group therapy" by either trained or untrained therapists are plausible. The main hypotheses appear to be supported by the data which were collected. However, there are a number of questions pertaining to the reliability and validity of the data, the degree of internal validity, and the extent to which generalizations can be made from the research. In essence, the hypotheses are partially verified, but more evidence within Poser's study as well as replicated studies in other situations would increase the reader's confidence in the findings presented.

Poser's conclusion regarding the necessity of training for group therapists is to be considered as a hypothesis which needs verification in future studies. Certainly, conclusions concerning the comparisons of trained and untrained therapists require more detailed information. Yet, serious questions are raised from this study with respect to what constitutes group therapy and with respect to what criteria of assessment should be employed to evaluate group therapy. In this regard, the study stimulates the need for more adequate conceptualization of the problem and for research which is geared to find answers to these problems.

2. How Identifiable, Accessible, and Manipulable Are the Independent Variables in this Study?

The variable of group therapy was operationalized with respect to the specifications of who should conduct therapy and for what periods of time. The specification of how therapy is to be conducted, and what is to take place in group therapy is not evident. Each therapist was instructed to do whatever he wanted to do. Thus, while the conditions under which therapy is conducted can be identified and manipulated, there is insufficient information to determine whether the procedures of therapy *per se* can be identified and manipulated. It appears that the conditions of having group meetings with patients can be specified, and to this extent the variable of "group therapy" may be accessible. The crucial problem for using knowledge pertains to the content of group therapy, and this cannot be generalized because it is unknown in this study.

3. In What Areas of Social Work Practice Might Knowledge Generated from the Poser Study Be Useful, Either Directly or Indirectly?

The most direct application pertains to the area of group work or group treatment with schizophrenic patients. The notion is that group treatment might lead to some therapeutic gains, but more fundamentally the question pertaining to the efficacy of group treatment by trained or untrained workers must be considered. Research in group work *per se* which pertains to the relative effectiveness of trained versus untrained personnel, such as volunteers, should be conducted. The findings from the Poser study cannot be generalized so that one could say that it is as appropriate to use or not to use volunteers as trained workers; however, the hypothesis could be entertained seriously.

More indirectly, the findings from this study generate concerns regarding the use of professional personnel in mental hospitals. If it is maintained that lay personnel such as volunteers are as effective as trained personnel in regard to group therapy with certain types of patients, then hospital administrators might consider more effective ways in which they could deploy their personnel to other functions.

With respect to research concerned with either group therapy or individual therapy, the issue of "placeboid effects" is paramount. This study provides further evidence that in addition to no treatment controls, research concerned with the efficacy of therapy should also attempt to control for potential "placeboid effects."

4. What Implications Might this Study Have for Considerations of Manpower in the Mental Health Field?

This study in and of itself may lead to the question of how much manpower is necessary for the mental health professions which attempt to treat patients in mental hospitals. It is well documented that there are shortages of psychiatrists, psychologists, and social workers. Yet the findings in this study are inconclusive in regard to who should conduct group therapy. The findings are suggestive in that it is possible that training may not need to be as extensive as believed by various professionals. However, this knowledge is at the level of hypothesis formulation.

Since the publication of the Poser study there have been a number of investigations which have dealt with the relative effectiveness of lay and professional personnel. To place the Poser study in the context of other findings, the student is referred to Carkhuff's (1968) review of the literature. Carkhuff presents a body of evidence which suggests that lay counselors can be beneficial in helping patients. Carkhuff's review of the research literature, which includes Poser's study and a number of other investigations, lends more credibility to the possibility that lay counselors can be effective. If this conclusion is true, it has serious implications for the use of manpower in contemporary society. Specifically, it may be possible that jobs can be created for people to serve as helping persons without receiving extensive education. This may relieve some of the pressures regarding shortage of mental health personnel, and at the same time may create opportunities for people who do not currently have jobs.

5. *What Further Hypotheses Pertaining to Group Treatment Might Be Developed from this Study?*

In addition to replicating the main hypotheses of this study, the reader may generate hypotheses which include more specific aspects of internal control. From an assessment of this study these following hypotheses are suggested:

A. Irrespective of training in group therapy, therapists with "accurate empathy" are more likely than therapists with "non-accurate empathy" to be effective with psychotic patients with respect to post-hospital adjustment, psychological test performance, and hospital ward adjustment.

B. Volunteer group workers with no previous experience are as "effective" as professional group workers in the counseling of mental patients with respect to outcome criteria of in-hospital and post-hospital adjustment.

C. The age of group therapists is associated with the psychological test performance of their patients.

D. There are no significant differences in the effectiveness of group therapists with chronic schizophrenics, as a function of either the patient's or the therapist's sex.

RECOMMENDED REFERENCES

Problems in Research Design and Sampling

HESS, IRENE; RIEDEL, DONALD C.; and FITZPATRICK, THOMAS B.; *Probability Sampling of Hospitals and Patients* (Bureau of Hospital Administration, The University of Michigan, Ann Arbor, 1961), pp. 7–25.

PARLOFF, MORRIS B., and RUBENSTEIN, ELI A., "Research Problems in Psychotherapy" in *Research in Psychotherapy*, Eli A. Rubenstein and Morris B. Parloff (eds.), The National Publishing Company, Washington, D.C., 1959, pp. 276–92.

KIESLER, DONALD J., "Some Myths of Psychotherapeutic Research and the Search for a Paradigm," *Psychological Bulletin*, 65:2 (February, 1966), pp. 110–36.

Statistical Concepts

BLALOCK, HUBERT M., JR., *Social Statistics* (New York, McGraw-Hill Book Company, Inc., 1960), "Introduction to Inductive Statistics," pp. 89–96; "Difference-of-means Test (T-Test)," pp. 169–76; "Analysis of Covariance," pp. 359–82.

EDWARDS, ALLEN L., *Statistical Methods for the Behavioral Sciences* (New York, Holt, Rinehart and Winston, 1960), "The T-Test for the Means of Independent Samples," pp. 246–75.

Implications of Psychotherapy Research

BERGIN, ALLEN E., "Some Implications of Psychotherapy Research for Therapeutic Practice," *Journal of Abnormal Psychology*, Vol. 71, No. 4, 1966, pp. 235–46.

PATTISON, E. MANSELL, "Evaluation Studies of Group Psychotherapy," *International Journal of Psychiatry*, (October, 1967), pp. 333–43.

CARKHUFF, ROBERT R., "Differential Functioning of Lay and Professional Helpers," *Journal of Counseling Psychology*, Vol. 15, No. 2, 1968, pp. 117–26.

A Study of Anchoring Effects in Clinical Judgment

by BEN A. ORCUTT

The study of clinical judgment is of fundamental concern in social casework. Casework clinicians continually exercise judgment as they appraise the inflow of varying information about clients in order to arrive at some kind of global estimate of the nature of the client's problems, personality, and adaptive capacities. The process of judgment is not only central to diagnosis; it is also inherent in every aspect of ongoing treatment. It is essential, therefore, to understand more about the cognitive processes involved in judgment and the aspects of functioning that open up tendencies to bias and distortion.

The problem with which this study is concerned is how clinical judgment in casework may be affected by different contexts in which judgments are made; that is, how varying "frames of reference" developed about a client may lead different judges to infer strikingly different characteristics about the same client and thus bias their judgment.

To approach this problem it was possible to employ concepts and methods used in psychophysical judgment. Context effects that may bias judgments in casework can be investigated partially through studying a basic process in judgment known as anchoring. An anchor is defined as a standard or a force that influences perception of other stimuli. This concept, developed in classical psychophysical studies of judgment in psychology, refers to the influence of extreme stimuli, or anchors, on stimuli that are some distance from the anchoring stimuli. For example, in psychophysics a study may include how experience in judging very loud tones (anchoring stimuli) influences the judgment of tones of more moderate loudness. In the clinical situation, the concept of anchoring may refer to how experience in judging cases extreme in pathology (anchors) will tend to bias judgment or perception of cases of moderate pathology. In this connection, two different directional phenomena have been found to operate in anchoring—assimilation and contrast. That is, the anchor creates an effect in which the stimulus is per-

SOURCE: Reprinted from *The Social Service Review*, Vol. 38, No. 4 (December, 1964), pp. 408–17, by permission of The University of Chicago Press, and the author.

ceived either as more like the anchor than it actually is (assimilation), or less like the anchor (contrast).

Some of the earliest psychophysical studies, such as those of Volkmann,[1] Hunt,[2] Postman and Miller,[3] and Helson,[4] demonstrated that anchoring effects distort perception in the judgment of simple sensory stimuli. That is, when an extreme stimulus or anchor is introduced and judged in comparison with previously judged stimuli, judgments of the previously judged stimuli tend to be in contrast to the newly introduced anchoring stimulus. Having clearly demonstrated this with sensory materials, McGarvey[5] showed that the same effects would occur with verbal materials and social value dimensions. Hovland[6] and others have also demonstrated these effects in attitude studies.

In view of the increasing body of research indicating that anchoring effects occur in reference to sensory, social, and attitudinal materials, it is logical to question whether these same phenomena also exist in clinical judgment. Two previous studies using clinical materials report ambiguous findings. A study by Arnhoff[7] failed to find anchoring effects, while studies by Campbell, Hunt, and Lewis[8] report the presence of anchoring effects.

The purpose of the current study was, therefore, to explore further whether anchoring effects exist in clinical judgment and, if so, to determine the nature of these effects. The study was designed to answer three major questions:

1. Will significant differences occur in the judgment of identical mod-

---

[1] John Volkmann, "The Anchoring of Absolute Scales," *Psychological Bulletin*, XXXIII (November, 1936), 742–43.

[2] William A. Hunt and John Volkmann, "The Anchoring of an Affective Scale," *American Journal of Psychology*, XLIX (January, 1937), 88–92, and "Anchoring Effects in Judgments," *American Journal of Psychology*, LIV (July, 1941), 395–403.

[3] Leo Postman and G. A. Miller, "Anchoring of Temporal Judgments," *American Journal of Psychology*, LVIII (January, 1945), 43–53.

[4] Harry Helson, "Adaptation Level Theory," in *Psychology: A Study of Science*, ed. Sigmund Koch (New York: McGraw-Hill Book Co., 1959), I, 565–621.

[5] Hulda Rees McGarvey, "Anchoring Effects in the Absolute Judgment of Verbal Materials," *Archives of Psychology*, No. 281 (New York, May, 1943).

[6] C. Hovland, O. Harvey, and M. Sherif, "Assimilation and Contrast Effects in Reactions to Communication and Attitude Change," *Journal of Abnormal and Social Psychology*, LV (July–November, 1957), 244–52.

[7] Franklin N. Arnhoff, "Some Factors Influencing the Unreliability of Clinical Judgments," *Journal of Clinical Psychology*, X (July, 1954), 272–75.

[8] Donald J. Campbell, William A. Hunt, and Nan A. Lewis, "The Effects of Assimilation and Contrast in Judgments of Clinical Materials," *American Journal of Psychology*, LXX (September, 1957), 347–60; and Donald J. Campbell, Nan A. Lewis, and William A. Hunt, "Contexts Effects with Judgmental Language That Is Absolute, Extensive, Extra-Experimentally Anchored," *Journal of Experimental Psychology*, LV (March, 1958), 220–28.

erately disturbed behavior depending on whether it is judged in the context of a high anchor (extremely disturbed behavior) or a low anchor (mildly disturbed behavior)?

2. Will differences in judgment be in the direction of displacement away from the anchor (contrast)?

3. As sequential judgments are made, will anchoring effects be dissipated; that is, will judges tend to correct distortion and judge more accurately?

METHOD

In order to study anchoring effects in clinical judgment, it was necessary to devise stimulus materials that were extreme enough to provide an anchoring context within which more moderate stimuli could be judged. Stimuli were needed that would have known scalar values on some meaningful clinical dimension. It was considered that pathological behavior could be scaled as high or low in value, depending on the extremity of the pathology. Middle-range pathological behavior could be judged within an anchoring context of mild or extreme pathology to determine the effect of the anchors on judgment.

The experiment required more restricted or limited stimulus materials than the quantity of sociobehavioral information characteristically acquired in the casework interview. It was essential, however, that the materials reflect the kinds of behavior ordinarily observed or reported in the interview. Aggresssion and dependency were selected as two behavioral dimensions on which to standardize the stimulus material. Use of these two dimensions would facilitate investigation of whether similar effects would occur with different behaviors. It was recognized that aggression and dependency are not strictly independent behavioral categories; however, for purposes of the experiment, they were defined as being as distinctly different as possible.

PATHOLOGY SCALE. As evaluation of a client's behavior and social dysfunctioning is inherent in casework diagnosis and treatment, it was desirable to standardize the stimulus material on a dimension of pathology and to provide a scale for judgment. It was assumed that pathological behavior could be ordered on a single continuum, from very mild to extreme. For judgment of behavioral stimuli, a twenty-point graphic rating scale was used, with "very mild maladjustment" as the lowest category and "extreme maladjustment" as the highest category.

STIMULUS MATERIAL. The material to be judged consisted of brief "cases" or clusters of social behaviors attributable to an adult male. Each case was constructed from either aggressive or dependent behavioral items derived from a large pool of items. These items had been previously judged individually on the pathology scale by eleven social caseworkers, twelve psychiatrists, and ten second-year casework students in a psychiatric field setting. The items covered the entire range of the scale. Arbitrarily, items were considered high in pathology when their judged mean values ranged from 15 to 20 on the scale. They were considered moderate in pathology when their mean values ranged from 7 to 14 and low when they ranged from 1 to 6 on the scale.

Each item consisted of a single sentence describing an instance of aggressive or dependent behavior. The following is an example of an aggressive item:

When the waiter brought him his hamburger rare instead of well-done, he roared profanities and threw the plate on the floor.

An example of a dependent item follows:

The only way he could muster enough courage to get to his job was for his wife to help him dress himself, buy his bus fare, put him on the bus, and keep telling him that he was "doing fine."

Items with the greatest interjudge agreement of mean scale values[9] were selected from the three ranges of the scale indicating high, middle, and low pathology. Four items from each range were then combined to form a case. Thus, twelve cases were assembled and presented as stimulus material to subjects in the experiment. These twelve cases consisted of four cases drawn from each range of the scale—high, middle, and low. Half of the cases in each range were composed of aggressive behaviors, and half were dependent behaviors.

To further standardize the cases, seventy-four graduate social work students, divided into three separate groups, judged cases drawn exclusively from the high, middle, or low scale range. Table 1 presents the mean judgments and standard deviations of the high, low, and middle cases as judged exclusively by the three groups of students. Their ratings assured that the combined items that formed the cases reflected mean values equivalent to the individual items. These judgments also provided mean scale values for high,

---

[9] Mean judgments of each of the three groups were essentially equivalent. Psychiatrists were slightly more variable in their judgments than were caseworkers and students.

middle, and low cases under non-anchored conditions, which could
be compared with judgments under anchored conditions in the
experiment.

EXPERIMENTAL DESIGN. The study was designed to demonstrate the
effect of alternating extreme anchors upon a series of clinical judgments of moderately pathological behavior. It was desirable not
only to study judgments of moderately pathological behavior
within different anchoring contexts but also to study these judgments in sequential phases so as to determine whether anchoring
effects, if they occurred, would persist over a series of judgments.
This had not been investigated in anchoring research other than
that by Levy,[10] who found that contrasts occurred in social judgment but tended to dissipate over a time sequence. It was necessary
also to provide for judgment of different moderate cases within
identical anchoring contexts, on each behavioral dimension, so as to
determine whether different cases might contribute to differences
in judgment.

In order to allow for the systematic variation of anchors,
behaviors, and middle cases and to demonstrate anchoring effects
over a series of judgments, an experimental design was constructed,
with four phases. In each phase, judgments were to be made on a
triad of cases, either two high or two low cases followed by a case of
middle range. The high or low cases served as anchors, which were
alternated with each phase. That is, for each group of judges, if the
anchor cases in the first phase were high, those in the second phase
were low. Cases in the first and second phases covered the same
behavioral dimension, and those in the third and fourth phases
covered the other behavioral dimension. For example, if cases in the
first and second phases dealt with aggressive behavior, those in the
third and fourth phases dealt with dependent behavior.

It was also necessary that the design provide for counterbalancing
the orders of presentation of the triad of "cases" within the four
phases. More explicitly, counterbalancing allowed three major conditions to vary: (1) initial high or low anchoring stimuli, (2) a
different middle case with identical anchors, and (3) aggressive or
dependent behavior presented initially. To accomplish this, eight
experimental groups were required. Table 2 presents in detail the
construction of the design in which the variables of high and low
anchor cases, different middle cases, and aggressive and dependent
behavior are systematically varied. By this method of counter-bal-

10 Leon Levy, "Adaptations, Anchoring, and Dissipation in Social Perception," *Journal of Personality*, XXIX (March, 1961), 94–104.

ancing, it was possible for half of the groups to receive high anchors first and half to receive low anchors first on each dimension. Also, it was possible for half of the groups to receive the high and low anchors with one middle case, while half received the identical anchors with another middle case. It was also possible for half of the groups to receive aggressive behaviors in the first two phases and dependent behaviors in the second two, whereas the other half had a reverse ordering. Twenty-two subjects were randomly assigned to each of the eight experimental groups.

TABLE 1

MEAN PATHOLOGY JUDGMENTS OF HIGH, LOW, AND MIDDLE CASES JUDGED EXCLUSIVELY BY THREE SEPARATE GROUPS OF STUDENTS

Cases	Aggressive Behavior		Dependent Behavior	
	Mean	Standard Deviation	Mean	Standard Deviation
High	18.21	2.68	16.47	3.75
High	16.79	4.38	14.26	4.29
Low	5.00	4.92	6.16	5.19
Low	5.11	5.11	5.89	5.33
Middle	11.63	3.51	11.59	3.67
Middle	10.00	4.25	10.18	4.10

SAMPLE. A total of 176 first-year social work students, drawn from the Columbia University School of Social Work and the School of Social Welfare of the University of California, Berkeley, during the latter part of the 1960–61 academic year, were used as subjects for the experiment. Seventy-four graduate social work students in their first or second year at Columbia University or in

TABLE 2

EXPERIMENTAL DESIGN INDICATING THE COUNTERBALANCED ORDER OF CASES OF AGGRESSIVE AND DEPENDENT BEHAVIOR SCALED AS HIGH, MODERATE, AND LOW IN PATHOLOGY* AS PRESENTED TO EIGHT EXPERIMENTAL GROUPS IN FOUR SEQUENTIAL PHASES

Group	Phase 1	Phase 2	Phase 3	Phase 4
	Aggressive Behavior		Dependent Behavior	
I	HHM_1	LLM_2	HHM_1	LLM_2
II	LLM_1	HHM_2	LLM_1	HHM_2
III	HHM_2	LLM_1	HHM_2	LLM_1
IV	LLM_2	HHM_1	LLM_2	HHM_1
	Dependent Behavior		Aggressive Behavior	
V	HHM_1	LLM_2	HHM_1	LLM_2
VI	LLM_1	HHM_2	LLM_1	HHM_2
VII	HHM_2	LLM_1	HHM_2	LLM_1
VIII	LLM_2	HHM_1	LLM_2	HHM_1

* H = high case; L = low case; M_1 = middle case; M_2 = middle case.

their first year at New York University during the spring and fall semesters of 1961 had served as comparative groups for judgment of cases under non-anchored conditions.

RESULTS

In order to determine the presence, the direction, and the persistence of anchoring effects, three different analyses were used which related to the three questions posed for study, as follows:

1. Will significant differences occur in the judgment of identical moderately disturbed behavior depending on whether it is judged in the context of a high anchor (extremely disturbed behavior) or a low anchor (mildly disturbed behavior)? If anchoring effects occurred, judgments of the middle case in the context of a high anchor would be expected to differ significantly from judgments of the middle case in the context of a low anchor. To identify these differences, analysis of variance using the method of orthogonal comparisons was applied to the data. Though the high and low anchor conditions were the major experimental effect to be considered, it was also possible to isolate the variance due to possible differences in judgment of the two middle cases *within* each type of behavior and possible differences in the middle-case judgments *between* the two types of behavior. Computations for each phase of the series of judgments indicated highly significant differences ($p < .001$) between middle-case judgments depending on the anchor in each phase, with the exception of Phase 3. Applying the t-test as a more stringent measure, differences due to the anchor were significant[11] in Phase 3 on the aggressive behavioral dimension. No significant differences were found attributable to the behavioral dimensions, or to the middle cases, with the exception of the two middle cases on the dependency dimension in Phases 2 and 3. Some less equivalence could be attributed to these cases. Table 2 presents a summary of the results of these orthogonal comparisons in the four phases of the experiment. The results clearly demonstrate that the anchoring context contributed significantly to differences. in judgment of the middle cases across two behavioral dimensions.

2. Will differences in judgment be in the direction of displacement away from the anchor (contrast)? The presence of anchoring effects having been clearly established, the second analysis examined the directional differences of these effects and determined whether the anchoring distortion was in the direction of contrast or assimilation. This depended on whether the mean

_____
11 Unless otherwise indicated, the level of significance is .05.

judgment on the anchored middle case deviated significantly from the mean judgment on the non-anchored middle case in a direction away from the anchor or toward the anchor.

In every instance middle-case judgments in Phase 1 were made in the direction of contrast to the anchoring context; that is, they deviated from the non-anchored middle-case judgment in a direction away from the anchor. In two of the eight groups this deviation was significant.

In Phase 2, the anchor in the triad was changed from high to low or from low to high, depending on whether the anchor in the first phase was high or low. All eight groups now judged the middle case in an assimilative direction toward the anchor; that is, their judgments deviated from the non-anchored mean judgments in a direction toward the anchor. In four of the eight groups this deviation was significant.

TABLE 3

SUMMARY OF RESULTS OF ORTHOGONAL COMPARISONS OF MIDDLE-CASE JUDGMENTS IN THE FOUR PHASES

Source of Variation	Degrees of Freedom	Phase 1		Phase 2		Phase 3		Phase 4	
		Mean Square	F Ratio	Mean Square	F Ratio	Mean Square	F Ratio	Mean Square	F Ratio
Between groups.....	7	100.28	5.17*	153.42	10.52*	38.42	2.10†	210.29	15.35*
H-L (aggressive)‡...	1	301.92	15.58*	418.91	28.71*	38.23	2.09	871.92	63.64*
H-L (dependent)§..	1	280.10	14.45*	418.91	28.71*	57.28	3.13	486.92	35.54*
M_1-M_2‖	1	4.10	.21	4.55	.31	2.91	.15	.28	.02
M_3-M_4#	1	67.38	3.47	198.00	13.57*	86.01	4.70†	39.56	2.89
A-D**	1	44.00	2.27	1.11	.76	22.55	1.23	.09	.006
Residual	2	1.12	.05	16.26	1.11	31.01	1.70	36.61	2.67
Within groups.....	168	19.38	—	14.59	—	18.29	—	13.70	—

* $p < .01$.
† $p < .05$.
‡ High vs. low aggressive cases.
§ High vs. low dependent cases.
‖ Middle case₁ vs. middle case₂ (aggressive).
Middle case₃ vs. middle case₄ (dependent).
** Aggressive vs. dependent.

In Phase 3 of the series, the anchor was shifted back to a scale value equivalent to the anchor in Phase 1. However, a new behavioral dimension was introduced—that is, aggressive instead of dependent behavior, or vice versa. Though five of the groups deviated from the non-anchored mean judgments in an assimilative direction, assimilation and contrast were not clear. Judgments in this phase tended to correspond more nearly with the non-anchored mean judgments. In only one group was there significant deviation.

This latter finding might have led to a belief that subjects were now beginning to correct the distortion created by the anchors and to judge more accurately, after having experienced and judged the middle case in the context of both high and low extremes of the scale. However, the results in Phase 4 tended to repudiate this theory. Here, the most striking evidence of an assimilation tendency occurred. In five of the eight groups, the anchored middle case was judged significantly different from the non-anchored middle case and in the direction of the anchor.

3. As sequential judgments are made, will anchoring effects be dissipated; that is, will judges tend to correct distortion and judge more accurately? The third and final analysis dealt with the question of dissipation of the anchoring effects over a series of judgments. The above results clearly indicate that anchoring effects were present and continued to persist throughout the series, though losing some effect in Phase 3, when a second behavioral dimension was introduced. However, to analyze the sequential deviation across four phases, the test for contrasts among means was applied.[12]

The results indicated no significant difference between middle-case judgments of Phases 1 and 2, but a significant difference between Phases 1 and 3. The failure to achieve significant difference between Phases 1 and 2 can be explained as a result of the tendency for subjects to evidence contrast on the initial phase, with subsequent evidence of assimilation on the second phase. Judgments would necessarily fall within a similar scalar range. Had there been a tendency, however, for judges to be consistent in their judgments across the series, Phase 3 would not have been judged significantly different from Phase 1. Judgments were also found to be significantly different between Phases 2 and 3 and between Phases 3 and 4. These findings may be interpreted as further evidence of the sequential shifts in judgment in the direction of the anchor after tending to show contrast in the initial phase. It is thus clearly evident that anchoring effects persisted throughout the four phases.

PARTIAL REPETITION

There was a possibility that results of the study might be associated with lack of training and experience in students. The study was partially replicated with thirty-two experienced caseworkers to determine whether similar distortions might also occur in judgments of experienced practitioners. Only two experimental groups were studied. One received high anchors initially, and the other

---

[12] Wilfred J. Dixon and Frank J. Massey, *Introduction to Statistical Analysis* (New York: McGraw-Hill Book Co., 1957), p. 153.

received low anchors. Results indicated that, under the condition of initial high anchoring, judgments of students and caseworkers followed almost an identical curve throughout the four phases, with the exception that caseworkers did not clearly evidence contrast on the initial judgment (Phase 1). However, under the condition of initial low anchor, practitioners strikingly showed evidence of the operation of contrast on Phase 1, but their subsequent judgments in the series tended to approach the non-anchored mean judgments. This finding suggests the possibility that, though practitioners, like students, initially distort judgments in relation to the anchor, they may tend to correct these distortions over time and judge more accurately. More comprehensive research will be needed to clarify this possibility.

DISCUSSION

The study clearly demonstrates the presence of anchoring phenomena in clinical judgments. It identifies a possible source of error in clinical diagnostic assessment, and it lends additional support to the assumption of generality of anchoring effects in perception. That is, responses influenced by anchoring stimuli may obey certain laws or principles that occur independent of the specific stimulus material being judged. Furthermore, this study shows that, when alternate anchors were used, judgments were initially distorted in the direction of contrast and were generally modified by assimilation tendencies.

The present study suggests that subjects' judgments of pathology of "cases" represent comparisons in their experience. That is, the behavioral stimuli were judged with reference to other related behaviors, events, intensities, both present and past, that converged in experience to form a pathological dimension.

Considering these concepts as a frame of reference, one may ask whether current theoretical formulations relative to anchoring phenomena offer any explanation for these biasing effects. Helson's adaptation-level theory, which suggests that there is a shift in perception, presumably predicts how the aggregate of previous experience "pools" to form the basis for a given response or judgment. It postulates that one uses the entire experience range of his scale, or the stimulus magnitudes to which he is accustomed as a "frame of reference," which "pools" to form an adaptation level or an average, a standard or a base, from which a judgment or a response is made.[13] Helson's theory, derived from experiments on anchoring, predicts a shifting of this average or adaptation level away from and

---

[13] Helson, "Adaptation Level Theory," *op. cit.*

in contrast to the anchoring stimuli and thus does not predict the findings of this study beyond Phase 1. Similarly, Volkmann's scalar extension theory, which assumes that the extreme anchor operates to stretch the perceptual scale like a rubber band, so that a moderate case stimulus would be displaced away from or contrasted to the extreme anchor, is equally insufficient to explain the assimilation results subsequent to Phase 1.[14]

Theoretical formulations of Sherif and Hovland,[15] as well as Peak,[16] predict that contrast or assimilation distortions in anchoring occur as a function of the distance that the anchor is varied from the experimental stimuli. Shorter distances tend to produce assimilation tendencies whereas greater magnitudes tend to produce contrasts. Contrary to these latter predictions, in the present study both contrast and assimilation effects were found without experimentally varying the distance between the anchor and the middle case.

Though the present study was essentially descriptive, an important principle was isolated which appears to contribute generally to anchoring effects in clinical judgment; that is, that judgments of "cases" of behavior located at the extremes of the scale are characterized by relative constancy, whereas judgments of those located in the middle range show variability. With the characteristic tendency of moderate judgments to vary, there is increased likelihood that these behaviors or cases will vary as a function of the anchor. From the findings, it is also evident that the judgments of cases serving as anchors at the extremes of the scale do shift slightly as a function of the middle case, but on the whole these judgments remain more stable than do the middle case judgments.

Explanation of the initial tendency for contrast to occur may derive from the fact that the anchor served as a standard of comparison in perception. The anchor defined either the more-pathological or the less-pathological end of the scale, depending on whether a low or high anchor was introduced first, with the middle case defining the opposite end of the scale. Subjects thus tended to perceive a two-category scale of a sick-well dimension, with the middle case being perceived as farther out on the scale than it

---

14 Volkmann, "Scales of Judgment and Their Implications for Social Psychology," in *Social Psychology at the Crossroads,* eds. G. H. Rohrer and M. Sherif (New York: Harper and Sons, 1951), pp. 273–74; *see also* Volkmann, "The Anchoring of Absolute Scales," *op. cit.*

15 M. Sherif, D. Taub, and C. Hovland, "Assimilation and Control Effects of Anchoring Stimuli on Judgments," *Journal of Experimental Psychology,* LV (February, 1958), 150–55.

16 Helen Peak, "Psychological Structure and Psychological Activities," *Psychological Review,* LXV (November, 1958), 325–47.

actually was (contrast). If, after judging the initial middle case in this range, subjects had attempted to remain consistent in their judgment across the series, the middle case judgment would not have shifted on Phase 3. However, the fact that it shifted significantly supports the interpretation of assimilation tendencies in subsequent judgments.

It appears that the assimilation that occurred was a function of a grouping effect. Subjects tended to group the middle case and the two anchor cases perceptually, with loss of discrimination. Thus, they were judging in essentially two categories, high and low. The variability of the middle case would tend to accentuate this tendency. The effect of the anchor was to stimulate assimilation of the more-moderate behavior of the middle case. For example, one subject's comment illustrates such a process. When questioned about how she arrived at her judgmental estimates, she said that she saw the three cases as a "unit."

SUMMARY

In order to demonstrate the existence of anchoring effects in clinical judgment and to study directional distortions, 176 social work students were asked to make judgments of maladjustment on previously scaled moderately pathological clinical materials in the context of alternated anchors in a sequence of four phases. These anchors reflected either severe or mild pathology; the clinical materials were either aggressive or dependent behaviors. The results indicated significant distortions of judgments attributable to anchoring. Anchoring effects took the direction of contrast in initial judgment but followed a trend toward assimilation subsequently in the series. In exploration of whether these results might be related to students' lack of training and experience, a partial replication of the study with 32 experienced caseworkers demonstrated that practitioners and students distort similarly, but results suggested a possible tendency for practitioners to correct their distortion over a time sequence. Anchoring effects thus appeared to occur from a tendency to perceive the moderate stimulus in the context of anchoring stimuli in terms of a two-category scale on a sick-well dimension and subsequently to group these stimuli perceptually with a loss in finer discrimination.

In conclusion, this research has isolated some interesting elements of clinical judgment bias and posed some new directions for further inquiry. It is important to study further whether the direction of anchoring effects is contingent upon the experimental design and to determine whether anchoring reflects shifts in scalar values or actual shifts in how stimuli are perceived. It is important to demonstrate further the persistence of anchoring effects with a variety of clinical and casework judgments within designs that approach the more normal interview situation. This study is a logical first step in this direction. A few simple principles have been isolated which contribute in part to a step-by-step process of formulating a general theory of judgment.

Exercise for the Reader:
Assessment of the Orcutt Study

CLASSIFICATION

1. What is the specific purpose (s) of the study?
2. What research methods does the author use to accomplish his purpose?
3. Why is the study classified as experimental? How does it differ from exploratory and quantitative-descriptive studies?
4. Should the study be sub-typed as a field experiment or as a laboratory experiment?

EVALUATION

Problem Formulation

1. How does the author use literature pertaining to judgment to conceptualize the problem for study?
2. How are anchors and anchoring effects conceptually and operationally defined?
3. What are the major questions and implicit hypotheses of the study? What are the independent and dependent variables?
4. To what extent do the specific major questions of the study relate conceptually to the more general problem of clinical judgment in casework?
5. What potentially influencing variables, other than the independent and dependent variables, did the author conceive of in his conceptualization and research design?

Research Design and Data Collection

1. What are the major characteristics of the experimental design used in this study?
2. What are the major assumptions in regard to the use of aggressive and dependent behavioral items in this design?
3. What variables are and are not controlled in the design?
4. To what extent are the stimuli used for the study standardized?
5. In what way is the response dimension of pathology appropriate as opposed to the use of response dimensions of aggressive and dependent behavior?
6. Referring to Table 1, to what extent are the pathology judg-

ments made by students similar for items of aggressive and dependent behavior?

7. What sampling procedures were employed for the selection of behaviors, items, and judges?

8. How were students assigned to different experimental groups, and to what extent were the groups comparable?

9. What procedures were used for obtaining the judgments of students, and to what extent were potential biases in the data collection minimized?

10. What alternative research designs could the researcher have used?

Data Analysis and Conclusions

1. Referring to Table 2, to what extent are there anchoring effects as a result of high and low anchors for aggressive and dependent behavior?

2. Referring to Table 2, to what extent are the middle cases used for different groups comparable? In what way would non-comparability affect the interpretations of data from this table?

3. Referring to Table 2 and the author's interpretation of data, why are there no significant differences in Phase 3 as a result of high and low anchors? Are there alternate explanations for this phenomenon?

4. What is the contribution to the study by the author's "partial repetition"?

5. How does the author use the literature in attempting to explain the findings of his study?

6. Are the author's conclusions regarding anchoring effects in clinical judgment consistent with the data presented in the study?

7. Has the purpose of the study been achieved?

UTILIZATION

1. To what extent is the study of clinical judgment of importance to social casework?

2. Are the concepts of "high and low anchors," "contrast," and "assimilation" identifiable, accessible, and manipulable?

3. In what way(s) can potential errors in clinical diagnosis and ongoing treatment be avoided as a function of information obtained from this study?

4. To what extent can the findings of this study be carried over into actual practice?

5. In what other areas of judgment and decision making in social work might the findings of this study be potentially useful?

6. What practice principles can be generated from this study and what hypotheses does the study suggest for further research that is relevant for practice?

RECOMMENDED REFERENCES

Problems in Research Design

HUNT, WILLIAM A., and JONES, NELSON F., "The Experimental Investigation of Clinical Judgment," in A. J. Bachrach (ed.), *Experimental Foundations of Clinical Psychology*, New York: Basic Books, 1962, pp. 26–51.

HUNT, J. MCVICKER, "On the Judgment of Social Workers as a Source of Information in Social Work Research," in *Use of Judgments as Data in Social Work Research*, Ann W. Shyne (ed.), New York, National Association of Social Workers, 1959, pp 38–54.

Statistical Concepts

BLALOCK, HUBERT M., JR., *Social Statistics*, New York: McGraw-Hill Book Company, Inc., 1960; "Analysis of Variance," pp. 242–72.

EDWARDS, ALLEN L., *Experimental Design in Psychological Research*, New York, Holt, Rinehart and Winston, 1960 (rev. ed.); "Multiple Comparisons in the Analysis of Variance," pp. 136–57.

Implications of Clinical Judgment Research

BIERI, JAMES, ATKINS, ALVIN L., BRIAR, SCOTT, LEAMAN, ROBIN LOBECK, MILLER, HENRY, and TRIPODI, TONY, *Clinical and Social Judgment*, New York: John Wiley and Sons, Inc., 1966; "Anchoring Effects in Judgment," pp. 109–46; "Empirical and Conceptual Analyses of Anchoring," pp. 147–81.

TRIPODI, TONY and MILLER, HENRY J., "The Clinical Judgment Process: A Review of the Literature," *Social Work* (July, 1966), pp. 63–69.

Chapter 6

Assessment
of Quantitative-Descriptive
Studies

The Role of the Social Worker in a Child Protective Agency

by ANDREW BILLINGSLEY

Social workers are currently paying more attention to, and trying to improve services for, families in which children are receiving substandard care. Such services have received new impetus as the various states began to implement the 1962 Amendments to the Social Security Act. This paper is concerned with the social worker's role in providing these services. It reports part of a larger study carried out in a statewide voluntary nonsectarian child protective agency in Massachusetts and, for comparative purposes, in a large metropolitan voluntary nonsectarian family counseling agency in the same state. In general, the study was concerned with a comparative analysis of role performance, role orientations, and role satisfaction in these two settings. This paper will focus more narrowly on some selected aspects of role performance and role preference (which is one type of role orientation) among social caseworkers in the two settings.

This presentation will be organized as follows: First, the focus of the analysis reported here will be specified; this will be followed by a statement of the rationale of the study, the methods used, the findings, some possible implications of the findings, and, finally, a brief summary.

Focus

The focus of this paper may be stated by raising four questions: First, what do professional social caseworkers do in a child protective agency? Second, what would they like to do? Third, what is the relationship between what they do and what they would like to do? And, fourth, to what extent are the actual and preferred activities of caseworkers in a family counseling agency the same or different from those of the caseworkers in a child protective agency?

Rationale

Why did it seem important to engage in a description of the role of

Source: Reprinted by special permission of the author and of Child Welfare League of America from *Child Welfare, Vol. XLIII*, No. 9 (November, 1964), pp. 472–79.

the social worker in a child protective setting, and why was a family counseling agency selected as a modified control group? A number of social work leaders have urged on our profession a series of studies of social work practice in different settings. Harriet Bartlett has put the matter as follows:

> Social work has been slower than many professions in analyzing its practice. Progress is urgent for several reasons. There is great need to identify the characteristics of social work as a professional practice in order to determine its goals and place in society, and to plan appropriate programs and services. Furthermore, the development of an educational curriculum without an equivalent system of concepts and theory relating to practice is producing an imbalance in the profession. There are also pressing questions regarding the criteria for professional competence, which are needed to build a system of professional certification.[1]

It seems important that we examine the nature of social work practice in different kinds of settings in order to increase our own understanding of reality. Then we as a profession can preserve what needs preserving, change what needs changing, and better prepare social work practitioners for the realities they must face in their efforts to help people in different situations and under the sponsorship of different kinds of agencies.

Child protective services are concerned with problems of neglect and abuse of young children and are focused primarily on work with unmotivated parents, or at least with parents who do not typically come to the agency asking for help with this problem.[2] This kind of work presents some distinct challenges to the social workers and the agencies involved, and to the profession in general.[3] A comparative analysis seemed appropriate as one way of describing the realities confronted by social workers in this setting.

METHOD

How did we go about collecting and analyzing data for this aspect of the study?[4] The sample of 110 respondents comprised 20 super-

[1] Harriet M. Bartlett, *Analyzing Social Work Practice by Fields* (New York: National Association of Social Workers, 1961), p. 7.
[2] *Child Welfare League of America Standards for Child Protective Service* (New York: Child Welfare League of America, 1960), p. 6.
[3] For a brief description of some of the dilemmas facing child protective services, *see* Dolores M. Schmidt, "The Protective Service Caseworker: How Does He Survive Job Pressure?" *Child Welfare*, XLII (1963), 115–19, 130.
[4] For a complete description of the methodology of the study, including its rationale and limitations, *see* Andrew Billingsley, *The Role of the Social Worker in a Child Protective Agency: A Comparative Analysis,* unpublished doctoral dissertation (Waltham, Mass.: Brandeis University, 1964).

visors and 41 caseworkers in the child protective agency (henceforth abbreviated CPA), plus 10 supervisors and 39 caseworkers in the family counseling agency (FCA). With the exception of executives and part-time workers, this sample included the entire professional casework staff in each agency. This paper will report only on findings concerning role performance and role preference among caseworkers in the sample.

Role Performance

As used in this study, the concept "role" encompasses the view that individuals in given positions behave according to the expectations held by relevant others.[5] Role performance refers to the behavioral element of what these caseworkers do on the job. Role perception is used here as a special type of cognitive orientation toward the job. Both are held to be influenced by the norms and expectations of the social work profession and of the agencies in which the respondents work.

Role performance was defined as the range of activities engaged in by social workers during the course of a usual work week, and the relative amount of time they devote to these activities. To examine these, we used an activities time study, adapted from a method used by John Hill in a study of the Family Service of Philadelphia.[6] Specifically, respondents in both agencies were asked to report to the research staff all the activities they engaged in and the amount of time they spent in each during five full working days spread over a period of five weeks in January and February 1963.

Role Preference

Our approach to the study of what respondents would prefer to do was conceptualized in terms of appreciative orientations. This concept is borrowed from Talcott Parsons.[7] Orientations are attitudes toward something.[8] Appreciative orientations are attitudes toward something based on standards of gratification.[9] We were interested

---

5 Neal Gross, Ward S. Mason, and Alexander W. McEachern, *Explorations in Role Analysis* (New York: John Wiley & Sons, 1958), p. 17.

6 John G. Hill and Ralph Ormsby, *Cost Analysis Method for Casework Agencies* (Philadelphia: Family Service of Philadelphia, 1953).

7 Talcott Parsons and Edward A. Shils, eds., *Toward a General Theory of Action* (Cambridge, Mass.: Harvard University Press, 1951).

8 Theodore M. Newcomb, "The Study of Consensus," in Robert K. Merton, Leonard Broom, and Leonard S. Cottrell, Jr., eds., *Sociology Today* (New York: Basic Books, 1959), p. 279.

9 Parsons and Shils, *op. cit.*, p. 60.

in attitudes of social workers toward their jobs. The concept "appreciative orientations" aims to express the extent to which role performers find their tasks gratifying.[10] Specifically, we asked the caseworkers in our sample to indicate, in advance of the activities time study, the relative proportion of their time they would ideally prefer to spend on a wide range of activities if they were free to allocate their working hours in any way they wished.

Role Deprivation

The discrepancy between how caseworkers allocate their time and how they would prefer to allocate it was conceptualized as role deprivation, which was measured by comparing their preferred and actual time allocations over the range of activities associated with their job. The concept "role deprivation" was developed by Norman Berkowitz and his associates as a result of a study of the role of the professional nurse in outpatient departments of general hospitals.[11] The concept suggests that people whose job requirements diverge substantially and systematically from their preferences are thereby deprived of the opportunity to express their essential professional calling and are in a state of role deprivation.

HYPOTHESES

In accordance with our view that the role of the social worker is influenced by both his profession and the particular agency in which he works, the study advanced several hypotheses about role performance and role orientations. We thought that:

Role performance would be related significantly to agency setting. That is, the pattern of activities would be different in the two agency settings. The specific direction of these differences was also specified in advance.

---

10 David G. French, *Social Work and Social Science: An Analysis of Their Relationship*, unpublished doctoral dissertation (Ann Arbor, Mich.: University of Michigan, 1960), pp. 76–77.

11 Norman H. Berkowitz, Mary F. Malone, and Malcolm W. Klein, "An Overview of Role Deprivation and Its Application to the Out-Patient Department Nurse," paper presented at the Rhode Island State Nurses' Association and the Rhode Island League for Nursing Joint Convention, East Providence, Rhode Island, October 1960. In operationalizing this concept, however, we have departed from the procedures suggested by these authors. They have measured the discrepancy between ideal role conception and perceived role performance, whereas our procedures measure the discrepancy between ideal role conception (as expressed in the workers' preferences) and actual role performance (as elicited by our role performance instrument). The latter measure seemed to us a closer approximation of the "ideal" vs. the "reality." It seemed also to capture somewhat the element of "reality shock" involved in the transition from education to practice.

Appreciative orientations would be related significantly to agency setting. That is, the pattern of preferences for activities would be different in the two agencies. The direction of these differences was also specified in advance.

Initially, no hypothesis was advanced about role deprivation. This finding was an instance of serendipity[12]—an unexpected finding—which grew out of the fact that one of the initial hypotheses was not supported by the data.

FINDINGS

Now let us turn to some of the specific findings. First, it is apparent from Table 1 that the patterns of role performance are different for caseworkers in the two agencies. (What is not reported here is that

TABLE 1

MEAN NUMBER OF HOURS PER WEEK FCA AND CPA CASEWORKERS SPEND IN THE FOLLOWING ACTIVITIES

Activity	Mean Hours per Week		
	FCA	CPA	Difference
A. Contact with Clients	16.49	10.51	−5.98*
Clients in the office	11.40	1.88	−9.52*
Clients outside office	2.47	7.63	+5.16*
Telephone with clients	2.40	1.00	−1.40
Letters to clients	.26	.07	− .19
B. Contact with Community Representatives	2.76	7.76	+5.00*
Direct contact with collaterals	.73	3.29	+2.56*
Letters to collaterals	.14	.39	+ .25
Telephone with collaterals	1.88	2.42	+ .54
Court activities	.00	1.70	+1.70*
C. Supervision and Consultation	6.84	5.97	− .87
Conference with supervisor	1.35	1.40	+ .05
Case conference and consultation	1.28	1.64	+ .36
Supervising others	.77	.00	− .77
Staff and committee meetings	.73	.72	− .01
Professional seminars, etc.	1.65	.88	− .77
Reading client records	1.06	1.33	+ .27
D. Administrative and Clerical	5.60	4.25	−1.35
Case recording	4.45	3.80	− .65
Statistical and other reports	1.15	.45	− .70
E. Travel	2.09	6.44	+4.35†
F. Other Activities	8.39	5.82	−2.57†
Lunch	3.77	3.75	− .02
Informal activities	3.15	1.80	−1.35
Miscellaneous	1.44	.60	− .84

* p < .0005 by one-tailed t test.
† p < .02 by two-tailed t test.

[12] Merton defines serendipity as "the discovery through chance by a theoretically prepared mind of valid findings which were not sought for." *See* Robert K. Merton, *Social Theory and Social Structure* (rev.; Glencoe, Ill.: The Free Press, 1957), p. 12.

the patterns of role performance for supervisors in the two agencies also differ systematically and significantly.)

Table 1 shows that the essential distinction between the two agencies in this respect is that social casework practice in the family counseling agency is primarily office centered, whereas practice in the child protective agency is primarily field centered. FCA caseworkers spend the bulk of their working hours in the agency seeing clients, supervisors, and consultants and doing clerical work, whereas CPA respondents spend the bulk of their working time in the community seeing clients and other community representatives and traveling.

Specific differences may be cited. Caseworkers in the FCA spend a greater portion of their time in direct contact with clients than do caseworkers in the CPA. Caseworkers in the FCA spend an average of about 16.5 hours per week in this activity, whereas those in the CPA spend about 10.5 hours per week. Caseworkers in the CPA spend a greater portion of their time than do FCA caseworkers in contact with persons in the community other than the client. FCA respondents spend only about three hours per week in such community-centered activities, whereas CPA caseworkers spend about eight hours per week. Of the time spent seeing clients, FCA caseworkers spend the greater portion seeing clients in the office, and CPA caseworkers spend the greater portion seeing clients outside the caseworker's office. This is generally in the client's home, but sometimes in places of employment, schools, and occasionally, courts and taverns.

Caseworkers in both agencies spend about the same amount of time—roughly six to seven hours per week—in professional supervision and consultation. Caseworkers in the FCA spend about five and a half hours per week in clerical activities, which is about an hour per week more than CPA respondents spend in this activity. CPA respondents spend about six hours per week in travel—four hours per week more than FCA workers spend in this activity. FCA caseworkers spend about two and a half hours more in miscellaneous activities than do those in the CPA.

The differences referred to here were all found to be statistically significant. In short, it does seem that there are two distinct patterns of role performance in the two agencies. These descriptions are limited, of course, by their quantitative nature. But to the person at all familiar with social work, they are suggestive of the qualitative differences present in these two different casework roles.

The second major set of findings has to do with appreciative orientations or preferences for activities. These data are presented in Table 2. The essential finding in Table 2 is that caseworkers in both agencies prefer to spend the bulk of their time—about 19 hours per week—in direct contact with clients. There is no differ-ence between the two groups in this respect. This preference for direct interaction with clients has been characterized as reflecting a "client-centered orientation." Professional social caseworkers in both agencies seem to be essentially client centered. Our hypothesis of agency difference in this respect obviously overstated the inde-pendent influence of different agency settings on so basic a pro-fessional attitude as that reflected in this client-centered apprecia-tive orientation.

TABLE 2

MEAN NUMBER OF HOURS PER WEEK FCA AND CPA CASEWORKERS PREFER TO SPEND ENGAGED IN THE FOLLOWING ACTIVITIES

	Mean Hours per Week Preferred		
	FCA (N = 34)*	CPA (N = 31)*	Difference
Contact with clients	18.9	18.8	− .1
Community contacts	3.1	5.3	+2.2†
Supervision and consultation	8.7	6.6	−2.1‡
Clerical activities	3.4	3.2	− .2
Travel	1.2	3.0	+1.8§
Lunch and miscellaneous	5.3	4.0	−1.3¶

* Incomplete reporting made it necessary to eliminate some respondents.
† t = 3.94, df = 63, p < .0005 (one-tailed test).
‡ t = 2.97, df = 63, p < .01 (two-tailed test).
§ t = 3.73, df = 63, p < .0005 (one-tailed test).
¶ t = 2.31, df = 63, p < .05 (two-tailed test).

Table 2 also shows that, next to seeing clients, caseworkers prefer to see their supervisors, consultants, and other professional col-leagues. FCA caseworkers prefer to spend better than eight and a half hours per week in this activity—two hours more than CPA respondents. In both groups, preferences for other activities are relatively slight, though CPA caseworkers do prefer to spend more time in community contacts and travel than do their counterparts in the FCA, who express a greater preference for miscellaneous activities than do CPA caseworkers. The strong preference for see-ing clients and the desire to minimize other activities support the view that this may be the essence of the professional casework enter-prise.

The question that now arises is, what is the relationship between role performance and appreciative orientation? What, in other words, is the relationship between patterns of role performance and patterns of role preference? The data relevant to this question appear in Table 3.

TABLE 3
MEAN DISCREPANCY BETWEEN NUMBER OF HOURS PER WEEK FCA AND CPA CASEWORKERS
PREFER TO SPEND AND ACTUALLY SPEND ENGAGED IN THE FOLLOWING ACTIVITIES

Activity	Mean Discrepancy Between Preferred and Actual Hours per Week*	
	FCA (N = 34)	CPA (N = 31)
Contact with clients	−2.4	−8.3
Community contacts	− .4	+2.5
Supervision and consultation	−1.9	− .6
Clerical activities	+2.2	+1.1
Travel	+ .9	+3.4
Lunch and miscellaneous	+3.1	+1.8

* Actual time allocations were subtracted from preferred, so that the minus sign suggests respondents prefer to spend more time than they do on a particular activity and the plus sign indicates they prefer to spend less.

Several observations may be made to summarize the findings in Table 3. First, it is apparent that some role deprivation exists in both agencies. Second, it is apparent that role deprivation is greatest for both groups in the area of direct contact with clients. Both groups, in other words, would like to spend a greater portion of their time in direct contact with clients than they are now able to do. Third, the role deprivation in this area of client contacts is greater for caseworkers in the CPA than in the FCA. Whereas the discrepancy for FCA caseworkers is about two and one-third hours per week, it is about eight and one-third hours per week in the CPA.

Fourth, caseworkers in the CPA feel that they would prefer to spend less time than they now do in community-centered activities. Fifth, in the area of professional supervision and consultation, caseworkers in the FCA exhibit greater role deprivation than their counterparts in the CPA. Finally, in order to spend more time in what they consider essential, rewarding professional activity, respondents in both agencies would like to spend relatively less time than they now do in clerical activities, travel, and other miscellaneous activities.

Table 3 does not, however, provide us with an overall statement of the extent of role deprivation in the two agencies. In order to arrive at such a statement each respondent was given a role deprivation score that expressed the total amount of discrepancy between how he now spends his time and how he would ideally prefer to spend his time. All of these scores were then arranged in a frequency distribution, and a median was computed. Respondents with role deprivation scores above the median were considered to exhibit high role deprivation, and those with scores below the median were considered to exhibit low role deprivation. Then, respondents in the FCA and the CPA were compared to see how many from each group fell into the high and the low categories. These data appear in Table 4.

TABLE 4
NUMBER OF FCA AND CPA CASEWORKERS EXHIBITING HIGH AND LOW ROLE DEPRIVATION

Agency Setting	Extent of Role Deprivation	
	High	Low
FCA (N = 34)	9	25
CPA (N = 31)	24	7

$\chi^2 = 14.86$, df = 1, p < .001 (one-tailed test).

It is apparent from Table 4 that role deprivation is significantly more prevalent among professional social caseworkers in the child protective agency than among their counterparts in the family counseling agency. Whereas 26 percent of FCA respondents exhibit high role deprivation, 77 percent of CPA respondents may be so classified. This suggests that the reality of practice in the child protective setting departs more strikingly from the preferences of these professional social caseworkers than does the reality of practice in the family counseling setting.

IMPLICATIONS

It is difficult to draw inferences from the limited analysis reported in this paper, even for the two agencies under study. It is impossible to generalize for the whole population of child protective agencies and family counseling agencies in the country or for the profession in general. To the extent, however, that these findings support theoretical and other more general observations about the social work profession, it is possible to suggest that such accumulated knowledge may have implications for social casework practice and for social work education.

These findings have been interpreted as supporting our basic theoretical proposition that different kinds of social situations exert different influences on the attitudes and behavior of their participants. In other words, it may be said that the reality of practice in different kinds of social work settings requires differential patterns of role performance and role orientations. Failure to adjust to these differences subjects the caseworker to a certain amount of role deprivation.

There are then, two possible implications of these findings that seem plausible. First, the different patterns of role performance in the two agencies seem to reflect different role requirements on the part of caseworkers in these two kinds of settings. It seems likely that professional caseworkers are more adequately prepared by their formal education and their informal professional culture for practice in a family counseling setting than for practice in a child protective setting. The distinctive feature of child protective services is that they attempt to reach out and bring professional social work help to families who are, for the most part, involved in a multiplicity of psychological and social problems, and who are not motivated in a professional sense to come to the agency for help with their problems. These are likely to be lower-class clients. It is not so easy—sometimes it is not even possible—for caseworkers working with clients such as these to overlook the sociocultural and other non-psychological aspects of these client problems and to concentrate on the psychological aspects as it might be in work with motivated clients who come to the office seeking help with their problems. Other findings of this study show that respondents from the CPA tend to be more aware of the relevance of sociocultural factors in the diagnosis and treatment of client problems than do respondents from the FCA.

Although differences in role requirements in different kinds of situations are to be expected and should not necessarily be viewed with alarm, they do deserve the kind of concerted attention our profession is beginning to pay to them. Professor Kermit Wiltse has observed that one of the basic tenets of professionalism is that different problems should be treated differently. It may be that we do not meet our professional and social responsibility by confining our best professional efforts to work with mildly neurotic clients with interpersonal problems they can identify and who are sufficiently motivated to come downtown to the caseworker's office for three or more interviews. Differences in role requirements in different settings should be given more systematic attention, not only in the professional education of social workers, but also in the nature of their work assignments and rewards.

It may be, for example, that caseworkers in a child protective setting should have smaller workloads, greater opportunity for professional learning through seminars and the like, and greater tangible rewards for what appears to be a more difficult job. In view of the importance of community work by caseworkers in this kind of setting, this aspect of their performance should receive the same kind of recognition as is given to their casework.

A second set of implications is stimulated by the client-centered appreciative orientation exhibited by professional caseworkers in both agencies. It is apparent that interaction with clients on a one-to-one basis is the heart or the essence of the professional casework enterprise. All other job activities are secondary from a professional perspective. But from an agency perspective or the perspective of client needs in situations of neglect and abuse, some other activities become of considerable importance and demanding of staff time. It must be emphasized that this dilemma is not unique to the specific agencies in this study. A similar situation faces professional social caseworkers in probation and parole,[13] corrections,[14] and other public agencies dealing with unmotivated clients.[15] Nor is this type of discrepancy between the professional orientation and actual conditions in the field unique to social workers. Professor Everett Hughes has observed that, in every profession, there are certain required activities that are not central to the professional's conception of his role and that professionals generally do not like.[16] This situation is likely to be heightened when professionals work in formal organizations.[17] Schoolteachers who go to work in lower-class neighborhoods[18] and nurses who go to work in outpatient clinics[19] are two examples of professionals who must adjust to conditions and engage in activities on the job for which they have not been adequately prepared in professional school.

As we have seen the kind of role deprivation to which the respondents in the child protective agency are subjected is not new. The question is, however, when do these secondary or ancillary activities become so necessary to carrying out the professional func-

---

[13] Lloyd E. Ohlin, Herman Piven, and Donnell M. Pappenfort, "Major Dilemmas of the Social Worker in Probation and Parole," in Herman D. Stein and Richard A. Cloward, eds., *Social Perspectives on Behavior* (Glencoe, Ill.: The Free Press, 1958), p. 254.

[14] Elliot Studt, "Casework in the Correctional Field," *Federal Probation*, XVIII, No. 3 (1954), 19–26; *Training Personnel for Work with Juvenile Delinquents* (Washington, D.C.: U.S. Government Printing Office, 1954); "Treatment of Persons in Conflict with Authority," in *Proceedings of the 1956 Social Work Progress Institute* (Ann Arbor, Mich.: Social Work Progress Institute, 1956), pp. 1–23; Donald R. Cressey, "Professional Correctional Work and Professional Work in Correction," *NPPA Journal*, V (1959), 1–15; Clarence C. Schrag, "Some Foundations for a Theory of Corrections," in Donald R. Cressey, ed., *The Prison* (New York: Holt, Rinehart and Winston, 1961), pp. 346–57; and Donald C. Gibbons, "Some Notes on Treatment Theory in Corrections," *Social Service Review*, XXXVI (1962), 295–305.

[15] Kermit T. Wiltse, "The 'Hopeless' Family," *Social Work*, III, No. 4 (1958), 12–22.

[16] Personal communication.

[17] Robert D. Vinter, "The Social Structure of Service," in Alfred J. Kahn, ed., *Issues in American Social Work* (New York: Columbia University Press, 1959), pp. 242–51. *See* also: Henry J. Meyer, "Professionalization and Social Work," in Kahn, *op. cit.*, p. 338; and Harold L. Wilensky and Charles N. Lebeaux, *Industrial Society and Social Welfare* (New York: The Russell Sage Foundation, 1958).

[18] Howard S. Becker, *Role and Career Problems of the Chicago Public School Teacher*, unpublished doctoral dissertation (Chicago: University of Chicago, 1951).

[19] Berkowitz, Malone, and Klein, *op. cit.*

tion that they should be incorporated into the professional role? It may be also, that the non-client-centered activities that are primarily administrative and clerical should be reduced and turned over to some extent to less highly skilled and educated personnel.

The non-client-centered activities that involved work with persons in the community other than the client, however, should not necessarily be accorded the same disposition. In short, community work may be so central to the function of helping neglected children and their families that it should be systematically built into the role of the social worker, rather than diminished, in spite of the fact that professional social caseworkers may currently react negatively toward this activity. Perhaps a way should be found to enhance the attractiveness and status of this community-centered activity. Three ways that suggest themselves are: (1) better preparation by the graduate schools for the community aspect of social casework, (2) better training of caseworkers by the agencies that employ them, and (3) greater rewards for this component of their jobs.

Summary

This paper has reported some findings in the study of role performance, role orientation, and role deprivation exhibited by social caseworkers in a child protective agency and in a family counseling agency. The pattern of role performance in the two agencies was found to be systematically different, with performance in the family counseling agency centered in the caseworker's office, and performance in the child protective agency more nearly divided between clients and community. The appreciative orientation of these respondents was not found to differ; respondents in both agencies exhibited a client-centered orientation, preferring to maximize the time spent in direct contact with clients. The discrepancy between role performance and appreciative orientation, defined as role deprivation, was found to exist in both groups to some extent, and to be greatest in the area of interaction with clients. At the same time, however, role deprivation was found to be significantly more prevalent among caseworkers in the child protective agency.

These findings have been interpreted as supporting the theoretical view that the attitudes and behavior of individuals are influenced by the groups or subsystems with which they are meaningfully associated. These data are also consistent with the general view that the conditions of social work practice differ in different types of settings.

ASSESSMENT OF QUANTITATIVE-DESCRIPTIVE STUDIES

These findings seem to imply, therefore, that more attention must be given both to the nature of the job assignments and job rewards in a child protective setting such as the one examined and to the nature of formal professional preparation for this type of social casework role.

An Assessment
of the Billingsley Study

1. What Are the Specific Purposes of the Study?

The author conducted this study for two major purposes: (1) the description of the role of caseworkers in providing services to families in two social service agencies; (2) the testing of hypotheses which relate agency context to the role orientation and role performance of caseworkers. The agencies studied were a statewide voluntary non-sectarian child protective agency in Massachusetts and a large metropolitan voluntary non-sectarian family counseling agency in the same state. From the information provided by the author, the agencies were similar in that they were both voluntary, non-sectarian agencies serving families. The major identifiable difference in the agencies is the fact that the geographical area covered for the child protective agency is statewide, while the family agency provides services only to a metropolitan area. Other differences are suggested by the author in his assertion that child protective services require a different type of professional contact than family counseling services due to differences in client problems.

The first purpose of the study is stated in the form of questions the author seeks to answer: What do professional caseworkers do in a child protective agency? What would they like to do? What is the relationship between what they do and what they would like to do? To what extent are the actual and preferred activities of the caseworkers in a child protective agency and a family counseling agency similar or different? In seeking answers to these questions, the author conceptualizes his research problem in terms of the role performance, appreciative orientations or role preferences, and role deprivation of caseworkers in the two social agency settings. The second and primary purpose of the study is the testing of two major hypotheses which utilize the role concepts identified above. These hypotheses predict the relationship between the role performance of caseworkers and agency context, and between appreciative orientations and agency context.

Implicit in these two purposes of the study is the intent of the author to provide data which will serve as a basis for considering changes in agency policies and procedures geared to increasing caseworkers' satisfaction with their jobs. The author is particularly concerned with providing data which will help to meet the challenges of providing child protective services to families involved in neglect and abuse, such as working with unmotivated parents. He therefore proposes a study of the "realities" of practice in a child protective agency. In order to increase the understanding of reality in this type of agency, the author also selected a family counseling agency for comparative study. This allowed for the collection of descriptive data regarding the activities and orientations of caseworkers in two different agency contexts, as well as for the testing of hypotheses using the agency context as the independent variable.

2. What Research Methods Does the Researcher Use To Accomplish His Purposes?

The research reported is a part of a larger study which included a sample of 110 respondents. The total sample comprised supervisors and social caseworkers selected from the two social agencies. The complete description of the study methodology is not included in this article, as the author cites the reference to the larger study. The present report is based on data collected from the 80 caseworkers in the sample. Executives, supervisors, and part-time workers are not included in this analysis. The sample, then, consists of 41 caseworkers from the child protective agency and 39 caseworkers from the family counseling agency. Data were collected on role performance and role preferences of the caseworkers in the two agencies. In order to measure role performance, an activities time study was employed, whereby respondents reported on the time they engaged in specified activities during five working days spread over a period of five weeks. In advance of the collection of role performance data, caseworkers were asked to indicate the relative proportion of their time they would ideally prefer to spend on a range of specified activities. This measurement was conceptualized as "appreciative orientations," defined as an expression of the extent to which the caseworkers found their various activities gratifying. To measure the concept of role deprivation, the author compared the data on appreciative orientations to the role performance data of the caseworkers in each agency, with the difference used to represent a measure of role deprivation.

3. How Should the Study Be Classified and How Does It Differ from Other Major Research Approaches?

This research is classified as a quantitative-descriptive study. It does not meet the requirements of an experimental study, although it has as one of its purposes the testing of hypotheses. The sampling procedures are not appropriate for an experimental study; there is no manipulation of an independent variable, and no control group of agencies or respondents. The author's reference to the family counseling agency as a "modified control group" is misleading, as there is no indication as to what "control" is provided by the inclusion of a family counseling agency. The agency setting represents the independent variable in the hypotheses being tested, but there is no randomization procedure used for the selection of caseworkers to represent the two agency contexts. The author gives as a rationale for including two types of agencies the desire to describe the realities of practice in different settings. However, the reader is left with the question of why these particular agencies were selected, and in what ways the rationale for their selection is related to the hypotheses being tested.

Although the study cannot be classified as experimental, the methods employed are empirical and therefore they meet one of the qualifications for a quantitative-descriptive study. The measurements of the concepts are specified, and the data are systematically collected from the caseworkers in the two agencies. The measurement employed is the report by respondents of the number of hours per week spent on activities, and the number of hours preferred for these activities. Another requirement of the quantitative-descriptive study is that it have as a major purpose the testing of hypotheses or the quantitative-descriptions of variables. This study meets this requirement, and can be sub-typed as a hypothesis-testing study. The hypotheses posed for study are explicitly stated, and the data are collected to test the hypotheses. The data also serve the purpose of describing accurately the selected characteristics of caseworkers in the two agencies.

EVALUATION: PROBLEM FORMULATION

1. *How Does the Author Utilize the Literature in Conceptualizing the Problem for Study? What Major Concepts Are Formulated for the Study and How Are They Defined Conceptually and Operationally?*

The author has identified as his problem for study the examination of the nature of social work practice in different kinds of agency settings. In order to study practice, Billingsley utilizes the literature dealing with role concepts in building a conceptual framework for his investigation. He draws from the work of Gross, Mason, and McEachern to define role as a concept which "encompasses the view that individuals in given positions behave according to the expec-

tations held by relevant others." One problem in this definition is
that the reader cannot ascertain whether role is defined mainly in
terms of behavior or expectations. To overcome this ambiguity, the
definition of role by Thomas as constituting a set of expectations
held by relevant others regarding given positions (Thomas and
Feldman, 1967) might have been used in this study. Billingsley
appropriately notes the behavioral aspects of the concept of role
performance. However, he mixes the conceptual definition of role
performance with an operational definition when he states that
"role performance refers to the behavioral element of what these
caseworkers do on the job." In operationalizing the concept of role
performance, Billingsley clearly cites the way in which the concept
is measured, stating that role performance includes "the range of
activities engaged in by social workers during the course of a usual
work week and the relative amount of time they devote to these
activities."

Billingsley defines role perception as a special type of cognitive
orientation toward the job, and then moves to the use of the concepts of role preference and appreciative orientations. What the
caseworkers would prefer to do on the job is conceptualized as
"appreciative orientations," a concept borrowed from Parsons, and
defined as "attitudes toward something based on standards of gratification." Billingsley introduces the concept of appreciative orientations in order to capture the notion of the extent to which performance of tasks is gratifying to caseworkers. However, this aspect
appears to be assumed in the measurement of the concept. Appreciative orientations are measured in terms of the ideal preferences of
caseworkers regarding the proportion of time they would like to
spend on a range of activities.

It appears that the concept of role preference is more consistent
with the measurement of ideal preferences than the concept of
appreciative orientations. References to authors who deal with
these concepts are cited, but the reader needs to read the selections
in order to adequately understand the appropriateness of the concepts for this study. The concepts of role performance and appreciative orientations are employed in the two major hypotheses of the
study, and while they are somewhat lacking in conceptual clarity,
they are operationally defined for the purposes of this study.

A third major concept employed in the study is role deprivation.
In providing a conceptual definition of role deprivation, the author
cites the work of Berkowitz concerning the role of the professional
nurse. The concept of role deprivation is suggested for individuals
whose job requirements vary from their job preferences. In such

circumstances, the individual is thought to be prevented from expressing his professional calling and to be in a state of role deprivation. This concept is operationally defined as the discrepancy between how caseworkers allocate their time and how they would prefer to allocate it. The variable was measured by comparing preferred to actual time allocations in each of the activities studied. Billingsley explains in a footnote that he chose not to follow the procedures used by Berkowitz for measuring role deprivation, and introduced his own procedures. This was due to the fact that the Berkowitz instrument dealt with perceived role performance and Billingsley was able to use a measure of actual role performance.

In his formulation of the problem for study, Billingsley cites literature relevant to his definitions of major concepts, but the conceptual definitions remain somewhat unclear and fuller development would have been helpful to the reader. The operational definitions are clearly stated so that the procedures will provide quantitative data. The conceptualization of role deprivation implies dissatisfaction and difficulties in adjustment on the part of caseworkers when there is an inconsistency between ideal and actual role performance. This assumption is questionable, leaving the validity of the concept of role deprivation in doubt.

In considering the concepts proposed for the study and the way in which they are operationalized, the reader should recognize that only single dimensions of the concepts are measured. Additional measurements of role performance might have included qualitative dimensions of the activities performed by the caseworkers, such as the types of problems encountered, and quantitative measures such as the amount of time spent with each case assignment. The author indicates that quantitative differences are suggestive of qualitative differences in the role performance of workers in different agency settings. This suggests that inclusion of qualitative aspects of practice would have strengthened the import of the study findings.

2. What Hypotheses Are Proposed for Study and What Are the Independent and Dependent Variables in the Hypotheses?

The two major hypotheses in the study were: (1) Role performance would be related significantly to agency setting; (2) Appreciative orientations would be related significantly to agency setting. In both hypotheses the independent variable is agency setting. The dependent variable in the first hypothesis is role performance; in the second, appreciative orientations. While the author states that the direction of differences for the two agencies were specified in advance, he does not state the direction expected. The direction can be ascertained by the reader by examination of the tables which present the study findings. In each case where a one-tailed "t" test is employed, the direction can be identified by noting the differences in mean number of hours for selected activities, with the agency setting with the largest mean number of hours representing the agency *expected* to have the largest amount of time for the activity under consideration. For example, the family counseling agency caseworkers are expected to spend more time in contacts with clients than caseworkers from the child protective agency. There appears to be no theoretical framework from which the direction of these predictions is derived. A general theoretical statement is offered by the author as a rationale for conducting the investigation, namely that "the attitudes and behaviors of individuals are influenced by groups or subsystems with which they are meaningfully associated."

However, this theoretical view is not developed in the research, and is not directly related to the hypotheses. In fact, predictions regarding role performance might have been made on the basis of practical differences of geography between the two agency settings since the one agency (FCA) is in a large metropolitan area and the other (CPA) is statewide. An alternative way of presenting the hypotheses would have been to state within the hypotheses the direction of the differences expected. For each of the major dimensions of role performance, such as contact with clients, contact with community representatives, supervision and consultation, administration and clerical, travel, and other activities, specific predictions could have been made prior to the study. Thus, a typical operational hypothesis would state that caseworkers in a family counseling agency would be likely to spend more time in contacts with clients than caseworkers in the child protective agency. Another example would be the hypothesis that caseworkers in the child protective agency would be likely to spend more time in travel than caseworkers in the family counseling agency. It also would have been helpful to the reader to have the researcher's rationale for his hypotheses.

3. What Assumptions Are Made by the Author in Regard to the Selection of the Variables for Study?

The author implicitly assumes that the geographical area to be covered by caseworkers in each of the agency settings does not influence the relationship between agency setting and role performance, and between agency setting and appreciative orientations. Review of the activities of the caseworkers indicates that the geographical area should have been taken into account, as it is likely to be an important contingent variable in relation to the findings. The author could have controlled this factor, or explicitly stated his assumption in regard to its potential influence and his rationale for not introducing it as a control variable.

From the author's description of the child protective agency, it appears that clients were sought out for service, while family counseling clients were likely to seek help voluntarily. In addition, the types of problems dealt with by the agencies are assumed to be the same, while in fact they may be considerably different, e.g., the child protective agency may stress investigation of complaints and conformity to community norms, in contrast to the stress in the family counseling agency of helping individuals with psychological problems. These factors would be expected to influence the amount of time spent with clients, collaterals, and in travel.

A potential contingent variable which could have been taken into account is the educational level of the caseworkers. The researcher could have introduced this variable as a control in analyzing his findings, or have explicitly made the assumption that education was not a relevant factor. The author refers to the caseworkers as professional, which implies equality of education, but this is not clearly established in the research report.

While the author does not explicitly state his assumptions regarding the selection of variables for study, we have identified some implicit assumptions and have noted the desirability of making assumptions explicit and of introducing possible contingent variables into the study. Introduction of such variables would be expected to provide a more stringent test of the study hypotheses.

EVALUATION: RESEARCH DESIGN AND DATA COLLECTION

1. *Is the Quantitative-Descriptive Approach Appropriate for Investigating the Study Problem?*

Given the problem as stated by the author, the quantitative-descriptive approach is appropriate for the investigation of role performance and role preferences of caseworkers in social agencies. The experimental approach is not realistic for the study of this problem, due to the difficulties in randomization procedures for assigning caseworkers to different agency settings. The variables proposed for the study are amenable to measurement, and procedures are provided by the author for systematic collection of data. Explicitly stated hypotheses guide the inquiry, although they lack in theoretical foundation. While the author suggests cause-effect relationships are inherent in his hypotheses, he has not sufficiently taken into account contingent variables related to the hypotheses, nor has he clearly shown that the independent variable precedes the dependent variable in time. Thus, evidence is not provided to support the testing of cause-effect relationships. However, the author is in a position to examine the association between the major variables included in the hypotheses. The author's two major hypotheses, his examination of the relationship between agency setting and role deprivation, and his operationalization of the concepts, provide the essential guidelines and procedures for conducting a quantitative-descriptive study.

2. What Sampling Procedures Were Employed in the Study?

Two agencies were selected for this study, both from within the state of Massachusetts. From the description of the agencies by the author, we would expect different kinds of problems confronting the caseworkers in the two agencies, different demands on travel, and differences in the location of service, e.g., office or community. The agencies are similar in that they both deal with families in which children receive inadequate care. It would have been helpful to the reader if the author had specified the agency characteristics which were expected to make a difference in the findings, and a rationale for the selection of the two agencies. The two agencies were not systematically selected from a larger group or population of family serving agencies, and hence do not constitute sample units of a known population. The author notes the limitations inherent in his procedure for selecting agencies for study when he states that he cannot generalize to child protective agencies or family agencies.

With the selection of two agencies for study, Billingsley elected to study all full-time caseworkers within each agency, with the exception of executives. The author also studied supervisors in the agencies, but for the purposes of this report these data are not included. While the author does not indicate the reason for separating the analysis of findings on supervisors from findings on caseworkers, he implicitly assumes that they differ in the amount of time they spend in activities such as contact with clients, supervision, and administrative duties.

The respondents in this study included 41 caseworkers from a child protective agency and 39 caseworkers from the family counseling agency. There is no indication whether the workers in each agency were employed in a central office or in branch offices, a characteristic which may have influenced their role orientations and role performance. It is also not clear whether or not the caseworkers have master's degrees in social work or not, and there is no indication of their experience in social work practice. While the reader is not provided with information about these characteristics of the caseworkers in the study, it is clear that the author does not use a random sample of caseworkers, as the study group is made up of the total population of caseworkers in the two social agencies.

The implications of these sampling procedures for the study are that generalizations cannot be made to other social agencies or to other professional caseworkers. Yet, the author is in a position to describe accurately the activities and preferences of the caseworkers studied, and to make comparisons between agencies.

3. How Were the Data Collected and How Were Potential Sources of Bias Taken into Account?

Data on the amount of time caseworkers spend on all their daily activities were obtained by use of an activities time instrument. The details of the instrument are not reported, such as the intervals of time recorded, e.g., every half hour or every hour. The author indicates that his instrument is an adaptation of a procedure developed by Hill in Philadelphia, but there is no indication of how the two study instruments differ. The author attempts to avoid bias in measurement by not focusing only on a single week, which might be influenced by the time of the month or other idiosyncratic occurrences. To accomplish this goal he collects data on one day in each of the five weeks.

In order to measure appreciative orientations, the caseworkers were asked to indicate the proportion of time they would ideally like to spend on a range of activities. Data on appreciative orientations were collected in advance of the time study of actual role performance. The author does not indicate why he chose to collect the data in this order. The caseworkers were given a range of categories and asked for time preferences for these activities. This procedure may have influenced the types of activities reported on in the activities performance study, and the data on preferences may not be independent of the role performance data. We do not have any indication of the amount of time which elapsed between collection of data on appreciative orientations and role performance, but the fact that a defined amount of time elapsed is indicated by the five week collection period for role performance data. Therefore the potential influence of the collection procedures for appreciative orientations may have had a differential influence on role performance data collected at the five different times. One possible alternative would have been for the author to counterbalance the collection of the two kinds of data, which would have allowed for analysis of the effects of measurement procedures on the data.

One source of bias which may enter into the study findings results from incomplete reporting on the part of some of the respondents. The reader has to assume that the data in Table 1 are from 41 CPA caseworkers and 39 FCA caseworkers, described previously as constituting the study population, but this is not specified in the table. In Table 2 the author indicates a loss of respondents in regard to activities preferences due to incomplete reporting. Fifteen respondents are lost, constituting 19 percent of the total group. One way of increasing the validity of the findings would have been to make attempts to get the caseworkers to fully complete their reporting. Although there is no indication that such attempts were made, the author could have checked data collection instruments for incomplete data on appreciative orientations and asked respondents to supply the missing data. If there was a loss of respondents on the role performance aspect of the study, this could have been handled to some extent by the researcher's checking the time reports the day after their completion. Since bias may enter into the findings as a result of the loss of respondents, the author could have examined the salient characteristics of the non-respondents (individuals giving incomplete data) and compared them to the individuals giving complete data. This would have provided a partial check on the likelihood that the findings are influenced by the loss of respondents.

4. To What Extent Did the Author Attempt To Increase the Reliability and Validity of the Measurements in the Study?

The author collected data on role performance over a period of five weeks, taking one day per week as the basis for reporting activities, in an effort to increase the validity of the data. There appears to be no attempt to increase the reliability of the measurements. One alternative would have been to select a sample of the respondents and to ask them to complete part or all of the activities instrument one or two days after the initial measurement. Another alternative effort to increase the validity of the instruments would have been to alternate the order of collecting data on role preferences and role performance. Yet another alternative would have been to introduce measures of role preference and role performance in addition to the measure of hours per week. From Table 1 it appears that the activities were sufficiently delineated so that they would be comparable between the two agencies. However, additional explication of the activities would appear to have increased the validity of the data. This could have been done in the instructions to the caseworkers along with the data collection instrument. The author does not indicate any efforts to prevent contamination of data by the possible interchanges between caseworkers as they completed their reports.

The measurement of role deprivation is based on manipulation of data collected regarding appreciative orientations and role performance. Actual time allocations were subtracted from preferred proportions of time for activities to determine the measurement of role deprivation for the workers in the two agencies. This measurement assumes that a discrepancy in score is an indication of lack of opportunity of a professional to engage in his calling and assumes such discrepancy places an individual in a state of role deprivation. The question is raised as to the validity of the concept of role deprivation in relation to its measurement. It may have been more appropriate for Billingsley to have simply referred to the discrepancy between ideal and actual scores, rather than to introduce the notion of role deprivation. The measurement in relation to the concept does not appear to have validity. It is appropriate, however, for Billingsley to compute the discrepancy score, and relate these scores to the type of agency setting for the purpose of seeking relationships between the variables.

EVALUATION: DATA ANALYSIS AND CONCLUSIONS

1. *What Statistics Are Employed in the Study and Are They Appropriate to the Data and the Assumptions of the Study?*

The "t" test is employed for the data analysis in Tables 1, 2 and 3. Since there was no systematic sampling of agencies or respondents, this statistical test is unnecessary. It is not clear that the assumptions necessary for the test are met, such as the assumption of a normal population. Since the sampling procedures preclude any generalizations, it is not necessary to employ statistical tests with these data.

Thus the statement by the author in regard to the findings of Table 1 is inappropriate, as he states "the differences referred to here were all found to be statistically significant." It would have been sufficient to use descriptive statistics, i.e., to show the mean hours in each activity. Thus, examination of Table 1 reveals a number of differences between the agencies, as well as a number of similarities. In Table 4 the author makes appropriate use of the chi-square test to examine the relationship between agency setting and role deprivation, as the assumptions for this non-parametric test are met by the study data.

2. Are the Hypotheses Supported by the Data?

The first hypothesis deals with differences in agency settings with regard to role performance. While Table 1 indicates differences in some areas, and similarities in others, all the categories cannot be assumed to be equivalent in significance and relevance to the study problem. Major differences are found in the category of contacts with clients, with the FCA workers spending more time with clients than the CPA workers. Table 1 also indicates that clients are more likely to be seen by FCA workers in their office, in contrast to the location of contact for the CPA workers out of the office. Thus for selected categories of activities, the first hypothesis is supported by the data to the extent that the findings go in the direction predicted. However, it should be noted that in some sub-areas, such as telephoning, letters, supervision and consultation, and administration and clerical activities, the hypothesis of differences is not supported.

Data in Table 2 are related to the second hypothesis. Differences are expected in regard to appreciative orientations of workers in the two agencies. According to the use of one-tailed tests in Table 2, the direction of differences was predicted for community contacts and travel, but no conceptual basis for such predictions is given in the research report. When the author states his hypotheses, he indicates that direction was predicted in advance, but examination of Table 2 reveals use of two-tailed tests on some items and one-tailed tests on others. For items where there is no difference, the reader cannot ascertain the direction of the author's predictions. A major item in Table 2 is the preferences for contacts with clients, where the author finds no differences between agency settings. He implies that his second hypothesis is not supported. However, in 4 of the 6 comparisons, differences between the agencies are found.

In Table 3, the author examines the relationship between agency setting and role deprivation, finding that role deprivation exists in both types of agencies. The author locates the specific areas where the most deprivation occurs, e.g., direct contact with clients. In order to compare agencies, an overall deprivation score was devised by the author by separating the caseworkers into two groups—high and low—in terms of role deprivation. The author makes use of the chi-square test to support his prediction that the CPA will have higher role deprivation than the FCA. This prediction is assumed from the use of the one-tailed test, although earlier in the paper the author notes that no prediction was made in advance of the test, and he indicates that the findings regarding role deprivation were ones of serendipity. The use of the chi-square statistical test is appropriate for data in Table 4 and indicates that the two groups of caseworkers did not come from the same population.

3. Were Possible Contingent Variables Accounted for in the Analysis of the Data?

The author does not introduce potentially contingent variables into the analysis, either explicitly as assumptions or as control variables through cross tabulations. Variables such as the education, experience of the workers, the location of the workers in relation to clients, and differences in problems presented to the caseworkers, could have been specified and controlled as contingent variables. It is reasonable to believe that some of these factors may strongly influence and/or explain the findings of the study.

4. What Were the Author's Principal Conclusions? Are His Claims Consistent with the Data?

The author's principal conclusions are found within the discussion of data for each table. The author emphasizes the differences in Table 1 concerning the role performance between caseworkers in the child protective agency and the family counseling agency. Practice is primarily office centered for the FCA workers and field centered for the CPA workers. Additional specific differences in role performance are cited, and the data support the author's contention that two different patterns obtain for the caseworkers in the two agency settings. However, the author does not take similarities sufficiently into account in his analysis. In addition, based on his limited data he assumes that these patterns differ in qualitative as well as quantitative ways.

The author implies that because he found selected differences in activities between CPA and FCA workers that his first hypothesis is confirmed, although this is not made explicit. It is suggested by his emphasis on the differences which he found to be statistically significant. However, due to questions regarding the relevance of the statistical tests to his data it would be more appropriate to think in terms of support in the direction of the hypothesis rather than confirmation of it.

In discussing data from Table 2 the author concludes that the independent influence of agency context is not sufficient to overcome the client centered orientations of caseworkers in each of the agencies. The data therefore fail to support the hypothesis that the caseworkers' appreciative orientations would differ in regard to contact with clients. However, orientations in regard to four other areas are found to be different, e.g., community contacts and travel were more preferred by CPA workers than by FCA workers; supervision and consultation, clerical, lunch and miscellaneous were more preferred by FCA workers.

The author draws from data in Tables 3 and 4 to suggest a principal conclusion of the study, that the reality of practice differs most from preferred practice in the CPA agency. This conclusion is consistent with the data, but does not take into account the assumptions the author makes about the relative importance of the various activities reported by the caseworkers. However, this can be detected by noting the highest to lowest mean number of hours in which activities are engaged in and preferred, which indicates to some extent the relative importance of the activities. Thus, the discrepancy scores in Table 3 suggest that CPA workers would prefer to spend more time with clients and in supervision and consultation, and less time in all other activities, with the greatest discrepancy occurring in regard to client contacts (−8.3).

5. What Are the Implications of the Findings as Defined by the Author?

According to the author, this study has implications for social casework practice and for social work education. First, the author suggests that the different social agency settings make different role requirements on their caseworkers, as evidenced by reports on role performance. He attributes this to the differences in clients seen by the caseworkers in the two agencies, and the style of casework practice, i.e., reaching out versus office located, psychologically oriented versus socio-culturally oriented practice. Secondly, the author suggests that caseworkers are more adequately prepared by education and professional culture to perform in family counseling settings than in child protective settings. The author presents no evidence to lead to this conclusion, although he could have obtained evidence in this area from the caseworkers in the study. Given what the author believes is a practice problem area of great importance, namely the differences in role requirements which emerge from different social contexts, the author suggests that the problem can be met to some extent by changes in professional education and in the reward and assignment system of the agency. The author considers ways to reduce role deprivation on the part of workers in child protective agencies, which appears to be a major focus in the study. He assumes that because workers in child protective services report a large amount of time in community work, that this work is important to them. He assumes that community work is not given sufficient recognition by superiors. However, this assumption is not linked to any evidence presented in the study. In fact Table 2 shows that CPA workers prefer only 5.3 hours per week in community contacts, third to client contacts and supervision.

The second set of implications identified by the author concerns his findings on appreciative orientations and the fact that caseworkers in both agencies prefer to spend the major proportion of their time in contact with clients. The author sees this as a problem particularly for the child protective agency worker, whose tasks center around situations of neglect and abuse, requiring community contacts and travel. The author states his bias when he says workers have not been prepared for these activities in school, and therefore suffer from role deprivation. The author is particularly concerned about the non-client centered activities which require dealing with other people, as contrasted to clerical duties. He assumes that professional caseworkers react negatively to what he calls community work. He believes these attitudes can be overcome by changes in professional education, in agency training, and in reward systems. However, the data do not suggest that negative attitudes prevail toward community work, but only that a greater proportion of time should ideally be spent with clients, and less on community contacts, and on non-client activities such as in clerical, lunch, and travel activities. It appears that we also have an expression of the author's bias that social and cultural factors should be emphasized more in the caseworker's performance, and that the casework "treatment" should either extend beyond the individual client, or at least take into account social systems such as the family and the community. The author makes the implication that contacts with people other than the client should be increased by the caseworkers, particularly in child protective work.

6. *To What Extent Did the Author Accomplish His Purposes as Set Forth for the Study?*

The author reached his objectives by finding out how caseworkers in a statewide protective agency and in a large urban family counseling agency differ with regard to what they do with their time while on the job; how they would prefer to spend their time; and the differences between what they do and what they would like to do. Based on these questions, the author sought to test two major hypotheses. He was able to provide some evidence supporting selected aspects of the hypothesis concerning differences in role performance. There was a lack of support for differences in major aspects of appreciative orientations, such as preferred contacts with clients. We have pointed out some ways in which a stronger test of the author's hypotheses might have been made, such as the introduction of potentially contingent variables and explication and measurement of the characteristics of the independent variable of agency setting. An implicit purpose of the study appears to have been the seeking of systematic data to provide a foundation for recommending changes which could be made in the child protective agency. We have raised questions as to whether or not the proposed changes, such as education and rewards, can be based on the data presented in the report. The author's discussion suggests that changes in agency procedures and caseworker's attitudes and behaviors was one of the purposes of conducting the study. In this regard, the study does not appear to have provided sufficient evidence for making agency changes.

UTILIZATION

1. *What is the General Level of Knowledge of the Conclusions Made in This Study?*

Due to the sampling procedures employed in the study, the knowledge derived is not at the level of empirical generalizations. However, the methods for collection and analysis of the data provide the author with a number of verifiable observations about the role performance and orientations of caseworkers in two social agencies. Since the theoretical scheme alluded to by the author is not well developed, the interpretation of the facts is based mainly on the author's perception of the problems arising for caseworkers and agencies when there are discrepancies between role preferences and role performance. While we have pointed out some of the possible limitations of the author's interpretations, the study's major contribution is the provision of accurate descriptions of the variables under study. The facts established by the study provide an understanding of the "realities" of practice in the two agencies studied, and allow for a limited examination of hypotheses identified by the author.

> 2. *In What Ways Are the Variables of Role Performance, Appreciative Orientations, Role Deprivation and the Agency Setting Identifiable and Manipulable for Practice Purposes?*

Billingsley suggests that changes in agency expectations and rewards can be made which will bring about changes in both role performance and appreciative orientations of caseworkers. The discrepancy between role performance and role preferences appears to be manipulable, although there are no data in the study which point to ways in which such change can be brought about. Billingsley suggests some ways which involve education of the caseworkers, and greater recognition and rewards for the non-client directed activities of the workers. It is not clear that any of these manipulations would result in a change in role deprivation *per se,* as the relationship between discrepancy of role performance and orientation is not clearly related to the notion of role deprivation. It is clear from the study that role performance differs according to the agency context, but we must speculate as to how changes in agency practices, policies, and procedures, might bring about changes in caseworkers' performance or orientations. As measured by mean number of hours, these variables are subject to manipulation by agency and/or workers. The study suggests that changes must be made by the agencies if the discrepancies, designated as deprivations, are to be eliminated.

> 3. *To What Areas of Social Work Practice Might the Knowledge Gained in This Study Be Useful, Either Directly or Indirectly?*

The study is suggestive of different role requirements for different positions in social agencies, which may be influenced by the type of agency. It points to the fact that caseworkers with a professional orientation which emphasizes interpersonal change and does not take into account cultural and environmental factors may not be very well satisfied in an agency such as CPA. One implication raised by Billingsley is the need for a different kind of education for professional caseworkers so that they can adjust better to the requirements of agencies like CPA, i.e., reaching-out casework, working with members of the community in behalf of the client, and so forth. Perhaps the more relevant implication is that the findings alert social caseworkers to differences in agency settings and requirements, so that the assumption is not made that they are all the same. Billingsley rightly does not make this assumption, and shows by his research both similarities and differences in the two types of agencies he studied. On the other hand he assumes that the training of caseworkers is the same, and that this factor leads them to view community work negatively. It may be that caseworkers with different kinds of educational experience will view their role requirements differently, and the study needs to be expanded if it is to supply information which can be used as guidelines for practice.

The facts provided in this study are directly useful for the administrators of the two agencies studied. The administrator is in a position to view the activities of his caseworkers in terms of the time they spend on a range of activities, and he may then consider manipulation of the agency requirements in order to more effectively reach agency goals. For example, he may make the judgment that administrative and clerical activities such as case recording are taking up an unduly large amount of the caseworkers' work hours, and consideration might be given to more efficient recording. Data from studies such as this are also directly useful for the individual caseworker. He is in a position to relate his own record of activities to the mean hours of the total group of caseworkers in the agency. He may find that the time he spends in community contacts is much higher, or lower than his fellow workers. He may want to consider if this is a result of his own style of work, or of his particular kind of client load, or other influences on his work pattern. For this use, data would need to be supplied to the caseworkers in addition to that presented in the research report.

The data suggest to the agency administrator the need for further study of role deprivation in terms of the satisfaction caseworkers have with carrying out their agency responsibilities. This may not only vary according to orientations toward work performance, but may be influenced by how long the worker has been in the agency, the commitment the worker has to working with a particular type of client, professional commitment on the part of the worker, and the clarity with which assignments are made to the worker.

Agency administrators can make use of this study by following the data collection procedures for measurement of role performance and role preferences. We have indicated the desirability of modifications in the procedures to maximize validity, but the general

procedures used by Billingsley are suggestive for use by an administrator for agency operations and planning.

4. To What Extent Does the Context in Which the Research Was Carried Out Impose Limitations on the Utilization of the Findings of This Study?

There are a number of characteristics of the agencies under study
which are unknown to the reader, as the specific factors which make
up the agency context are not identified. However, the fact that one
agency extends services to clients throughout a state suggests that
travel time will differ from that required by a large metropolitan
agency servicing a limited area. Differences in the agencies in
regard to the area covered also affect the location where clients
are seen by caseworkers, and it would be expected that clients
would be seen outside the office when contacts must be made statewide. Another difference in the agencies studied is the type of
clients served. As the author indicates, more collateral contacts are
necessary for particular types of problems with which the caseworkers in the child protective agency work. These differences are
not clearly stated or taken into account in the study. The usefulness
of the findings would have been more general for social agencies if
controls had been introduced for the variables we have mentioned,
and the specific characteristic of the agency thought to bring about
differences explicated more precisely as the independent variable.
The facts about the role performance of caseworkers in these
agencies, and their role preferences, are suggestive to other agency
personnel that quantitative differences may obtain between
agencies in regard to the specified range of activities. The findings
are therefore useful to caseworkers who may have assumed that the
nature of the work in social work practice does not vary. While this
may not be the case for many social workers, the range of differences in the activities specified would be instructive in consideration of taking or changing job positions.

Some of the limitations in the use of the knowledge from the
study might have been overcome by improved sampling procedures,
both in the selection of agencies for study, and in the selection of
respondents. Modifications in the research would have required
more time, effort, and money to bring the study to the point of
providing empirical generalizations through more adequate tests of
the hypotheses under study. With modifications the usefulness of
the findings could have extended beyond the two agencies in which
the research was done to a range of family and child welfare

agencies. With the present findings, the study is suggestive of further research on what Billinglsey has rightly noted as a serious need in social work practice, i.e., the study of the realities of practice and the factors which influence practice. Included in Billingsley's discussion of implications of the study are a number of leads for the development of hypotheses dealing with professional education, in-service training, task assignments, orientations toward the content of preferred casework practice, philosophical and theoretical approaches to treatment, and reward systems of different agencies for meeting role requirements.

RECOMMENDED REFERENCES

Problem Formulation

BILLINGSLEY, ANDREW, "Bureaucratic and Professional Orientation Patterns in Social Casework," *Social Service Review*, 38 (December, 1964), pp. 400–07.

THOMAS, EDWIN J., "Role Conceptions and Organizational Size," *American Sociological Review*, 24 (February, 1959), pp. 30–37.

————, and FELDMAN, RONALD, "Concepts of Role Theory," in E. J. Thomas, ed., *Behavioral Science for Social Workers* (N.Y.: The Free Press, 1967), pp. 17–50.

Research Design and Data Collection

CHEIN, ISIDOR, "An Introduction to Sampling," in Claire Selltiz, Marie Johoda, Morton Deutsch, and Stuart Cook, *Research Methods in Social Relations* (rev. ed.), (New York: Holt and Co., 1959), pp. 509–45.

HILL, JOHN G. and ORMSBY, RALPH, *Cost Analysis Method for Casework Agencies* (Philadelphia: Family Service of Philadelphia, 1953).

Statistical Concepts

BLALOCK, HUBERT M., *Social Statistics* (New York: McGraw-Hill Co., 1960), Chapter 13, "Two-Sample Tests: Difference of Means and Proportions," pp. 169–86; Chapter 15, "Nominal Scales: Contingency Problems," pp. 212–41.

————, *Causal Inferences in Nonexperimental Research* (Chapel Hill: University of North Carolina Press, 1961), pp. 128–43, "Reducing the Effects of Confounding Influences."

Power Balance and Staff Conflict
in Correctional Institutions

by MAYER N. ZALD

Many observers have noted that correctional institutions are con-flict-prone organizations. Powelson and Bendix,[1] and Weber,[2] among others, have described in detail the conflicts that develop between professionally trained treatment personnel—psychiatrists, social workers, and psychologists, and lay personnel—cottage parents, attendants, or guards. These conflicts arise out of the incompatible requirements of custodial and treatment goals. A custodial goal requires the staff to attempt to control and contain clients and leads to punitive control techniques and to authoritarian staff-inmate relations; whereas a treatment goal requires the staff to attempt to encourage positive individual change and, given contemporary theories of treatment, leads to an emphasis on nonpunitive control of inmates and to permissive and close staff-inmate relations. Since correctional institutions vary in the relative dominance of custody and treatment in their goals, it seemed likely that institutions might differ in their level and pattern of staff conflict. Using data from a comparative study of five correctional institutions for delinquents,[3] we attempt in this paper to account for some of these differences.

The goals of a correctional institution for delinquents can be located on a continuum[4] whose poles are custody and treatment, and will probably not be at either pole of the continuum, since

SOURCE: Reprinted from *Administrative Science Quarterly*, Vol. 7, No. 1 (June, 1962), pp. 22–49. Reproduced by permission of the author and the journal.

[1] Harvey Powelson and Reinhard Bendix, "Psychiatry in Prisons", *Psychiatry*, 14 (1951), 73–86.

[2] George H. Weber, "Conflicts between Professional and Non-professional Persons in Institutional Delinquency Treatment", *Journal of Criminal Law, Criminology, and Political Science*, 48 (1957), 26–43.

[3] This study is part of a larger study of correctional institutions for delinquents being conducted under the direction of Robert D. Vinter and Morris Janowitz at the University of Michigan under a grant from the National Institute of Health (M–2104). The data reported here are drawn from my "Multiple Goals and Staff Structure: A Comparative Study of Correctional Institutions for Delinquents" (Ph.D. dissertation, University of Michigan, 1960). I am indebted to the Elizabeth McCormick Memorial Fund of Chicago, which also supported the study, and to Harrison White, Charles Perrow, and Anthony Kallet for their comments on an earlier draft of this paper.

[4] For a discussion of the differences between custodial and treatment mental hospitals *see* Milton Greenblatt, R. York, and E. L. Brown, *From Custodial to Therapeutic Care in Mental Hospitals* (New York, 1955).

society usually requires some attempt to implement both goals. Different positions on the goal continuum are reflected in the role requirements and role strain on the staff.[5] Furthermore, and this is our main point, the position of an institution's goals on the continuum is a determinant of the *level* of conflict and of the *pattern* of conflict among the organization's employees.

As in any organization, conflict in correctional institutions occurs when there is competition for control of the operating practices and policies of the institution. This may include competition for control of the rules and policies governing staff-inmate relations or, more subtly, for control of the frame of reference used to define situations. Conflict within large-scale organizations is usually non-violent and often covert, because membership in an organization restricts the legitimacy of property destruction, interpersonal violence, and overt refusal to follow directives. When we speak of conflict in correctional institutions, therefore, we are speaking of felt but not accepted frustrations or goal blockages of particular employees or groups of employees created by practices of other groups within the organization.

While conflict may develop over salaries and working conditions or out of personality incompatibilities, here we are concerned with the conflicts specific to correctional institutions for delinquents and caused by their goals and structure. Briefly, we see the *level* of conflict in an institution as a function of several factors: (1) the extent to which organizational goals lead staff groups and individuals to pursue incompatible policies, (2) the degree of ambiguity in the relation of administrative means to organization ends, (3) the extent to which organizational behavior cannot be routinized but instead requires continuous choice and new decisions, and (4) the degree of interdependence of staff groups.

We conceive of the *pattern* of conflict as a function of the power balance among staff groups (such as cottage parents, social service workers, and teachers), the degree of interdependence and intercommunication among groups, and the differences in attitudes and values of these groups. Basic to our concept is the notion that the power of groups is related to the goals of the organization. In custodial institutions cottage parents are likely to have more power, and operational policies will be directed toward maintaining their

---

5 For a discussion of differences in role requirements in prisons *see* Donald R. Cressey, "Contradictory Requirements in Complex Organizations", *Administrative Science Quarterly*, 4 (1959), 1–19. *See also* Oscar Grusky, "Role Conflict in Organization: A Study of Prison Camp Officials", *Administrative Science Quarterly*, 3 (1959), 452–72; and George H. Weber, "Emotional and Defensive Reactions of Cottage Parents," in D. R. Cressey, ed., *The Prison: Studies in Institutional Organization and Change* (New York, 1961), pp. 189–228.

position; in treatment institutions social service workers are likely to make many of the major decisions.

Organizational conflict was one of several problems investigated in this comparative study.[6] Both public and private, and large and small institutions were included in the study. The goals of the institutions studied were at different points along the continuum. Questionnaires were completed by employees (staff) and inmates; historical documents and official records were examined; and observations of organizational procedures and extended unstructured interviews with key executives were conducted. In this paper we rely primarily on data obtained from the staff questionnaire and on observations and extended interviews.

First we briefly describe each of the five institutions studied to provide the reader with a perspective on the data. Second, we discuss the hypothesis pertaining to the level, or amount, of organizational conflict. Third, we present a paradigm for predicting patterns of staff conflict and data which test these predictions. Finally, we consider the implications that our discussion of conflict in treatment institutions has for organizations in general.

DESCRIPTION OF INSTITUTIONS

The position of the goals of each institution on the continuum, the institution's size, and its control (public or private)[7] are presented in Table 1. We now briefly characterize the major orientation of each institution to provide a background for the data pertaining to conflict.

Dick[8] Industrial School stressed *discipline* in its program and had

---

[6] For a statement of the hypotheses of the larger project *see* Robert D. Vinter and Morris Janowitz, "Effective Institutions for Delinquents: A Research Statement", *Social Service Review*, 33 (1959), 118–31.

[7] *See* Zald, *op. cit.*, pp. 48–54, for a description of the process of selecting institutions for the study and a comparison of our sample to the universe of institutions. For the measurement of institutional goals *see ibid.*, pp. 84–114. To recapitulate briefly the selection process and the measurement of goals, institutions were initially selected on a reputational basis so as to maximize comparison of custodial and treatment institutions. An attempt was also made to have both public and private and large and small institutions in the study so that these important variables could also be taken into account. The purpose of our selection was to emphasize comparison, not to represent the universe of institutions. The reputations of institutions, our initial criterion for selection, are obviously composites of goals and operating programs. To measure goals independently, we used official documents, executive perspectives on goals, and staff perceptions of goals. Placement of an institution on the goals continuum was dictated by the interrelation of all three measures for each institution.

[8] The first two or three letters of each name refer to some salient aspect of the institution's program (serving as a mnemonic device). False names are used to preserve anonymity, which was guaranteed.

the most custodial goals of the institutions in the sample. Its rehabilitation program was summed up in its motto "Firmness, Fairness, and Faith," and the superintendent, a former state legislator and physical education instructor, felt that a program of hard work and discipline was more effective than any clinical treatment program. In fact, he insisted that he would not hire professionally trained social workers, because he thought they would disrupt institutional discipline. All persons working with boys were allowed to punish them physically, and major sanctions were applied to those who ran away—their heads were shaven and they were beaten with a paddle; they were put into an isolation cell and given only bread and water, and in addition were started over again on their term of confinement.

Although some efforts had been made to broaden the vocational training program, no other aspect of Dick's program had changed in recent years. The institution continued to operate with traditional means of rehabilitation—discipline, hard work, and limited education—governed by a basically custodial set of decision criteria.[9]

TABLE 1
CHARACTERISTICS OF INSTITUTIONS STUDIED

Goals	Size	
	Small	Large
Custodial		Dick Industrial School 260 boys 65 staff members Public
Mixed ..:.........................	Regis Home 56 boys 13 staff members Private	Mixter Training School 400 boys 177 staff members Public
Treatment	Inland School 60 boys 40 staff members Private	Milton School for Boys 200 boys 117 staff members Public

Regis, run by a Catholic *religious* order and *Mixter,* a *mixed-*goal institution which had benign custodial policies, were located close together on the center of the goals continuum. We consider Mixter to be closer to the center of the continuum because of its multiple emphasis on custody *and* treatment. On the other hand,

9 Of the three public institutions in our sample, Dick was the only one not under some form of civil service; all staff members could be politically appointed (except for the teachers who were under merit service). Although there is not a direct relationship, it is likely that the more urbanized a state and the more educated its residents, the greater the chance that it has an effective civil service *and* institutions with treatment goals. Put another way, it is unlikely for treatment goals to find support in a poor and "backward" state.

Regis was operated more like a residence and was not confronted to any great extent with the problem of implementing multiple goals of custody and treatment.

Regis was a small institution which stressed care and guidance in its official goal statements and attempted to provide a controlled environment for its clients. The boys went to school at some twenty schools throughout the city in which Regis was located, and the staff considered one of their prime objectives to be that of helping the boys to do better in school.[10]

The superintendent of Regis, though willing to have professional treatment personnel on his staff, insisted that their orientation be sympathetic to that of the religious order. In practice this meant that Freudian orientations were suppressed because the Freudian orientation was believed to be overpermissive, especially with regard to sexual behavior. In some respects, however, the program of Regis resembled that found in treatment institutions, since attempts were made to provide a wide range of activities which the boys would enjoy.

Where Regis was a small, private institution, which could select its clients and could send a boy back to court if he did not obey the rules, Mixter was the largest public institution in its state and was for some counties their last resource in handling delinquents. Mixter was often criticized by its neighboring citizenry and the press because of its high truancy rate. Mixter was benign in its custodial policies, refusing to allow its staff to use repressive sanctions. Its other major emphasis was on containing and controlling the clients, which limited it to low-risk rehabilitational programs.

The superintendent of Mixter, an educator who had been employed in both military and civilian prison systems, felt that he had continually to accommodate himself to custodial pressures, both from relevant external publics and from many of his staff members. Internally, the head of cottage life, who had a consistently custodial perspective,[11] was perceived by staff members and executives to be second in command to the superintendent, although not officially so designated.

---

[10] Since there was no attempt to contain delinquents at Regis, its inclusion in the study might be questioned. In order to have a variety of institutions of different sizes and goals a small institution emphasizing containment was sought. Since none was available, excluding Regis would have left an important gap in our comparisons. Its small size allows us to make comparisons with Inland, and its emphasis on respect, obedience, and education reflects a parallel with older concepts of rehabilitation; it must, however, be considered as a special case. The important comparisons are between Dick, Mixter, Milton, and Inland.

[11] While Regis had no operating departments and Dick was just slightly departmentalized, Mixter, Milton, and Inland were fully departmentalized.

Compared to the other three institutions, Milton and Inland were both institutions with predominantly treatment goals. *Milton* was a medium-sized public institution that stressed the therapeutic *milieu* technique, attempting to rehabilitate the delinquent through his relationships with the staff and through a carefully planned educational program. To implement its milieu treatment philosophy, it had established cottage committees composed of cottage parents and social service workers to discuss and make decisions about the program of each client. Although officially a social service worker was in charge of each committee, a high degree of consultation was maintained.

The superintendent at Milton was a former journalist and state administrator. Although he was strongly committed to treatment goals, his major functions were to maintain a sound relationship with various external groups and to promote harmony among the employees. Major internal control was given to a psychiatrist, who was in charge of all staff-inmate activity, and who was deeply committed to the milieu philosophy. Because Milton was a public institution, it had to be somewhat more custodial than Inland, but its directors considered its custodial goal to apply explicitly only to a few extreme cases.

Inland focused on *individual* treatment in a one-to-one relationship with a professional as its major rehabilitative tool. Its chief executives considered Inland to be best fitted for the care of psychoneurotic adolescents who needed to be away from home, a definition in terms of psychological need rather than legal status.[12] A majority of its clients, however, were court-committed delinquents.

The superintendent, a former minister and teacher of sociology, and the assistant superintendent, a clinical psychologist, were both firmly committed to treatment goals, although the superintendent sometimes supported a more custodial orientation in public relations programs over the judgment of treatment personnel. Since the superintendent defined his major role externally and had tense relationships with the staff, major internal control fell to the assistant superintendent.[13]

To summarize, our final ranking of goals of the institutions places Dick's goals at the custodial end of the continuum—at least compared with the goals of other institutions in this sample. Regis'

---

[12] Inland called itself a "residential treatment center," indicating its attempt to change identification and affiliation from that of a correctional institution to that of an institution dealing with psychological problems of adolescent boys.

[13] On the inside-outside dichotomy in the executive role in treatment institutions *see* Zald, *op. cit.*, pp. 128–29, 143–54; also R. D. Vinter, "Juvenile Correctional Institution Executives: A Role Analysis," (mimeo., Ann Arbor, 1958).

goals come next, followed by Mixter's, which are here considered to be just to the custodial side of the center of the continuum (mixed-goal). Milton and Inland are clearly treatment institutions. The fact that one focuses on milieu treatment whereas the other focuses on individual treatment will be shown to be of major importance in accounting for the pattern of conflict.

LEVEL OF INSTITUTIONAL CONFLICT

We predicted different levels of conflict for institutions with different goals. In institutions with predominantly custodial goals, criteria of effectiveness—such as low runaway rates—are easily established; programs are highly routinized; and staff interdependence is low, centering mainly around transferring clients from one supervisor to another. We would thus expect little conflict among the employees of institutions with custodial goals. As a correctional institution takes on treatment goals, however, professional treatment personnel must be added to the staff. Their perspectives often clash with those of custodial personnel. Furthermore, criteria of effectiveness are difficult to establish for treatment goals, since the success of rehabilitation can be established only over a long period of time and the efficacy of alternative policies and ways of handling delinquents are difficult to determine. Mixed-goal institutions are, therefore, likely to have a higher level of conflict than more custodial institutions. Even when institutions have predominantly treatment goals, the difficulties of establishing objective criteria of success and of dealing with the behavior problems of inmates lead to a continuing debate over means. Similarly, the individualized planning and lack of routinization required by treatment programs result in constant discussion and decision making. Disagreements requiring adjustment occur continually. In predominantly treatment, as in mixed-goal, institutions, therefore, conflict is likely to be high.[14]

In order to obtain a quantitative measure of conflict, members of the staff of each institution were asked, "On the whole, would you say there is any tension between the following pairs of groups?"[15]

---

14 Initially we expected conflict to be lower both in institutions having a predominantly treatment and predominantly custodial orientation, hypothesizing that conflict was a function just of multiple goals. During the exploratory phases of the research we recognized the difficulty of resolving conflict in treatment institutions, and modified our hypothesis.

15 Of course, it is true that conflict may exist without perception of tension. If conflict is defined as direct competition for scarce goods or values, it is conceivable that conflict could exist without tension (psychological frustration), as in a game. However, if tension occurs between two groups it is highly probable that it is based

The pairs listed were: (1) "teachers and social service workers," (2) "social service workers and cottage parents," (3) "cottage parents and teachers," and (4) "employees and the superintendent."[16] Respondents checked a five-point scale ranging from "a great deal of tension" to "no tension at all."[17] (Percentage distributions for each pair in each institution are presented in Appendix A.)

In order to establish the over-all conflict level within each institution we excluded the "no" responses[18] and computed conflict indices by combining the amount of tension for pairs.[19] Two index scores were computed: the first index score included all four judgments of tension made by respondents; the second index score excluded the tension perceived between employees and the superintendent—it is a measure of intergroup tension. Conflict index scores are presented in Table 2.

These computations show that Dick and Regis tended to have lower tension index scores than Mixter, Milton, and Inland, thus tentatively confirming our hypothesis. Although size may account for some of the variation, the differences among the institutions cannot be attributed only to the size of the institution.[20] Dick had a larger staff than Inland but had a lower tension level; while Mixter was larger than Milton yet tended to have a slightly lower conflict level. Furthermore, although Mixter had over four times as

---

on some sort of conflict of interest. Furthermore, in common usage the two are often identified together. We use perception of tension as an indicator of underlying conflict.

[16] The same type of conflict question was used by Basil Georgopoulos and Arnold Tannenbaum in "A Study of Organizational Effectiveness", *American Sociological Review*, 22 (1957), 534–40. They found that conflict as measured by this type of question was inversely related to productivity, organizational effectiveness, and organizational flexibility in the divisions of a package delivery company.

[17] The data to be presented are based on self-administered questionnaires which all staff members were asked to complete; 85 percent or more of the staff who were asked to fill in questionnaires in each of the institutions filled them in, though not always completely. The questionnaire was distributed after the research staff had been around the institution for at least a week. Staff members were guaranteed anonymity.

[18] There was a high rate of "no" responses on the tension questions, partly because many staff members were unwilling to comment on the amount of tension between groups of the staff of which they were not a part.

[19] In computing the index, "a great deal of tension" is assigned a weight of 5, "considerable tension" a weight of 4, and so on. The equation for the index is given

by $T = \Sigma \dfrac{P_r W}{N_{pa}}$ where T is tension level, P_r is proportion, W is weight, and N_{pa} is the number of pairs. To illustrate for one pair, if 15 percent check "a great deal of tension" (5), 60 percent check "considerable tension" (4), and 25 percent check "some tension" (3), the score for that pair would be 3.90.

[20] Georgopoulos found a statistically significant positive correlation of .53 between size and tension (personal communication).

many staff members as Inland, its combined tension level for all pairs was approximately the same as that of Inland. Comparing Regis and Inland we find that the level of conflict appears to be similar, if we exclude the superintendent-employee pair from the data. The data from Regis, however, are not really comparable, since they are based on only two pairs, one of which is not internal to the institution.

Our observational impressions tended to confirm these findings about the level of perceived tension. Especially at Dick, conflict was muted, and in conversations with staff it was difficult to elicit comments on the amount or issues of conflict. At Inland, Milton, and Mixter the staff readily supplied the investigator with comments about the sources of conflict. Moreover, as noted earlier, field observations indicated that at Inland superintendent-staff relations were tense, while at Milton superintendent-staff relations showed little tension or conflict. The quantitative indices reflect these differences. Scores on the second index are lower than on the first index at Inland and are higher at Milton, reflecting the different degrees of tension between superintendent and employees at the two institutions.

The quantitative data are supported by our observational impressions. We conclude that the more custodial institutions in our sample did have a lower level of conflict than the mixed-goal or treatment institutions.[21]

PATTERN OF CONFLICT

A Power-Balance Model

The position of an institution's goals on the continuum is related not only to the level of conflict but also to the power balance and patterns of conflict among the staff. If teachers, cottage parents, and social service workers have somewhat divergent goals or perspectives within an institution, then conflict is most likely between those who are unable to control the situation and those who are perceived as being in control of the situation.

Our basic model of patterns of conflict in correctional institutions for delinquents, which we call the power-balance model, is as follows. Since custodial institutions give more power to cottage

---

21 This conclusion should not be taken to imply that all treatment institutions will always have high levels of conflict. Small institutions, especially, which are able to select personnel carefully, may avoid intense forms of conflict. Furthermore, conflicts over working conditions and other factors may change the level of conflict of an institution.

parents and to custodial perspectives than do treatment institutions we expect teachers and social service workers in custodial institutions to be in conflict with cottage parents but not with each other. The benign custodial institution, that is, the mixed-goal institution on

TABLE 2
COMBINED INDICES OF LEVEL OF CONFLICT

Conflict Index	Dick	Regis	Mixter	Milton	Inland
All pairs............	1.79	1.83	2.11	2.40	2.20
All pairs except superintendent	1.78	1.94*	2.11	2.58	1.98

* Based on only two pairs, (1) cottage parents and social service, and (2) Regis Home and schools.

the custodial side of the continuum, is likely to have a pattern of conflict similar to the custodial institution, differing only in that conflict is more intense. On the other hand, in individual-treatment institutions we expect teachers and cottage parents to be in conflict with social service workers but not with each other. In a milieu institution, where there is a greater sharing of power between cottage parents and social service workers and a team concept of organization, we expect teachers to conflict with cottage parents and social service workers, but there should be little conflict between cottage parents and social service workers. The model is summarized in the paradigm in Table 3, which gives our predictions for the level of conflict for each pair of staff groups in the various institutions.

TABLE 3
PARADIGM OF CONFLICT PATTERNS: PREDICTED LEVELS OF CONFLICT AMONG COTTAGE PARENTS, SOCIAL WORKERS, AND TEACHERS

	Conflict pair		
Institutional type	Cottage parents and teachers	Cottage parents and social service	Teachers and social service
	Conflict level		
Custodial and benign custodial.	High	High	Low
Individual treatment	Low	High	High
Milieu treatment..............	High	Low	High

Two preconditions underlie this model, and when these preconditions are violated exceptions to the predicted patterns may occur. First, it is assumed that conflict requires some minimal interdependence among groups, the lower the interdependence, the less the conflict. If groups have little intercommunication, however, their members may not recognize the conflict even though the groups may be interdependent. For example, in a custodial institution teachers may have a more rehabilitative orientation than cottage parents, but, since teachers are isolated, their feelings of being frustrated by cottage parents may not be apparent to others. Second, teachers, social service workers, and cottage parents are assumed to have conflicting perspectives and values. Organizational adaptation, however, may lead to the selection and socialization of personnel so that they accommodate to the dominant perspectives. For instance, the cottage parents at Inland and the social service workers at Dick had perspectives which supported the dominant orientation. In such cases conflict with dominant groups is not expected.

To evaluate the utility of our model we must examine the actual power balance among staff groups in the sample. We must also examine the amount of conflict between each of the pairs in a given power balance (e.g., how much tension was perceived between themselves by the cottage parents and the social service workers). We have used an arbitrary criterion of 30 percent or more in the "high" or "some" tension category for either partner to the conflict as representing high conflict. For instance, if 30 percent of the teachers in an institution perceive high conflict with cottage parents but only 10 percent of cottage parents perceive conflict with teachers it is still considered to be a high-conflict situation. Field observations are also used both to examine the issues of conflict and its form of expression, and to validate our questionnaire data.

The Power-Balance Model Tested

First, we must examine evidence for the assumption that power balances differ in institutions with different goals. Elsewhere we have discussed in detail the power balance actually found among staff groups;[22] here we touch only on the major trends. In general the data confirm our assumption of a relationship between institutional goals and the power of staff groups.

Table 4 presents the proportions of staff attributing high influence to cottage parents, teachers, and social service workers (counselors, social workers, psychologists).[23] It is clear that social service workers at the treatment institutions, Milton and Inland, were seen as having high influence by a larger proportion of staff than at other institutions. There is a decline in the perceived influence of

---

22 M. N. Zald, "Goals and Organizational Control Structures in Correctional Institutions for Delinquents" (forthcoming).

23 Respondents were asked: "How much influence do each of the following groups have in making decisions about *how the boys should be handled?*" A five-point scale was used.

cottage parent groups from Dick, the most custodial institution, to Inland, where individual treatment was stressed. At Milton, under the milieu principle, cottage parent influence was high. It is also clear that teachers were perceived as having little influence in any of the institutions.

TABLE 4

STAFF PERCEPTION OF POWER BALANCE

| Staff groups | Percent of staff perceiving groups as having high influence | | | | |
	Dick (N = 62)	Regis (N = 9)	Mixter (N = 155)	Milton (N = 108)	Inland (N = 37)
Cottage parents........	50	33	34	70	8
Teachers	23	—	11	17	19
Social service..........	38	22	49	76	76

In Table 4 there seems to be one exception to our assumption. At Mixter, the benign custodial institution, the internal ordering of groups indicates that a larger proportion of staff (49 percent) perceived social service workers as having great influence than perceived the cottage parents (34 percent) as having great influence. This must be seen, however, in the setting of the general policies and distribution of executive power at Mixter. There the head of cottage parents was second only to the superintendent in perceived power; twice as many employees perceived the head of cottage parents as having great influence as perceived the training director (the nominal second in command) or the head of social service as having great influence. Thus, while it is true that cottage parents were limited by rules and regulations, custodial definitions still reigned, although enforced through the head of cottage parents. While social service staff members might have been able to influence decisions about a boy's program, they had little official control over when a boy went home, and the social service department as a whole did not shape policy. Although the education and status of the social service worker carried some weight in any particular case, in terms of general policy, custodial cottage life requirements predominated. The influence pattern at Mixter was that which might be expected in an institution with goals near the center of the continuum.

Let us now look at the predicted and actual patterns of conflict in Dick, Mixter, Milton, and Inland. (Regis is excluded from this analysis since it did not have teachers.) The results are summarized in Table 5. Eight out of twelve predictions were correct: at Dick only one prediction was correct, at Mixter all three were correct, and at Milton and Inland two predictions in each were correct. The pattern of conflict in each of the institutions will now be discussed in detail. As we will show, three of the incorrect predictions resulted from the failure of the data to satisfy the predictions of the model, not from an inadequacy in the model.

TABLE 5

SUMMARY OF PREDICTED AND ACTUAL CONFLICT PATTERNS

	Conflict pair		
Institution*	*Cottage parents and teachers*	*Cottage parents and social service*	*Teachers and social service*
		Conflict level	
Dick			
Predicted	High	High	Low
Actual	High	*Low†*	*High*
Mixter			
Predicted	High	High	Low
Actual	High	High	Low
Milton			
Predicted	High	Low	High
Actual	High	*High*	High
Inland			
Predicted	Low	High	High
Actual	Low	*Low*	High

* Regis is excluded because it did not have three conflict pairs.
† Instances where predicted and actual outcomes are different are in italics.

DICK. From the power-balance model of conflict we expected social service workers and teachers in Dick, the custodial institution, to be in conflict with cottage parents but not with each other.

Although the general level of conflict at Dick was low, 40 percent of the teachers perceived "some" or "high" tension with cottage parents and 30 percent perceived "some" or "high" tension with social service. Neither cottage parents (9 percent)[24] nor social service workers (0 percent) perceived tension with the teachers. Furthermore, there was little perceived tension between cottage parents (18 percent) and social service (0 percent).[25] Thus, only the prediction of conflict between cottage parents and teachers turned out to be correct. However, by considering the amount of interdependence and the perspectives of staff groups, the deviations from the model in the other two cases can be explained.

What conflicts there were at Dick between teachers and cottage parents were based on the teachers' greater permissiveness and

---

[24] Wherever a percentage in parentheses follows a member of a conflict pair it refers to the proportion in the group who perceive "some" or "high" tension with the other group.

[25] At Dick there were 11 cottage parents, 10 teachers, and 2 social service workers who filled in the questionnaire.

interest in rehabilitative educational activity. These differences were evident in at least three areas of organizational activity: (1) cottage parents stressed control of client movement while teachers tended to be lax in their watchfulness (2) teachers felt educational activities should be given priority over work activities,[26] and (3) teachers felt some cottage parents were too harsh with the boys. These are standard custodial-treatment conflicts and need not be discussed further.

How do we account for the low conflict between cottage parents and social service and the higher conflict between social service and teachers? The issues between social service workers and cottage parents were, surprisingly, the reverse of what we would expect. For example, one cottage parent complained that the social service director and the chaplain did not spend enough time with the boys. He felt the boys needed counseling and wanted information which was not being provided by social service. The social service director, a former clothing salesman, and the chaplain supported custodial and disciplinary policies. These accommodations to the institution may also help to explain the conflict teachers felt with social service workers. Teachers and social service workers were, however, of similar educational and status backgrounds and interacted informally with each other. Little conflict was evidenced during the period of field observation, and it is not possible to conclude definitely that the nonrehabilitative orientation of the social service workers frustrated teachers' objectives.

It is likely that the accommodation of social service workers to the institution prevented the predicted pattern of conflict between cottage parents and social service workers from occurring at Dick. Since the social service director and the chaplain did not support a more permissive and rehabilitative program, a precondition for the operation of the power-balance model was not met. Moreover, the isolation of both teachers and social service workers from cottage parents minimized the emergence of overt conflict.

MIXTER. Mixter was a benign custodial type of institution, and, although the overall level of conflict was higher than at Dick, the pattern of conflict was expected to follow that predicted for cus-

---

[26] A general complaint of the school involved the institution's overemphasis on production. The principal of the school felt that clients too often were taken out of school to work on the farm. Sometimes whole classes would be put to work and sometimes just a few boys would be taken out, interrupting teachers' lesson plans and making it difficult to keep the boys at the same rate of progress. At all the institutions teachers complained about classroom interruptions, but, where in Mixter, Inland, and Milton boys were taken out of school to participate in social service activity, at Dick they were taken out to work.

todial institutions. As predicted, teachers (57 percent) and social service workers (88 percent) conflicted with cottage parents (15 percent, 30 percent), while teachers (28 percent) and social service workers (13 percent) had little conflict with each other.[27]

While, as at Dick, teachers perceived tension between themselves and cottage parents, overt conflict was not high, and cottage parents perceived less tension than did the teachers. The teachers had little formal or informal contact with the cottage parents and also had little influence in the institution. Furthermore, since they had little contact with the cottage parents, their only source of information about cottage parents was from the boys—who tended to tell "atrocity tales." They tended to work their seven-hour day and have little other involvement in Mixter, the issues of conflict between teachers and cottage parents being the traditional custodial issues.

By contrast, social service workers were in constant contact with the cottage parents and cottage-life department, and, although some social service staff supported the custodial program, the conflicts with cottage parents were more clearly evident than those of the teachers. Conflict between social service workers and cottage parents had been even more virulent during an earlier period, and this had led the superintendent to require that social service workers spend two hours a week in the cottages in order that they might learn to work with the cottage parents. To some extent, this led to an accommodation of the social service workers to the cottage parents, because the increased communication allowed them to appreciate the point of view of the cottage parents, not just of the boys. Few resources relevant to cottage parents were controlled by social service workers; therefore there was no reason for the cottage parents to accommodate to the social service workers. The conflicts between social service workers and cottage parents were also less than they might have been, because the head of cottage parents and his assistants handled many disciplinary problems without involving the social service workers. If the social service workers had been brought into these cases more often, they might have sided with the boys.

The pattern of conflict at Mixter conformed closely to what we expected. An important difference between Dick and Mixter, which helps account for the emergence of the predicted pattern of conflict at Mixter, lies in the greater power of social service staff. Mixter's social service workers were perceived by cottage parents as

---

27 At Mixter there were 35 cottage parents, 14 teachers, and 8 social service workers who filled in questionnaires.

a competing power, while at Dick social service workers did not present a threat to the dominant definitions or policies.

MILTON. The power balances at Mixter, Dick, and Regis differed sharply from those at Inland and Milton in that the power of social service and the importance of treatment goals were clearly established. Our model of conflict led us to expect little conflict between social service and cottage parents at Milton, because they shared power and made joint decisions, while we predicted high conflict between teachers and both cottage parents and social service workers. The data indicate high conflict between all three groups:[28] teachers (67 percent) and cottage parents (32 percent); cottage parents (48 percent) and social service (89 percent); and social service (67 percent) and teachers (67 percent).

The conflict between teachers and the cottage committees—social service workers and cottage parents—was clearly the result of the low power of the teachers. The teachers had not been fully incorporated into the structure implementing the milieu treatment philosophy and thus were unable to influence the decisions of the cottage committees directly. The teachers felt that often, when a boy was sent back to the cottage for disrupting the school, the cottage committees would neither discipline the boy nor tell the teachers what action had been taken. As a result, they felt that they were left without adequate information. On the other hand, some cottage parents felt that teachers sent boys back to the cottages too quickly and were not patient enough with the boys.

More important for evaluating the adequacy of our model were the factors contributing to the maintenance of conflict between cottage parents and social service workers. The difficulty of integrating all cottage parents into the milieu structure seemed to be an important factor. Although the cottage parents in charge of each cottage, the cottage mothers, and the day cottage parents worked closely with social service staff, cottage parents who worked in the afternoon and evening had to deal with large groups of boys armed only with an injunction to "understand before you act." The head cottage parents and recreation men sometimes helped the other cottage parents in the evening, but the afternoon and evening cottage parents were not in close contact with members of the social service staff. In general, then, it was difficult to bring all cottage parents into the committee structure.

Another factor contributing to the maintenance of tension was

---

[28] At Milton there were 38 cottage parents, 9 teachers, and 9 social service workers who filled in questionnaires.

the inability of this institution to pay adequate salaries to cottage parents, making it difficult to attract personnel with compatible attitudes. While Inland used only college men, Milton's larger size and its location prevented it from relying on college men alone; nor did the executives think this would be desirable.

Finally, the very operation of the cottage committees contributed to the maintenance of tension. Disagreements and differences in perspective were easily brought into the open and expressed. Differences of opinion about the role of discipline and authority were thus projected into sharp focus.

However, the cottage committees had been effective in lowering the over-all level of conflict at Milton. Staff members reported that the institution was much more stable at the time of the study than it had been several years earlier, when the "professionals" and the cottage parents were in open conflict. Many staff members claimed that the higher level of conflict between social service workers and cottage parents at an earlier time had been reflected in tension among the boys; in recent years there had been a decline in fighting, property destruction, and general "acting out."

There was a direct relationship between the length of service of cottage parents at Milton and the tendency to perceive tension. Of the eight cottage parents who had worked at the institution for less than one year, only two perceived high tension; of the nineteen who had worked there between one and six years, eight perceived high tension, while of the eight who had worked there more than six years, seven perceived high tension. It is possible that the cottage parents with seniority had been sensitized to perceive tension by the older issues and conflicts. Although our data indicate that there was still conflict, it appeared to be less virulent than previously and was more often a disagreement over means than the earlier disagreements over basic aims.

Unification of the cottage committee also had changed somewhat the bases of differentiation in the institution, and, therefore, the bases of conflict. Although social workers and psychologists retained their professional identities, to some extent they gave up their departmental identities. The new lines of differentiation were between cottage teams. Within the limits defined by the institutional schedule and facilities, each cottage established its own rules of procedure and did its own programming. Since the cottages had different age groups and diagnostic problems, different procedures were felt to be necessary for each cottage. Cottage parents were encouraged to adapt formal procedures to their special needs. The organization into cottage committees meant that, instead of the professionals uniting against the nonprofessionals, the professionals faced each other across the boundary of the team, and identifications within the cottage committees were not uncommon. Conflicts of this sort among professionals did not affect the operation of the individual cottage committees and, therefore, as compared to departmental conflicts, might be expected to contribute less to institutional instability.

INLAND. Because of Inland's focus on individual treatment we expected its teachers and cottage parents to conflict with social service workers but not with each other. The data indicate that there was little conflict between cottage parents (0 percent) and teachers (18 percent), while there was high conflict between teachers (56 percent) and social service staff (50 percent).[29] Contrary to our prediction,[30] however, there was little conflict between social service (0 percent) and cottage parents (0 percent). The model is thus only partially supported.

Conflict between teachers and social service at Inland involved issues central to an educational, as opposed to a psychotherapeutic, approach to rehabilitation. Although conflict had been somewhat lowered by indoctrinating teachers into psychodynamic theory, the "old guard" continued to believe that the clinical orientation was overly permissive and failed to establish occupational and life goals for the boys. Clinical focus on the resolution of psychological problems de-emphasized educational goals. Furthermore, even though the teachers admitted that the small size of classes at Inland was ideal for teaching, some continued to feel that their lack of authority and ability to discipline led to constant classroom disruptions and misbehavior.

While the teachers at Inland were in conflict with the social service staff, as expected, they were not in conflict with the cottage parents. Both teachers and cottage parents had little power in the institution, and, since they were not interdependent, there was little basis for strain or tension. Field observation revealed no overt conflict between cottage parents and teachers.

29 At Inland there were 7 cottage parents, 9 teachers, and 4 social service workers who filled in questionnaires.

30 As Harrison White has pointed out in a personal communication, a larger proportion of teachers than any other group in all of the sample institutions tended to perceive high conflict, while the proportion of cottage parents perceiving conflict was always less than any other group—regardless of the partner to the conflict. On the one hand, the teachers' overperception of conflict may reflect their isolation and sense of powerlessness. On the other hand, cottage parents' underperception of conflict may reflect their lower education and working-class origins, rendering them both less aware of interpersonal strain and less committed to ideological positions regarding appropriate institutional means.

Why, contrary to our prediction, was there little conflict between social service and cottage parents? The field observations indicated that cottage parents did feel themselves to be under strain; the strain, however, did not evidence itself in overt conflict for two reasons. First, conflict was avoided by hiring young cottage personnel who accepted the clinical, permissive orientation. Second, cottage parents tended to have closer informal relationships with the social service workers than with the teachers. Moreover, in contrast to Mixter, the weekly meeting of cottage parents and social service workers contributed to the accommodation of the cottage parents to the social service workers. The status of the social service workers, the youth of the cottage parents, and the clear-cut treatment goal minimized conflict.

Although the social service workers had close informal relations with the cottage parents, they had no responsibility for the supervision of cottage parents or the management of the cottages. Disciplinary problems were handled by the assistant director or the head of cottage life; as a result social service workers were freed from decisions which might have led them to conflict with the cottage parents. At Inland, then, the pattern of conflict departed from that predicted by our model largely because the cottage parents did not have a custodial orientation.

SUMMARY AND CONCLUSIONS

Two major conclusions may be drawn from this analysis of the level and pattern of institutional conflict. First, we may tentatively conclude that the level of conflict in correctional institutions is a function of their multiple goals, their vaguely specified means, the degree of interdependence of employee groups, and the degree of routinization. Mixed-goal and treatment institutions had a higher level of conflict than more custodial institutions.

Second, we have demonstrated the utility of a power-balance model of conflict in accounting for the patterns of conflict in correctional institutions. In eight out of twelve cases the conflict level between pairs was predicted by the power-balance model of conflict. In three of the cases in which the model was not successful in predicting the actual level of tension, its failure appears to have been not the result of the model, but of the data to satisfy the preconditions of the model. That is, since social service workers at Dick accepted the dominant custodial perspectives and cottage parents at Inland accepted treatment perspectives, the necessary precondition of divergent values was not met. In the case of Milton we failed to take into account the effect of heightened interdependence in raising the potential of conflict and the persistence of divergent views when few criteria were available to establish the efficacy of alternatives. Although the model cannot be applied without knowledge of the relation of organizational adaptations to the preconditions of conflict, such as staff interdependence and divergent values of staff groups, the power-balance model can be a useful tool in predicting the patterns of conflict. A word of caution may be in order, however; power balance among groups is directly related to differences in institutional goals. The pattern of conflict reflects the over-all power balance among executives as well as the power balance among specific groups.

The Problem-Solving Organization

Consideration of the conflict over means that existed in the two treatment institutions leads us to a view of organization and organizational conflict which has not been well conceptualized in the literature. Much has been written about the advantages of involving lower-level staff in decision making.[31] In situations in which rational criteria exist and in which routinized programs are possible, such involvement of lower-level personnel may be partly a fiction or at best feasible only for a limited range of decisions, for in organizations with routinized techniques major decisions are usually made in the higher echelons. To be effective, however, treatment institutions, particularly those operating on a milieu principle, may be forced to allow decision making to occur on lower levels.

In this respect, milieu institutions depart sharply from our usual conception of bureaucratic organization, which assumes that routinized procedures are used and that the discretion of lower-level personnel is sharply circumscribed. From this point of view bureaucracies are considered as tools or machines for achieving ends. If the environment of such organizations were relatively stable and technology did not change, organizations would operate routinely.

Such a model, of course, is rarely approached; changes in the sources of supply, in the amounts and kinds of market demands, in the labor market, and in technology require organizational adaptation. Nevertheless, even granting the pervasiveness of informal organization, some organizations, for periods of time, may operate relatively routinely. Furthermore, many of these adaptational problems may have few or no consequences for the rank and file of the

---

[31] For instance, Peter F. Drucker, *The Practice of Management* (New York, 1954).

organization. We would suggest that the philosophy of milieu treatment requires such institutions to be continually solving problems, and the rank and file of the organization must be involved in this process.

Treatment institutions in general, and milieu institutions in particular, must continually adapt resources to the therapeutic needs of their inmates. Techniques of handling inmates and programs for each inmate must be established and co-ordinated among staff members. Techniques must be changed as inmates change and react to staff behavior. In other words, the organization is not turning out a standardized product with standardized means; neither the tasks nor the techniques lend themselves to uniform definition.

Individualized planning and programming require a larger staff to participate in the making of decisions. Lower-level staff must be consulted so that they can provide information for decisions, and also to ensure staff motivation to carry out organizational policy. In treatment institutions the absence of objective indices of staff performance requires staff members to be committed to goals if executives are to be sure that organization goals are pursued. In a factory, on the other hand, objective indices of production allow control from above without great commitment of lower-level staff—production failures can be met by sanctions. One way to ensure staff motivation is to involve them in the decision-making process, but involving lower-level staff in decision-making may open up a wide range of problems for debate.

A third factor contributing to the problem-solving nature of milieu treatment organizations is the interpersonal basis of all service to inmates. As compared with organizations that turn out material products or offer only limited and specific services, the operation of milieu institutions, and correctional institutions in general, is based on interpersonal relationships. If these relationships are to be used for treatment gain, the organization must take into account the personalities and special competencies of, and attachments between, staff members and inmates. Where in many large-scale organizations the personalities and attachments of lower-level staff are considered to be irrelevant to organizational decisions, in treatment institutions staffing patterns and assignments must take into account and utilize the relationships existing between staff members and inmates. Personal criteria, therefore, enter into the realm of organizational decisions. On the executive level of many large-scale organizations, of course, such factors are likely to play a role, but in milieu institutions personality and interpersonal relationship factors are likely to enter into decisions even at the lowest level of the staff.

What are some of the consequences of operating as a continually problem-solving organization? Since there have been few if any, studies of organizations from this point of view, we can only speculate. First of all, in a problem-solving organization, at least as exemplified by milieu treatment institutions, decision making must be decentralized. If executives are actually to involve lower-level staff, more than token consultation must take place—real power to take action must be delegated. By careful selection and training of personnel, executives can ensure that lower-level staff members make decisions in accordance with over-all policy and goals. Despite this, some decisions will be made which the executive would have made

APPENDIX A
PERCEPTION OF TENSION BETWEEN GROUPS (IN PERCENT)

Conflict pair	Dick (N = 62)	Regis (N = 9)	Mixter (N = 155)	Milton (N = 108)	Inland (N = 37)
Cottage parents and teachers					
High tension*.....	3	—	7	9	—
Some tension......	13	22†	16	37	8
Little tension	29	44	32	32	49
No tension	37	33	23	5	27
Not answered	18	—	25	17	16
Cottage parents and social service					
High tension......	2	—	8	10	—
Some tension......	15	33	27	41	8
Little tension	27	33	26	28	46
No tension	37	33	15	9	32
Not answered	19	—	25	12	14
Teachers and social service					
High tension......	3	—	1	9	8
Some tension......	7	—	14	35	27
Little tension......	29	56‡	37	33	43
No tension........	44	44	23	9	11
Not answered......	18	—	26	13	11
Employees and superintendent					
High tension......	3	—	8	3	27
Some tension......	15	11	12	12	22
Little tension......	29	67	36	42	24
No tension........	37	22	21	30	14
Not answered	16	—	21	14	14

Probability < .05 for each of the first three pairs, > .05 for the last pair; determined by Difference in Proportions Test, comparing those checking "little tension" or more at Dick and Regis with those in similar categories at Mixter, Inland, and Milton.
* "High tension" combines "a great deal" and "considerable" tension.
† Regis Home and schools substituted here.
‡ Social service and director substituted here.

differently. Paradoxically, the organization must give up control over some areas to achieve organizational goals. Failure to delegate control over decisions may result in cynicism and staff apathy. Executive control must take the form of specifying the intent and aims of policy and setting the limits of staff discretion.

Secondly, problem-solving organizations are likely to be conflict-ridden organizations. The opening up of organizational decisions to discussion and debate raises, or maintains, the level of conflict in the institution. Even if overt conflict is raised or maintained in problem-solving organizations, however, some kinds of tension may be lowered—those tensions that result from feelings of injustice and misunderstandings and that lead to subversion of goals and avoidance of rules. In any event, the conflict that results in a milieu treatment institution with carefully selected and trained personnel is likely to be different from that of the mixed-goal institution. First, basic disagreement about goals is less likely and conflict and debate operate more to adjust disagreements about means to the agreed ends. Second, greater involvement on the part of lower-level staff can be used to further and promote organizational activities. Although the milieu institution or the problem-solving organization may have a high level of conflict, it may be that the conflict is of a kind that works in the service of institutionalized goals rather than as a brake and impediment to organizational effectiveness.

Exercise for the Reader:
Assessment of the Zald Study

CLASSIFICATION

1. What is the specific purpose of the study?
2. What research does Zald use to accomplish his purpose?
3. Why is the study classified as quantitative-descriptive, and how does it differ from experimental and exploratory studies?
4. How should the study be sub-typed?

EVALUATION

Problem Formulation

1. How does the author utilize the literature on organizational conflict in formulating the problem for study?
2. How does the author conceptualize custodial and treatment goals, and how are these types of goals defined operationally?
3. How does the author conceptualize and operationally define the concept of organizational conflict?
4. What are the major hypotheses of the study?
5. What are the independent and dependent variables in the study hypotheses?
6. What are the author's major assumptions regarding the selection of variables and hypotheses for study?

Research Design and Data Collection

1. To what extent are the institutions selected for study representative of a universe of institutions?
2. What types of evidence pertaining to the testing of hypotheses can be generated from the author's comparative design? What other sources of evidence are necessary?
3. To what extent are the institutions described in Table 1 appropriate for comparisons to test the author's hypotheses?
4. What types of data are collected, and to what extent are they reliable and valid?
5. In what way does the author utilize observational impressions of tension in the study institutions as data?

Data Analysis and Conclusions

1. To what extent do the data in Table 2 support the author's

hypothesis that custodial institutional goals lead to a low level of staff conflict?

2. Are the obtained relations potentially spurious, i.e., can they be explained by other variables that could be introduced into the analysis, such as the size of the institutions?

3. Describe the power-balance model developed by Zald. What assumptions does he make regarding the use of the model?

4. Is the power-balance model adequately tested in the study?

5. Are the data presented in the study consistent with the author's stated purposes of the research?

6. Are the conclusions presented in Table 5 and the author's summary warranted by the data?

7. How does the author explain findings on patterns of conflict which do not coincide with his predictions?

8. Are the statistics employed in the presentation appropriate to the data?

UTILIZATION

1. In what ways are the variables of organizational goals, level of conflict, pattern of conflict and distribution of power identifiable, accessible, and manipulable?

2. What is the general level of knowledge of the conclusions of this study?

3. To what areas of social work practice might such knowledge be useful, either directly or indirectly?

4. To what extent does the author's conceptualization of organizational conflict have implications for practice in treatment or milieu institutions?

5. What implications does the author's view of treatment institutions as problem-solving organizations have for the practice activities of psychiatrists, social workers, psychologists, and lay personnel, e.g., cottage parents, attendants?

6. How might the concepts used in this study be utilized in research directly relevant to a caseworker or group worker whose treatment orientations are in conflict with the goals of the institution in which he works?

7. How could agency administrators use the conceptual framework posed in this study for assessing agency operations and goals?

RECOMMENDED REFERENCES

Problem Formulation

CRESSEY, DONALD R., "Contradictory Requirements in Complex Organizations," *Administrative Science Quarterly*, 4 (June, 1959), pp. 1–19.

Vinter, Robert D., and Janowitz, Morris, "Effective Institutions for Delinquents: A Research Statement," *Social Service Review*, 33 (June, 1959) pp. 118–131.

Zald, Mayer N., "Organizational Control Structures in Five Correctional Institutions," *The American Journal of Sociology* (November, 1962), pp. 335–45.

Research Design and Data Collection

Street, David, Vinter, Robert D., and Perrow, Charles, *Organization for Treatment* (New York: The Free Press, 1966).

Chapter 7

Assessment
of Exploratory
Studies

Community Leadership:
A Case Study and Conceptual Refinement

by CHARLES M. BONJEAN

The phenomenon of power-leadership decision-making at the community level has received a great deal of attention from both sociologists and political scientists during the past decade.[1] Many of these investigations, especially those conducted by sociologists, have been criticized on the grounds that the method of investigation used—the reputational approach—is inadequate for several reasons.[2] (1) The

---

SOURCE: Reprinted from *American Journal of Sociology*, Vol. 68, No. 6 (May, 1963), pp. 672–81. Reproduced by permission of The University of Chicago Press, and the author.

This investigation involves one facet of community affairs in the Piedmont Industrial Crescent being studied by the Institute for Research in Social Science of the University of North Carolina under a grant by the Ford Foundation. The leadership studies are under the direction of E. William Noland, who suggested a number of revisions and modifications of this investigation. Revisions and useful suggestions were also made by Richard L. Simpson and Ernest Q. Campbell of the University of North Carolina.

1 Including Floyd Hunter, *Community Power Structure: A Study of Decision Makers* (Chapel Hill: University of North Carolina Press, 1953); Roland J. Pellegrin and Charles H. Coates, "Absentee-owned Corporations and Community Power Structure," *American Journal of Sociology*, LXI (March, 1956), 413–19; Charles Freeman and Selz C. Mayo, "Decision Makers in Rural Community Action," *Social Forces*, XXXV (May, 1957), 319–22; Robert O. Schulze, "The Role of Economic Dominants in Community Power Structure," *American Sociological Review*, XXIII (February, 1958), 3–9; Delbert C. Miller, "Industry and Community Power Structures: A Comparative Study of an American and an English City," *American Sociological Review*, XXIII (February, 1958), 9–15; Ernest A. T. Barth and Stuart D. Johnson, "Community Power and a Typology of Social Issues," *Social Forces*, XXXVIII (October, 1959), 29–32; Nelson W. Polsby, "Three Problems in the Analysis of Community Power," *American Sociological Review*, XXV (December, 1959), 796–803; Orrin E. Klapp and L. Vincent Padgett, "Power Structure and Decision-making in a Mexican Border City," *American Journal of Sociology*, LXV (January, 1960), 400–06; Arthur J. Vidich and Joseph Bensman, *Small Town in Mass Society* (Garden City, N.Y.: Doubleday and Co., 1960); Robert A. Dahl, *Who Governs? Democracy and Power in an American City* (New Haven, Conn.: Yale University Press, 1961), and Benjamin Walter, "Political Decision Making in Arcadia," in F. Stuart Chapin, Jr., and Shirley F. Weiss (ed.), *Urban Growth Dynamics* (New York: John Wiley and Sons, forthcoming).

2 By reputational approach, of course, is meant asking certain members of the community under investigation to list and rank the most powerful and influential leaders in the community. The approach has also been termed the "snowball technique" since one informant's nominees become the next informants. Critics of this technique include Robert A. Dahl, "A Critique of the Ruling Elite Model," *American Political Science Review*, LII (June, 1958), 463–69; Herbert Kaufman and Victor Jones, "The Mystery of Power," *Public Administration Review*, XIV (Summer, 1954), 205–12; Nelson W. Polsby, "The Sociology of Community Power: A Reassessment," *Social Forces*,

approach enables the investigator to find a monolithic power structure when, in fact, such a structure may not exist in the community. (2) Assuming there is a monolithic structure, this approach may lead to premature closure (not including all the leaders) or may lead to the inclusion of non-leaders. The problem is the cutoff point in the final list of nominees. (3) If the reputational approach is used, we must take into consideration inaccuracies in respondent perceptions. Private citizens, it is claimed, may be unreliable sources of information. (4) Interviewer and respondent may not agree on what is meant by "power." Certain questions used may not mean the same thing to both interviewer and respondent or there may be no consensus in regard to the meaning of the question among respondents.

The purpose of this investigation is to attempt to indicate how these shortcomings may be overcome through an extension of method and a refinement of concepts. The collection of additional data—sociometric and other—on a sample of community leaders so designated by the reputational approach makes it possible to probe group characteristics and internal differentiations of the sample. Analysis of the data indicates that reputational leaders are, in fact, meaningful groups and not artifacts of the operational measures in at least one community—Burlington, North Carolina. Because of the heuristic nature of this investigation no specific hypotheses will be tested, but one general hypothesis of an exploratory nature will be entertained: A conceptual refinement of the term "community leader" based on the method of investigation itself will lead to greater agreement among investigators, will satisfy to some degree the basic criticisms listed above, and may serve as a useful basis for comparative studies in the future.

THE COMMUNITY

Burlington, located in north-central North Carolina, has a population of approximately 33,000 (1960) and a suburban population of about 15,000 (1958 est.). Approximately 125,000 live in the city's trade area, which extends 8 miles to the west and 20 miles in all other directions. The population of the city increased slightly more than 33 percent between 1950 and 1960, an increase due primarily to industrial expansion and new industries. Eighty-eight percent of the population is native-born white, and 11.4 percent is Negro (1960).

XXXVII (March, 1959), 232–36; Raymond E. Wolfinger, "Reputation and Reality in the Study of Community Power," *American Sociological Review*, XXV (October, 1960), 636–44, and a number of the investigations listed in n. 1.

Primarily an industrial community, Burlington ranks sixth in the nation in hosiery production and leads the South in the number of hosiery plants. Of the city's seventy-eight industrial establishments, thirty are hosiery mills and fifteen others produce textile products. Among the 3,073 counties in the United States, Alamance, of which Burlington is the largest city, ranks 216th in the number of manufacturing plants and 203d in the number of industrial wage earners —well in the top 10 percent on both items. A total of 19,000 persons are employed in Burlington's industries.[3]

The city operates under the mayor-council type of government.

METHOD OF INVESTIGATION

The empirical objectives of the investigation have already been stated: to isolate a group of community leaders according to standard methodology and to further delimit this group on the basis of other measures. A two-step reputational analysis supplemented with sociometric and interaction data was used to attempt to fulfil these objectives.

The executive secretary of an established community association, was asked: "Who are the community leaders who really get things done around here?"[4] He was asked to rank up to twenty leaders in order of over-all influence and to specify those leaders he had worked with as well as the areas of participation.[5] Using his list as a starting point, interviewers asked each individual named by him to do the same. This was continued until new lists yielded many more duplications than nominations. After forty-five interviews it was evident that there was relatively high agreement in regard to sixteen community leaders and little agreement on the remaining one hundred nominations. Additional interviews would probably have had the same results—more nominations for the sixteen top leaders and more names to add to the remaining list of one hundred. According to Moreno, this assumption has general validity and may be termed the "sociodynamic effect":

It might be anticipated that increasing the chance probability of being chosen by allowing more choices within the same size population and thus lessening the chance probability to remain unchosen will gradually

---

[3] *Hill's Burlington and Graham City Directory* (Richmond, Va.: Hill Directory, Inc., 1958), pp. i–xiii.

[4] This was but one question included in a standardized interview schedule consisting of seventy-eight questions (both poll type and open end) and requiring from forty-five minutes to four hours to complete.

[5] Thirty specific activities were listed. They could be grouped into seven general participation areas: economic, welfare, livability, educational, political, philanthropic, and desegregational.

bring the number of unchosen to a vanishing point and likewise reduce more and more the number of comparatively little chosen.

However, in actuality, this does not take place. . . . The further choices allowed go more frequently to the already highly chosen and not proportionately more to those who are unchosen or who have few choices. The quantity of isolates and little chosen comes finally to a standstill whereas the volume of choices continues to increase for those at the upper end of the range.

The sociodynamic effect apparently has general validity. It is found in some degree in all social aggregates.[6]

Thirty-eight of the forty-five respondents became informants by naming individuals and ranking them. Their 116 nominations were tabulated and weighted—a weight of 20 assigned to each first-place choice, 19 to a second place choice and so on down to one for a twentieth-place choice. The total leadership score assigned to each of the 116 individuals mentioned consists merely of the sum of the weighted choices.

Leadership scores ranged from 350.5 for Neal Allen, the top leader in the community, to one for Mrs. Robert Cain, who received one twentieth-place vote.[7] Fourteen of the 116 persons mentioned received scores of more than 100 and two received scores between 90 and 100. No other person received a total leadership score higher than 70 and most were far below this score.[8] Thus, because of the high agreement regarding the selection of the first sixteen as leaders and because of the lack of consensus in regard to the remainder of the sample, it was assumed that, *if* a power elite existed in Burlington, these sixteen individuals would be the basic element of its membership.

Most power structure studies stop here in regard to the reputational approach. (Two exceptions, studies conducted by Robert O. Schulze and A. Alexander Fanelli, will be discussed briefly below.) But using the same data and analyzing them from a different standpoint may yield additional valuable information. Thus a second step in the data analysis is incorporated. In Burlington, of the forty-five informants, twelve were in the leader category (members of the top sixteen);[9] the other thirty-three were not. The second analysis

---

[6] J. L. Moreno *et al., The Sociometry Reader* (Glencoe, Ill.: Free Press, 1960), p. 36.

[7] "Neal Allen" and "Mrs. Robert Cain" are pseudonyms as are the names and affiliations of the other leaders and non-leaders specifically referred to in this investigation.

[8] It is impossible to include the full data here because of space limitations. The investigator will provide mimeographed copies of additional data or will answer more specific questions on request.

[9] Of the sixteen top leaders in Burlington, only twelve were interviewed. One died shortly after the study had started, one was not in the city during the time of the study, and, although the other two were interviewed, they asked to keep the schedule in order to complete some "difficult" questions and did not return it.

utilizes only the choices and rankings of ten of the twelve "leaders."[10] When this is done, a new picture emerges—the "power elite" has gained new members (because of high agreement among these twelve, but no or few nominations from the remainder of the informants) and assigns much less power to other nominees (because of no or few choices from the elite). This modification of the reputational approach does not incorporate an arbitrary cutoff point, and, at the same time, it reduces the likelihood of inaccuracies in respondent perception (in that the "judges" are determined by the first analysis). The wording of the question and the additional requirement for judges to list the nominees' spheres of influence seems to overcome the problem of ambiguity. The possibility of ambiguity and the desirability of judges is indicated by comparing leader and non-leader rankings (Table 1). That there is little agreement between the two sets of rankings is supported statistically, as Spearman's rank correlation for the two groups is .012.

TABLE 1
RANKING OF SIXTEEN LEADERS BY THEMSELVES AND BY NON-LEADERS

Leader	Total Sample (N = 38)	Leaders (N = 10)	Non-Leaders (N = 28)	Difference	Leader Type*
Neal Allen	1	1	2	− 1	v
James Barton	2	2	3.5	− 1.5	v
George Welles	3	10	1	9	s
Mike Reynolds	4	3	5	− 2	v
Tom White	5	9	6	3	v
R. V. Daniels	6	4	11	− 7	c
Terry Jones	7	13	7	6	s
Percy Roberts	8	17	3.5	13.5	s
Charles Martin	9	11	12	− 1	v
Thomas Mintler	10	14	9.5	4.5	s
A. G. Curtis	11	7	13	− 6	c
Richard Murphy	12	16	8	8	s
Harold Smith	13	5	14	− 9	c
Harold B. Green	14	6	15	− 9	c
LeRoy Barton	15	8	16	− 8	c
Harvey Harris	16	15	9.5	5.5	s
Dan Morley	—	12	—	− 5	c

* Leader types: *v*, visible; *s*, symbolic; *c*, concealed.

Two questions must be answered before further discussion. First, does this method imply an *a priori* assumption that a monolithic power structure does exist in the community? Second, have we really established a power elite?

In regard to the first question, it should be noted that this technique allows for disagreement as well as for agreement in regard to

---

10 Of the twelve leaders interviewed, two refused to rank leaders and to indicate those they interact with. Thus, sociometric choices and actual information regarding interaction are available for ten of the sixteen leaders.

leadership choices. If there were no leadership elite in the community we would expect little or no agreement in leadership selection. There is no reason to reject the assumption that the technique is able to indicate the absence of a power structure, as well as its presence.

Obviously, all of Burlington's 48,000 residents (including suburbs) could not conceivably play leadership roles, strictly on the grounds of accepted role definition. When one starts cutting down a population of this size by factors of two for sex (excluding females), perhaps three for age bracket (excluding those too old and those too young), X_1 for income sufficient to insure some leisure, X_2 for education and so on, the result *is* a limited group. The size of this group is unknown in Burlington, but it is reasonable to assume that it is *at least* 116 (based on nominations alone). The 445 choices made by the 38 informants *could* have been distributed evenly, indicating a power vacuum. In fact, they were not. Of the 445 choices, 201 were directed to the top sixteen nominees $(X = 12.6)$; the other 224 were directed to the remaining 100 nominees $(X = 2.24)$. Had there been the least possible agreement in leadership selection in regard to the leadership pool of 116, each nominee would have received almost four (actually 3.86) votes. Adopting 3.86 as the mean and 4.6 as the standard deviation (an estimate based on the range, which in this case is 22), an upper confidence limit of 4.97 (at the 99 percent level) may be computed. In other words, we may assume that choices are no longer random if we are able to isolate a number of individuals, each receiving five or more choices. As a matter of fact, the number of choices assigned to the judges selected by the first step of the method ranges from six to twenty-two. No one in the remainder of the "leadership pool" has more than four choices and most have only one. An informal analysis of rankings (as opposed to sheer number of choices) seems to indicate, even more convincingly, that a power vacuum does *not* exist in Burlington.[11]

At least two validity checks may be employed to ascertain whether or not the technique actually has established a power elite.

First, if most top leaders also select one another as top leaders and, second, if, in fact, they actually indicate that they interact with one another, it seems reasonable to assume that a *group* has actually

---

[11] These data were not subjected to the same sort of statistical analysis as described above because of time and cost limitations and because the first test was thought to be convincing enough to support the argument in question. The informal analysis was used merely as a quick check.

been discerned as opposed to a mere aggregate of individuals with similar characteristics.

By constructing a sociogram (Figure 1) showing the first three

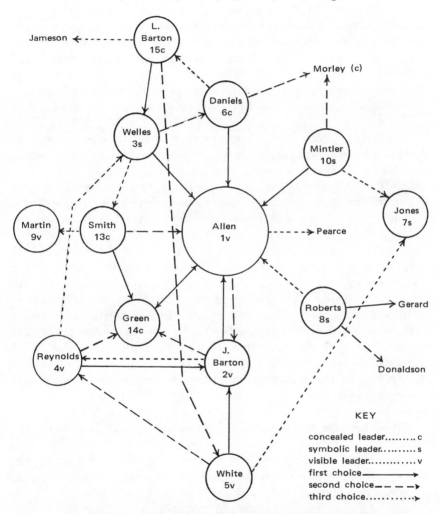

FIGURE 1. Leadership Ranking by Ten Leaders.
Uncircled Are Not Top Leaders.

leadership choices of the ten top leaders completing this section of the interview schedule, an index of the degree to which these leaders form a group is available. Of the thirty possible choices (ten leaders times three choices each), twenty-four are within the elite designated by the entire sample. Thus, the *ratio of interest,* one aspect of group cohesiveness, is .80.[12] This statistic (the number of in-group choices divided by the total possible number of such choices) is meaningful only when compared with that of another group. The only group available for comparison at this point is the remainder of our sample of informants. Of their eighty-four possible choices, forty-five are directed to the top sixteen (ratio of interest = .53). Assuming the remainder of our informants do not form a group and are not a part of the elite group, we have a basis for comparison and consequently can test for statistical significance of differences between proportions. In this case, a t-test yields $P <$ .001.

A second validity check, "interaction," also indicates that Burlington's power elite resembles a group more than it does an aggregate. As was indicated above, after listing and ranking leaders, each informant was provided with a check list of thirty community activities (although not all were found to be salient in Burlington) and was asked to indicate those individuals he "worked with" on each of the thirty activities. Significant here is the fact that a number of interaction patterns could be noted that *were not* connected with formal memberships.[13] For example, a cross-tabulation of responses indicates that five of the ten leaders say they have worked with one another regarding "who gets elected to municipal office," yet none hold offices themselves nor do they hold formal positions in a political party. Eight of the power elite name one another in the area of attempting to attract new industries to the community. All in all, interaction patterns *within* the leadership elite are discernible in twenty-one of the possible community activities. In each case the patterns involve between three and eight of the ten interviewed leaders.

Thus, because the data indicate mutual choices between members of the power elite as well as interaction within the elite, most of the sixteen leaders uncovered by the reputational approach may be considered as a group rather than merely an aggregate. It should be noted, however, that four of the top sixteen leaders—ranks 8, 10, 11 and 12 (see Fig. 1)—received no first, second, or third place choices within the power elite. It is apparent that their position in the leadership group is thus derived from one or both of two

---

[12] For a discussion of the ratio of interest and other statistics of social configuration *see* Moreno *et al., op. cit.,* pp. 19–51.

[13] This is not the first investigation conducted where interaction has been designated as a necessary "check." An "acquaintanceship scale" was used successfully by Schulze and described in a report published subsequent to the research described here (*see* Robert O. Schulze, "The Bifurcation of Power in a Satellite City," in Morris Janowitz [ed.], *Community Political Systems* [Glencoe, Ill.: Free Press, 1961], p. 51).

phenomena: their leadership score was a consequence of rankings beyond three by members of the elite *or* their leadership score was a consequence of high ranking by non-leaders. Also, several other individuals, not originally identified as elite members, were given such choices. This brings us more directly to the second step in data analysis—an attempt to determine differentiations *within* the power elite.

TYPES OF LEADERS

Assuming that the sixteen persons uncovered by the first step in data analysis are the most qualified to perceive others of their kind, the next step should be to compare the leaders as perceived by one another with how they are perceived by that proportion of the sample not designated as part of the power elite. Such a comparison would yield three possible leadership types: (1) The leader who is assigned approximately the same amount of power by both other leaders and non-leaders. (2) The leader who is assigned more prestige by leaders than by non-leaders. (3) the leader who is assigned more prestige by non-leaders than by leaders.

Leaders of the first type will be termed *visible leaders* because they are playing roles in the community that are perceived and known by the community at large. Leaders of the second type will be termed *concealed leaders* because they have more influence within the leadership circle or power elite, and consequently in the community in general, than the community at large realizes. Leaders of the third type will be termed *symbolic leaders* because they probably do not wield as much influence in the community as the community at large thinks they do.

Looking at the comparison of leaders shown in Table 1, all three types may be distinguished. Arbitrarily setting a rank variation of five (true limits of 4.5 or greater) as the point where leaders are classified as concealed or symbolic rather than as visible, there are five visible leaders, six concealed leaders and six symbolic leaders. Sixteen of the leaders, of course, were uncovered by the general reputational approach; but a seventeenth was located by the modification described here. Leader types are indicated on both the sociogram and Table 1 by the symbols "*v*" (visible), "*c*" (concealed), and "*s*" (symbolic).

For this differentiation to be meaningful, the next step is to determine whether or not there is a relationship between leader type and other variables. In attempting to locate differences between symbolic and concealed leaders, there are no patterns or trends in regard to age, type of business, number of employees, types of activities engaged in, memberships (including religion), or education.

There is, however, one basic difference between the two extreme types of leaders—symbolic and concealed. Four of the six symbolic leaders are members of prominent Burlington families—families that have lived in the city for several generations, that are wealthy, and that have passed the family business on to the person listed as a leader. Murphy (12), before his death, was the top officer in a hosiery mill that had been in his family for three generations; Roberts (8) is the second-generation administrator of his family's hosiery mill; Jones (7) inherited his father's automobile dealership, and Harris (16) is the member of a family possessing all of the characteristics except the last (inheritance of family business). Only Welles (3) and Mintler (10) differ in this respect from the other symbolic leaders. Welles's symbolic placement may be explained by the fact that he is paid by the city businessmen for work in community affairs. Thus he occupies a position highly visible to the community in general, but one of perhaps less importance in the sphere of policy formation and decision-making than in the actual execution of policy. Thus, this deviant case analysis seems to further validate the method proposed here. Only Mintler's placement as a symbolic leader is unexplainable. This may indicate a necessary change in method. The arbitrary rank variation set forth for classification as a concealed or symbolic leader was five (4.5 true limit). Mintler was a borderline case. The difference between leader and non-leader ranking was exactly 4.5. This may indicate that the arbitrary difference is set too low—perhaps, for example, the true limit should be raised to five.

The concealed leaders differ markedly from the symbolic leaders. Only one of the six concealed leaders *owns* a large business or industry and this leader, Congressman Green, founded his businesses himself, rather than inheriting them. In other words, his wealth is at least a generation newer than is the wealth of most of the symbolic leaders. His concealed status may also be due to the fact that he is the local power structure's link with a larger, more influential power structure at the state or national level.[14] As such, perhaps he would be more closely connected to the elite personnel and consequently more visible to them at the community level than to the remainder of the sample, who perhaps have a more macro-

---

14 *See* Floyd Hunter, *Top Leadership U.S.A.* (Chapel Hill: University of North Carolina Press, 1959) for a discussion that supports this tentative hypothesis.

scopic conception of his role. It is interesting to note that Allen, the leader receiving the greatest number of choices and highest ranks, ranked Green first. The other five concealed leaders do not own businesses—two are professionals and three are the local administrators of subsidiaries of state or national corporations. Five of the concealed leaders spent their childhood or longer outside of Burlington and thus, compared with the symbolic leader group, are relative newcomers. The outstanding observation is that none is from a traditionally prominent Burlington family. This suggests that non-leaders perhaps think more in terms of the status or class dimensions of stratification when asked to name community leaders, whereas leaders themselves are more apt to think in terms of the power dimension. It suggests further that non-leaders may not recognize changes in the leadership base or power elite but think instead that those who have always been powerful will probably continue to be so. In other words, individuals who have formerly ranked high on all three dimensions of social stratification—class, status, and power—may through time have lost, to some degree, one of these characteristics, but for several years a "halo effect" will operate to influence the general viewpoint. Schulze's Cibola findings lend some credulity to this hypothesis (economic dominants exerted sociopolitical power as well as economic power in the past, but currently have relinquished the former in that community).[15]

Critics of stratification studies continually remind us of the necessity to distinguish between class and status.[16] Studies of the third major aspect of stratification—power—face the same problem. High status or class position may lead to the assumption by informants of high power positions. Thus it becomes necessary to differentiate between three different types of community leaders—class (economic) leaders, status (reputational) leaders, and true power leaders. The *hypothesized* relationship between the methodological distinction of visible, concealed, and symbolic leaders to class, status, and power leaders, as suggested by this sensitizing exploratory investigation, is summarized in Table 2. Two important relationships should be noted: (1) the traditional reputational

---

[15] Schulze, in Janowitz (ed.), *op. cit.,* pp. 40–41.

[16] Including Paul K. Hatt, "Stratification in the Mass Society," *American Sociological Review,* XV (April, 1950), 216–22; Harold F. Kaufman, Otis Dudley Duncan, Neal Gross, and William H. Sewell, "Problems of Theory and Method in the Study of Social Stratification in Rural Society," *Rural Sociology,* XVIII (March, 1953), 12–24; Kurt Mayer, "The Theory of Social Classes," *Harvard Educational Review,* XXIII (Summer, 1953), 149–67; Gregory P. Stone and William H. Form, "Instabilities in Status: The Problem of Hierarchy in the Community Study of Status Arrangements," *American Sociological Review,* XVIII (April, 1953), 149–62, and others.

approach uncovers symbolic leaders who are actually not members of the power elite. (2) It may *not* uncover actual members of the power elite if these members rank low in either class or status.[17]

TABLE 2

HYPOTHESIZED RELATIONSHIP BETWEEN METHODOLOGICAL TYPES AND
STRATIFICATION COMPONENTS

	Class	Status	Power
Symbolic	High	High	Low
Visible	High	High	High
Concealed	Low	Low*	High

* The concealed leader may rank high in either class or status position, but not in both.

Thus, a second step needs to be added to the reputational approach if its use is to be continued in this type of study. The second step, of course, is the one that has been outlined here—the comparison of rankings by leaders and non-leaders and the classification of leaders into three types based on rank differences. This method itself is a useful heuristic device at the single case study level of investigation. When power studies reach the comparative level (examining two or more leadership structures simultaneously), it should be even more useful as it is one means of assessing one of the most controversial and central characteristics of such structures— their visibility. Are leaders and leadership behavior overt or covert? Furthermore, is this characteristic, the structure's visibility, related to community attributes?

The first question may be answered in regard to the case at hand. The second answer must be delayed until a uniform methodological approach is applied to the study of other communities. In Burlington, the leadership structure is partly visible and partly concealed. The structure's "star," Neal Allen, is visible. Although it is a subjective impression, it seems that one factor coinciding with Allen's number one rank in the community may be that he is a co-ordinator of community affairs. In other words, because so many of the other top leaders, each with his own specialized community interests, select Allen as the top leader, his function may be that of assigning priority to various projects (some visible and some concealed) and attempting to integrate and interrelate them. Support-

---

17 A. Alexander Fanelli ("A Typology of Community Leadership Based on Influence within the Leader Subsystem," *Social Forces*, XXXIV [May, 1956], 332–38), sets forth a method that enables the investigator to distinguish between the symbolic and visible leaders (he calls them prestige influentials and active influentials), but that ignores the possibility of concealed leaders. Schulze's distinction between economic dominants and public leaders (in Janowitz [ed.], *op. cit.*, pp. 19–80) has the same shortcoming, but obviously the economic public leader distinction has other merits and is thus not as comparable to the method being discussed as is the Fanelli distinction.

ing evidence is that he is a member of all important civic organizations but holds formal offices in none of them. Informants furthermore remarked, for example, "He really isn't active himself as far as *doing* things goes, but he certainly has more influence than anyone else in town." On the other hand most of the other top leaders (both visible and concealed) direct their activities toward only one or two institutional spheres of the community—usually economic plus one other. Other than Allen, only two leaders, Welles (3) and Reynolds (4) are active in more than two institutional areas of participation. In summary, Burlington's leadership structure may be seen as a network of overlapping subgroups, some visible and some concealed, co-ordinated by one central visible figure. This structure is not too unlike the smaller and simpler power structure described by Arthur J. Vidich and Joseph Bensman in Springdale and is similar to the structure described by Schulze in Cibola—three groups of dominants linked by two individuals occupying "dual statuses."[18]

Conclusion

Adding a second step in data analysis, interaction checks, and statistics of social configuration to the traditional reputational approach used in the study of community power-leadership decision-making and distinguishing between three types of leaders (1) takes account of and, to varying degrees, answers the criticisms of the traditional reputational approach, (2) serves as a heuristic device leading to more penetrating modes of analysis in itself, (3) emphasizes that structural characteristic—visibility—that has been a major source of disagreement and discussion, and (4) suggests interrelationships between the concepts "class," "status," and "power" that may later contribute to a more general theory of stratification.

The fact that all generalizations discussed above are based on, and derived from, only one case study obviously requires cautious interpretation. They are offered here only as material for hypotheses—hypotheses to be tested by this investigator in the near future in other communities and to be modified, improved, or rejected by other interested investigators.

---

[18] Vidich and Bensman, *op. cit.*, pp. 110–230, and Schulze, in Janowitz (ed.), *op. cit.*, p. 52.

An Assessment of the Bonjean Study

1. What Are the Specific Purposes of the Study?

Bonjean reviews the literature regarding the use of the reputational approach in studies of power, leadership, and decision-making. The reputational approach refers to a procedure by which members of a particular community are asked to list and rank leaders in the community with respect to their perceived power and/or influence. On the basis of his review, the researcher summarizes arguments which point to possible inadequacies in the use of this method:

a. It is based on an *a priori* assumption that a monolithic power structure exists, and can be determined through the reputational approach.

b. The point at which no more nominees are collected is arbitrary, and this may lead to either an over-inclusion or an under-inclusion of leaders in the sample obtained.

c. There may be inaccuracies, distortions, or biases in the respondents' perceptions regarding community leadership and influence.

d. The respondents may not have the same notions of such concepts as "power" and "influence"; thus, the data which are obtained may not be reliable and valid.

In view of the above possible inadequacies of the reputational method for assessing community leadership structures, Bonjean's explicit purpose is to demonstrate how the approach can be improved by extending the method and refining the concept of "community leader." In addition, a subsidiary purpose is to describe a way in which the proposed extension of the reputational method can be used to estimate the structure of the "power elite" in Burlington, North Carolina. An implicit objective is to develop hypotheses regarding types of leaders in a community.

2. What Methods Does the Author Use to Accomplish His Purposes?

One community in North Carolina was selected as the site for the study; and within that community one person, "the executive secretary of an established community association," was chosen as the initial informant for the first stage of the author's approach. The first informant was asked to identify and rank up to 20 leaders with respect to " overall influence." He was also asked to indicate those with whom he had worked and to specify the area of participation from a list of 30 activities. The list obtained from the first informant was then used as a device to locate other informants. The same procedure was repeated for each of the identified persons until there were fewer new nominations for leaders than there were duplications for persons already named. This procedure resulted in 45 respondents, of which 38 were used as the primary informants in the study. One hundred sixteen individuals were named by the informants, and leadership scores based on the rankings of all the informants were assigned to all of the persons nominated. A high leadership score reflected more agreement among the informants. Those 16 individuals with the highest leadership scores were regarded as the basic core of a "power elite," *if* a power elite existed in the community.

The second stage of the analysis focussed on the "leaders" and "non-leaders" who were available in the sample of 38 primary informants. Ten individuals were identified as having high leadership scores and as being among the 16 "leaders," while 28 individuals with low leadership scores were regarded as "non-leaders." The rankings of leaders and of non-leaders were compared to determine whether there appeared to be different sets of rankings between the leaders and the non-leaders. Following this step, Bonjean used two indices of group behavior to determine whether the 16 leaders could be regarded as a group: (1) the extent to which the sample of 10 leaders chose themselves as leaders, and (2) the extent to which the leaders indicated they worked with each other on a series of specified community activities.

Comparisons of the rankings of the 16 leaders by the sample of leaders and by the sample of non-leaders led to the development of a typology of leaders. Those leaders who received similar rankings by non-leaders and by leaders were classified as "visible leaders"; higher rankings by leaders than by non-leaders resulted in "concealed leaders"; and higher rankings by non-leaders than by leaders were used to identify "symbolic leaders." Additional data on selected characteristics of leaders were used to develop hypotheses regarding the relationship of leadership type to the concepts of class, status, and power.

3. Why Is the Study Classified as Exploratory?

The study is classified as exploratory because the primary objectives of the investigation are to refine concepts and to develop hypotheses for further research. This is different from the objectives of experimental and quantitative-descriptive studies concerned with the testing of research hypotheses. In addition, the purposes of the Bonjean study are distinct from those quantitative-descriptive studies which seek to describe accurately characteristics among designated populations or to search for quantitative relations for further testing. However, contained within the study are selected quantitative-descriptions of the single community being investigated, as well as quantitative-descriptions concerned with the rankings of community leaders.

Essentially, the investigation is focussed on an extension of a method for locating and identifying leaders within a single community, and there is no attempt to generalize the findings of the study to other communities. It is clearly not an exploratory study based on the experimental manipulation of independent variables. In fact, the primary focus of the study is on the elaboration of one variable, "community leader." The research is not classified as an exploratory study which uses a specific data collection procedure for developing ideas. The reason for this is that the research involves the use of several data collection procedures and also the study and extension of one procedure *per se.* Nevertheless, this study has features of exploratory studies which use specific data collection procedures, as well as selected aspects of quantitative-descriptions. Based on both the major objectives of the research and the methods employed (interviews with rankings, sociometric analyses, and selected demographic and qualitative-descriptions), this case study can be sub-typed as a combined exploratory-descriptive study.

EVALUATION: PROBLEM FORMULATION

1. *How Does Bonjean Use the Literature on Power, Leadership, and Decision-making in Conceptualizing the Research Problem?*

Bonjean refers to the literature on approaches which identify community leaders in order to study community power structures. He summarizes some of the shortcomings of the reputational approach, and he develops his research problem in an attempt to improve the reputational method. Bonjean emphasizes the procedures which were used as indicators of the concepts being investigated, but he does not articulate his conceptualization of the variables. Rather, it is implicitly assumed that the concepts are understood, and that they are intimately tied to the reputational approach. The references he cites, such as Dahl's *Who Governs*, and other available references, such as Polsby's *Community Power and Political Theory*, clearly point to alternative conceptions and methods for studying community power and leadership. For example, distinctions have been made between those who have available resources for the exercise of power and those who actually exercise power with reference to influencing specific decisions in selected issue-areas which are relevant to a particular community. Such authors believe that the study of leadership should be geared to *actual* decisions rather than to *perceived* influences of leaders. In this regard, it appears that Bonjean could possibly have considered some of these notions in both his conceptualization and operationalization of alternatives and/or extensions of the reputational approach.

Selected literature pertaining to sociometric analyses for the purpose of distinguishing a group from an aggregate of individuals is employed. The main emphasis appears to be in the use of methods and indices for identifying groups, rather than in the conceptualization of groups *per se*. In particular, little attention is given to the way in which an established group of leaders is indicative of the concept of power elite. The literature could have been used in greater detail to indicate various conceptions and assumptions pertaining to concepts employed in the research. Further, a greater use of the literature might have provided more refinements of a particular method, and, indeed, comparisons of alternative methods with respect to attempts to overcome the problems cited by various critics.

The major concepts used in the research were derived from the literature: community leadership, power elite, monolithic power structure, power, prestige, class, and status. The key concept in the study was "community leader." Bonjean derived relevant concepts from the literature, but he tended throughout his study to interchange such concepts as "power" and "prestige," as well as "leadership elite" and "power elite." Further, the concepts were not specified in sufficient detail for the reader to be able to discern to what extent the author regarded them as similar or different.

2. How Does the Researcher Conceptualize and Operationalize the Concepts of Community Leadership, Power Elite, and Power Structure?

Curiously, the concept of "community leader" was not specified.

Since a conceptual refinement of that concept was regarded as a major purpose of the study, the author should have indicated to what extent the concept would be refined as a function of his method. The reader is faced with the problem of attempting to determine the meaning of "community leader" as used by the researcher. Referring to the operational procedures, the reader can discern what aspects of community leadership are considered. First, one member of the community in an established association is selected. He is asked to identify and rank-order community leaders in regard to their overall "influence." The guiding question for identifying leaders was, "Who are the community leaders who really get things done around here?" Thus, it is implicit in the first operational stage that the informant has a conception of community leadership in regard to overall influence that might be shared by other informants. Further, reliance appears to be placed on the informants' *perceptions* of influence, rather than on *actual* behavior of the presumed leaders which results in decisions affecting the community. Informants' identifications of leaders may, therefore, be regarded as indices of actual behavior, but Bonjean offers no conceptualization in this regard.

The first informant is a source for other informants who are also asked to identify leaders, rank them, and to indicate in which areas of influence the leaders have participated. With respect to participation, it appears that it may be a necessary condition for influencing decisions; however, it may not be a sufficient condition. In essence, it seems that participation is assumed to be directly related to influence. The magnitude of such a relationship is unknown unless it is studied empirically with respect to specific decisions.

Agreement by the informants is used as the basic criterion for choosing the first group of leaders, and the leaders are separated from non-leaders by an arbitrary cut-off point in leadership scores. The implicit assumption is that agreement by interviewed informants regarding their perceptions of community leaders leads to the identification of a "leadership elite." Bonjean then implies that *if a power elite exists,* the identified community leaders would be the core members.

The researcher proceeds to build on the reputational approach by studying the rankings of leaders from a sample of identified leaders. It is assumed that the leaders can make more accurate perceptions of themselves. Those leaders with the highest rankings are assumed to be those leaders with "real power." Thus, it becomes apparent that perception of high ranking leaders is assumed to be an index of a power elite. In the research report Bonjean shifts the concept of power elite to be identical to the index of power elite provided by identifying community leaders. This is particularly evident when he shifts his attention from estimating a potential power elite in the first step of his analysis to determining types of leaders "within the power elite" in the second stage of his analysis. Further, he indicates that the criterion of agreement and of disagreement in the selection of community leaders is able to indicate the absence of a power structure, as well as its presence. In effect, he is arguing that the method does not imply an *a priori* assumption that a power structure exists in the community. In this regard, it does not appear that he deals with the question of a *monolithic power structure* adequately. In the first place, he has not articulated the concept. Secondly, he implies that his concept of "leadership elite" is equivalent to "power structure." Thirdly, the criterion of agreement for perceived leaders may not lead to the identification of leaders who actually exercise "power."

3. To What Extent Is the Concept of Community Leadership Refined According to His Conceptual Framework?

Bonjean refines the method for determining community leaders by analyzing the rankings of the leadership group identified in the first stage of the reputational approach and by adding sociometric analyses to determine whether the selected leaders actually form a group. However, he did not explicate his conception of "community leader," and it is difficult to determine whether the concept is refined, extended, or changed. His sociometric data are relevant for identifying a group of individuals who interact with each other, but it appears that this is changing the concept from "community leader" to a group of power elite. Yet, Bonjean did not state his purpose as refining that concept. Moreover it appears that he uses such concepts interchangeably throughout his research report.

It seems that Bonjean could have been more precise in his specification of concepts and that he could have incorporated notions posited by Dahl, Polsby and others in an attempt to link his methods more closely to a conceptual model of community leadership. As previously implied, he might have considered what conceptual distinctions have been identified in relation to "power" and to "leadership." Further, he could then have specified the way in which his indices of the concept correspond to the concept itself, i.e., a conceptual model might have led him to specify more precisely the extent to which his indices could be validated. This is especially important in relation to the inadequacies of the reputational approach which he attempts to overcome.

EVALUATION: RESEARCH DESIGN AND DATA COLLECTION

1. *Was the Design of Research Consistent with the Articulated Purposes of the Study?*

The research design was essentially that of a case study of leaders in one community. The design was appropriate for Bonjean's objective of attempting to demonstrate a refinement of the reputational approach. However, the plan of the research might have been extended so that more evidence pertinent to the stated inadequacies of the reputational method might have been provided. For example, in addition to the reputational approach, he might have used another method for determining community leaders. The two approaches could have been used to validate the designated community leaders from a single community. An example of a different method would be the "pluralist approach" which was used by Dahl and Polsby in studying community power in New Haven. An additional extension might have involved the comparison of the same method in two or more communities in order to yield potential ideas concerning differential patterns as a function of different types of communities. For example, the reputational approach, as outlined in the Bonjean paper, may be less valid in a larger urban community or in a smaller rural community.

2. *What Sampling Procedures Were Employed in the Study with Respect to the Selection of the Community and of the Community Leaders?*

The one community selected for study was a small Southern city, which was primarily an industrial community operated "under the mayor-council type of government." It appears to have been selected arbitrarily, perhaps due to its proximity to the University of North Carolina, and, perhaps, due to its relatively small size. The representative sampling of communities is not a crucial issue in Bonjean's investigation since he does not attempt to test a research hypothesis. Nevertheless, it is possible that he could have demonstrated a greater feasibility for using his method if more than one community had been studied. In particular, one might speculate about the possible differences in communities which have different types of local government.

More pertinent to the objectives of the research is the sampling procedure involved in selecting community leaders since it is claimed that they are identifiable as a result of the reputational approach and supplementary data. Specifically, the selection of the first informant appears to be crucial. In Bonjean's study, this informant was "the executive secretary of an established community association." Since this person could name up to 20 leaders, it is possible that he might have selected people who might have chosen him and each other as leaders. The resulting sample of leaders may include over-representations of friends and associates of the first person queried. The basic question is concerned with possible differences as a function of the initial informant. There were essentially 38 informants in this study. Would these same informants have emerged if the initial informant was the Mayor or some other individual? Bonjean did not present his rationale for selecting the first individual. Nevertheless, he had the data to indicate how many of the identified leaders were choices of the first informant and what the first informant's ranking of leadership was. Further, the investigator might have demonstrated that the identified leaders would be the same persons, irrespective of the first informant, by replicating the approach within the same community with two or more initial informants. It is possible that within small communities that the same leaders may be obtained, but in large communities one might hypothesize that different leaders would be selected, depending on the position of the first informant in the community.

Since the findings are discussed in relation to leaders and the "community at large," it would be helpful for the reader to have some idea regarding the extent to which these groups are representative of the community. Evidence in this regard might have been indirect, such as the demonstration of equivalent socio-economic characteristics for the sample of informants and for a random sample of informants selected from the community.

The sampling problem becomes more evident when it appears that only 10 of the 16 leaders identified in the study were able to give their full cooperation: one died; one was out of town; two did not return interview schedules; two did not provide sociometric and interaction data. Are the 10 leaders studied representative of the 16 leaders? Would the rankings of the 16 leaders have been different if all of the living "leaders" had participated? These questions probably could have been answered to some extent by the data which were already available to Bonjean. The essential point is that such problems were not considered in the presentation, and a consideration of such problems may have increased the reader's confidence in the validity of the method.

3. *What Specific Kinds of Data Were Collected?*

The primary sources of data were obtained from the respondents in the study who were subjected to a standardized interview schedule consisting of 78 questions. Respondents identified and ranked community leaders and indicated participation activities for the leaders. Most of the 78 questions were not presented in the article, but the author indicated that more detailed information was available upon request. Interaction data regarding the extent to which leaders worked together on specific activities were gathered. In addition, selected characteristics of the leaders were used although the data were not presented in the report.

4. *How Reliable Did the Data on Community Leadership Appear to Be?*

The respondents were asked to rank leaders on the basis of which leaders get things done in the community, and they were also asked to specify activities of participation for the leaders. Essentially, Bonjean used a criterion of reliability, i.e., agreement, in identifying the leaders; but on that basis the data from the non-leaders could be regarded as unreliable. Although agreement was used as a criterion for identifying leaders, no specific concern was devoted to the reliability of the questions themselves. Did all of the respondents conceive of leadership and of participation in the same way? Indications of reliability might have resulted from the use of procedures which ask the respondents to either define the concepts themselves or to check one of several alternative conceptions of, for example, community leadership. The greater the agreement obtained, the higher the interjudge reliability would have been.

5. *How Valid Were the Data Regarding the Concepts of Power Elite and Community Leadership?*

With respect to the validity of the data, Bonjean employs two procedures: sociometric analysis based on leadership choice and interaction data. He uses these devices in an attempt to validate whether or not his extension of the reputational approach has established a *power elite*. As was previously discussed, he offered no definition of the concept such that the reader could determine whether the data add to its validity. Nevertheless, it is clear that the "validity checks" which he employed served to establish whether or not the identified leaders could be regarded as a group. The device of demonstrating group activities appears to have been appropriate. However, it is difficult to understand in which way the notion of a group adds further to the concept of power. Presumably, there are many groups of people which could be identified in the community being studied, but having group characteristics does not necessarily increase the power of an aggregate of individuals. Hence, the notion of power is still dependent on the identification and ranking of community leaders. Further, the notions of agreement for selecting community leaders and for establishing a group based on the choices of leaders appear to be biased in favor of defining a monolithic power structure as a function of the methods employed. To add to the validity of the concept, one might specify independent indices of actual power on specific decisions in that community. Then one would attempt to demonstrate that the distribution of actual power for the individuals in the selected leadership group is much greater than the distribution of actual power in the non-leadership group. As implied by Polsby, little attention has been paid to the extent and duration of power by adherents to the view that power is hierarchically distributed in communities. In essence, Bonjean may have added the notion of group to his conception of "power elite," but he has not validated the notion of "power."

6. *What Is the Basic Assumption in the Second Phase of His Procedure in Which He Compares the Perceptions of Leaders and Non-leaders? Is this Assumption Plausible?*

The basic assumption is that those persons designated as leaders from the first step in the reputational approach are more qualified to make choices of "leaders" than are those who are not adjudged as leaders. It is implicit that the rankings of designated leaders comprise the most appropriate index of the power elite. It is plausible that leaders may know more about themselves on the basis of these assumptions: that the leaders do, in fact, form a group of individuals who exercise power as opposed to an aggregate of individuals who exercise power; that the chosen leaders are, in fact, "community leaders." However, these assumptions relate to the validity of the reputational method. Thus, Bonjean's assumption rests on the validity of the first stage of the reputational approach. The plausibility of the assumption would be increased if evidence, such as the actual distributions of power among the leaders and the non-leaders, were presented.

EVALUATION: DATA ANALYSIS AND CONCLUSIONS

1. *Are the Data Presented in Table 1 Consistent With Bonjean's Methodological Approach?*

Bonjean's second step in the reputational approach includes comparisons of rankings of 16 leaders by 10 of the leaders and 28 of the non-leaders. With respect to Table 1, the reader would be interested in the extent to which leaders agree among themselves. This information is necessary for the following reason: prior to the comparisons between the two sets of rankings presented in the table, one should have some indication of the reliability of the rankings within each group. If the reliability within each of the two groups is low, the comparison between groups might reflect unreliability in the rankings rather than true differences in rankings between the two groups. According to Bonjean's method of deriving leadership scores and rankings, it would appear that the set of rankings for non-leaders is less reliable than the set of rankings for the leaders. However, insufficient information is presented to substantiate this possibility. Thus, the use of rankings appears to be consistent with Bonjean's methodology, and information on the reliability of rankings for leaders and for non-leaders might have strengthened the author's conclusions regarding true differences in rankings between the two groups. For example, *if* the rankings had been derived from the average of the rankings of the leaders by all of the individuals in each of the two groups being compared, the reliability within each group might have been estimated by a statistic such as the coefficient of concordance. The higher the estimate of reliability within each group, the greater the reader's confidence regarding the reported differences in rankings.

The correlation which was obtained by Bonjean is of zero order (rho = .012), and it indicates that there is no relationship between the sets of rankings presented in Table 1. This allows the researcher to sub-divide the 16 leaders into either those with similar rankings by both groups or those with divergent rankings. If the correlation were of a high magnitude, the rankings would have been similar for both groups. This means that only one type of leader might be obtained by this method. Thus, the method for determining types of leaders is dependent on obtaining a correlation of low magnitude. To increase one's confidence in this method, it could have been replicated within another community. Nevertheless, the internal analysis of different types of leaders appears to have been an appropriate way to locate possible leadership types in this exploratory study within one community.

2. How Does Bonjean Develop Hypotheses Pertaining to Leadership Type and Stratification Components?

From the data presented in Table 1, Bonjean developed three types of leaders as a function of similarities and differences in the rankings of 16 leaders by "leaders" and by "non-leaders." Similar rankings were designated arbitrarily as rank differences of less than 4.5. Leaders with similar rankings by both "leaders" and "non-leaders" were regarded as *visible leaders*. Leaders who were ranked higher by "leaders" than by "non-leaders" were called *concealed leaders; symbolic leaders* were those leaders who were ranked higher by "non-leaders" than by "leaders."

Bonjean then used available data, such as age and education, to determine if there were any noticeable patterns among the leadership types he derived. Although the data were not presented, the procedure was appropriate in that he attempted to discern possible differences in types which could form the basis of hypotheses for subsequent research. He observed one difference between the symbolic and concealed leaders: the symbolic leaders, for the most part, were members of prominent families who had lived in the community for several generations; whereas concealed leaders were not from traditionally prominent families.

The author used the literature on social stratification to lend credibility to his observations, and he indicated that the components of class, status, and power should be distinguished. He did not attempt to define or to suggest appropriate indices for these concepts, but he did hypothesize relationships between leadership types and stratification components in Table 2. For example, symbolic leaders were hypothesized as having high class (economic) and status (reputational), but low "power." Essentially, the researcher attempted to define attributes of his three leadership types. The crucial problem in his development of hypotheses pertains to the distinction between "true power" and "prestige" or "status." In his use of the reputational approach, it appears that prestige was used as an index of power. Yet, in his development of hypotheses, "true power" is regarded as distinct from prestige. In view of this, it appears that the researcher might have made the necessary distinctions in the use of the concepts employed in his hypotheses. In this way the likelihood of further research would be enhanced. In effect, the hypotheses are not researchable until the concepts are explicated such that they are distinct from each other. Nevertheless, the researcher developed interesting hypotheses as a result of the combined usage of data from his study and the available literature; and further conceptualization and operationalization of the concepts could render the hypotheses researchable.

3. What Do the Sociometric Analyses Contribute to the Research?

The sociogram represents pictorially the first three leadership choices of 10 of the leaders, and it is used to demonstrate that the leaders form a cohesive group. It summarizes the data and gives an indication of potential interaction patterns. To the extent that group composition of the chosen leaders is relevant to the concepts of "community leadership" and "power elite," the sociogram is a useful addition to the presentation of data. Further, it can be used to generate questions about the reasons why members chose each other, and it appears that it was used appropriately by Bonjean in this regard.

In addition to the sociogram, the author also employed interaction data regarding the extent to which leaders participated with each other in specified activities. These data, although not presented in detail, are relevant to the notion of group, and they supported Bonjean's conclusions concerning the group structure of the "leaders."

For comparative purposes in this exploratory study, it might have been informative to have more data regarding the group structure or lack of group structure among the "non-leaders." Bonjean reported that the ratio of interest was higher for the leaders than for the non-leaders, and he assumed that the non-leaders did not form a group. Nevertheless, the ratio of interest was .53 for the non-leaders, and interaction patterns may have indicated that non-leaders were more of a group than an aggregate. However, it appears that Bonjean's conclusions regarding differences in group cohesiveness between the leaders and non-leaders are plausible.

4. Are the Author's Conclusions Consistent with the Data Presented in the Study?

Bonjean makes the general conclusion that all of his generalizations are based on one case study and are regarded appropriately as hypotheses. Yet within the community which was studied, he argues that his use of sociometric analysis and the extension of the reputational approach answers the criticisms of the traditional reputational approach. On the basis of his study, this does not appear to be the case. His conclusions concerning the group structure of the chosen leaders are consistent with the data. However, the extent to which those conclusions are relevant to the author's conception of "community leader" and of "power elite" is indeterminate from this report since the concepts are not defined. It appears that his indicators of "power" are based on perceptions of community influence by the informants in the research. There is no attempt to validate these measures against independent criteria of actual uses of "power." Further, his extension of the reputational approach seems to be based on the assumption that a core membership of the "power elite" can be identified by the reputational method. In essence, he is, in part, assuming the validity of the reputational approach. In this respect, it does not appear that Bonjean has provided sufficient evidence to validate the reputational method. In addition, his approach has aspects of arbitrariness in it, but the arbitrary nature of the method is less crucial than is the validation of the measurement of the concepts *per se* on independent criteria. If the researcher wished to demonstrate more adequately his assertions about the reliability of the data based on the perceptions of respondents, he could have attempted to demonstrate this by empirical means. Bonjean attempted to answer the critics' questions by a series of assumptions pertaining to the reliability and validity of the data. Thus, however plausible, he has not demonstrated empirically that his method overcomes the comments of critics as presented in the purposes of his study. Nevertheless, he did demonstrate how a method can be extended so that hypotheses for further research could be developed, and he posited hypotheses which are relevant for leadership types and stratification theory.

UTILIZATION

1. *What Is the General Level of Knowledge of Conclusions From this Study?*

The results from this exploratory study are in the form of hypotheses which would need further verification in subsequent research. The knowledge produced is essentially that of demonstrating a way in which the reputational method can be extended by internal analyses and the use of supplementary data pertaining to the potential group nature of community leaders. A set of concepts and assumptions are employed throughout the study; and they serve to sensitize the reader to conceptual problems regarding the use of the reputational approach, as well as to critical assumptions concerning the location of leaders in a given community.

It is evident in this study that the identifiability of the concepts, "community leader," "power elite," etc., is the primary reason for the research. The investigation was concerned with modifying a method for operationalizing the concepts, and, thus, rendering them more identifiable. Yet, the research is not conclusive in this regard. In fact, the identifiability of the concepts "community leader" and "power elite" appear to depend on the accessibility of those individuals who may exercise power and influence in a particular community. In view of these considerations, it would be premature to consider possible ways in which the variables discussed in this study might be manipulated in order to produce some set of potentially desirable consequences. However, questions derived from this study may be employed as sensitizing concepts.

2. To What Areas of Social Work Practice Might the Results of this Study Be Applied?

The knowledge dealt with in this research refers to the location of community leaders as a potential source of power in community decisions. It is not concerned with abnormal aspects of leadership, but rather is concerned more with the structure of a group of leaders who have influence at the community level. In this respect the knowledge is potentially relevant to those areas of social work which deal directly with community leaders, such as in social planning, administration, and fund raising activities. Further, those social workers who either deal directly with community leaders or require knowledge concerning the location of potential community leaders may gain some insights regarding the phenomenon of community leadership, as a function of having assessed this study. Therefore, the knowledge generated from this study may be relevant for community organizers and for group workers. In this regard, Wachtel (1968) has discussed two models of community power structure, the elitist and the pluralist, and has suggested that different strategies for community organization should be employed as a function of the type of power structure in the community. Thus, a strategy based on a coalition of diverse groups in a community may be more effective for producing change in communities which are characterized as having monolithic power structures. The reader is referred to Wachtel's work for a detailed consideration of alternative strategies for community organization based on an assessment of community power structure.

3. In What Way Can Bonjean's Use of Research Methods Be Used as a Practice Technique?

To the extent that community organizers and social planners are interested in estimating those individuals in a community who may be influential, the extension of the reputational method can be used as a device for locating such persons. This presumably might be of some importance in obtaining some understanding of the community in which organizing or planning activities might take place. The method, particularly if it is modified to deal with decisions with which the practitioner is concerned, can be used as a tool in conjunction with other devices for community assessment. It would serve as a means by which practitioners might become sensitive to the location of potential leaders. In addition, the use of sociometric analyses may provide an indication as to which leaders might work together with respect to specific planning or organizing activities.

4. As a Result of Analyzing This Article, to What Problems Might Practitioners Become Sensitive?

If there are different types of community leaders as posited by Bonjean, then the implication is that practitioners should not assume that high socio-economic status for an individual necessarily implies that he has influence regarding decisions which affect community residents. The practitioner should gather as much information as possible regarding who has been involved in making decisions, and he should be sensitive to the notion of differential leadership types.

In regard to notions about power structure, the practitioner should be aware that he may be making similar assumptions to those made by researchers. In particular, the practitioner should attempt by observation and other indirect means to validate his assessment of the community both prior to and during his plan of intervention. For specific activities, a group of leaders may or may not be involved in the exercise of power. Further, these considerations require that the practitioner be more specific regarding who is deemed to be influential in a particular community. Thus, although the practitioner becomes sensitive to abstract notions pertaining to leadership, power elite, prestige, etc., he also should become aware of the indicators of such concepts at the concrete level of community decisions with which he is concerned.

5. As a Function of Analyzing This Article, What Hypotheses Can the Reader Develop?

In addition to the hypotheses posited by Bonjean, the practitioner may develop hypotheses such as the following:

a. Leaders identified by the extension of the reputational

approach are more likely to influence decisions related to social planning activities than are other individuals in the community being studied.

b. Symbolic leaders are less likely than either visible or concealed leaders to be influential in community decisions regarding the allocation of resources for social agencies.

c. The smaller the size of the community, the more likely it is that community leaders can be characterized as a group with respect to interaction patterns.

RECOMMENDED REFERENCES

Research Design and Data Collection

DAHL, ROBERT A., "A Critique of the Ruling Elite Model," *American Political Science Review,* LII (June, 1958), pp. 463–69.

LINDZEY, GARDNER, and BORGATTA, EDGAR F., "Sociometric Measurement," in *Handbook of Social Psychology, Vol. 1, Theory and Method,* Gardner Lindzey (ed.) (Reading: Addison-Wesley Publishing Company, Inc., 1954), pp. 405–48.

Statistical Concepts

BLALOCK, HUBERT M., "Ordinal Scales: Rank-order Correlation," and "Two-Sample Tests: Differences of Means and Proportions," *Social Statistics* (New York: McGraw-Hill Book Company, Inc., 1960), pp. 317–24 and pp. 176–81.

Community Power and Leadership

POLSBY, NELSON W., *Community Power and Political Theory* (New Haven: Yale University Press, 1963), Chapters 1, "The Relevance of Political Theory to Community Power," pp. 3–13; 5, "Power and Social Stratification: Theory or Ideology," pp. 98–111; 6, "How to Study Community Power: The Pluralist Alternative," pp. 112–21.

WACHTEL, DAWN DAY, "Structures of Community and Strategies for Organization," *Social Work* (January, 1968), pp. 85–91.

WALTON, JOHN, "Substance and Artifact: The Current Status of Research on Community Power Structure," *American Journal of Sociology* (January, 1966), pp. 430–38.

Introducing Institutionalized Retardates to the Community

by JOSEPH J. PARNICKY and LEONARD N. BROWN

The period of transition from institutional to community living has long been recognized by practitioners in the field of mental retardation as a time of special stress and adjustment. The incidence of and reasons for readmission have pointed up the institutionalized retardate's need for social competence and community acceptance. These impressions from practice have been affirmed in follow-up research. In a comprehensive survey of studies reported on by Windle, Stewart, and Brown, the chief reason for community failure of subnormals released from institutions was given as difficulties of interpersonal relationship.[1] Gunzburg further substantiates the need to prepare the retardate more adequately in social skills, stating they may need more help in this area than in vocational training.[2]

The impressions at the Johnstone Training and Research Center, Bordentown, New Jersey, drawn from individual case reviews and surveys of students returning from community placement, point up

---

Source: Reprinted with permission of the authors and of the National Association of Social Workers, from *Social Work*, Vol. 9, No. 1 (January, 1964), pp. 79–85.

[1] C. D. Windle, E. Stewart, and S. J. Brown, "Reasons for Community Failure of Released Patients," *American Journal of Mental Deficiency*, Vol. 66 (1961), pp. 213–17. Studies on which the authors reported, all published in the *American Journal of Mental Deficiency*, were: D. L. Brown, "The Working Convalescent Care Program for Female Patients at the Rome State School," Vol. 56 (1952), pp. 643–54; R. D. Collmann and D. Newlyn, "Employment Success of Educationally Subnormal Ex-pupils in England," Vol. 60 (1956), pp. 733–44; M. Craft, "Withdrawals from License in Mental Deficiency," Vol. 63 (1958), pp. 47–49; and G. Tarjan and F. Benson, "Report on the Pilot Study at Pacific Colony," Vol. 57 (1953), pp. 453–62. Others, variously published, were: W. E. Fernald, "After-Care Study of the Patients Discharged from Waverly for a Period of Twenty-five Years," *Ungraded*, Vol. 5 (1919), pp. 25–31; N. O'Connor, "The Successful Employment of the Mentally Handicapped," in L. T. Hilliard and B. H. Kirman, eds., *Mental Deficiency* (London, England: Churchill, 1957), pp. 448–80; H. W. Potter and C. L. McCollister, "A Resume of Parole Work at Letchworth Village," *Proceedings of the American Association for Study of the Feeble-minded*, Vol. 31 (1926), pp. 165–88; G. De M. Rudolph, "Improvement in Mental Defectives in Colonies," *Journal of Mental Science*, Vol. 96 (1950), pp. 272–75; and R. J. Stanley and H. C. Gunzburg, "A Survey of Residential Licenses from a Mental Deficiency Hospital," *International Journal of Social Psychiatry*, Vol. 2 (1956), pp. 207–13.

[2] H. C. Gunzburg, "The Place of Further Education in the Rehabilitation of the Adult Subnormal," *Proceedings of the London Conference on the Scientific Study of Mental Deficiency*, Vol. 1 (1960), pp. 251–57.

similar needs and difficulties. Cohen reported that for the most part the reasons for students' return to institutions were social rather than vocational. These included lack of judgment with regard to social norms, poor attitude on the job, lack of readiness for employment or difficulty in adjustment, and severe problems at home. Besides these factors, it was also noted that the stigma-rejection pattern in the community toward the institutionalized retardate presented barriers to acceptance that intensified the problems of adjustment.[3]

In a recent statement by the Vocational Rehabilitation Administration recognition is given to such findings, especially in its statement of the goal in rehabilitation of the mentally retarded as

. . . to provide conditions and circumstances that permit the retarded person to perform the activities of daily life and to learn how to behave socially and vocationally in such a manner that he may compete successfully within that segment of his milieu that is within normal limits.[4]

Providing Introductory Experiences

In order to achieve this goal institutional programs must provide introductory experiences within the community, experiences with which the retardate can cope successfully and that are part of a progression leading to independent living off the institution grounds. One of the aspects of community life for which the retardate needs preparation is the varying degree of acceptance he may experience, including possible rejection and hostility. Disabilities are variously defined culturally and, since our society places a high premium on normality, retardation is unacceptable to many.

This is evident even within the social welfare services. In response to the handicap, the community may react by restricting the availability of community resources, which in turn may contribute further to the social disability of the retardate. When community services exist, they are often more segregated than is necessary and limit the handicapped person's interaction with the more normal population.[5]

From the point of view of the residential program, what is needed is a program of community reintegration *during* institu-

---

3 J. S. Cohen, "An Analysis of Vocational Failures of Mental Retardates Placed in the Community After a Period of Institutionalization," *American Journal of Mental Deficiency*, Vol. 62 (1960), pp. 371–75.

4 M. A. Seidenfeld, *Mental Retardation: A Further Assessment of the Problem*, Rehabilitation Service Series No. 63–62 (Washington, D.C.: U.S. Department of Health, Education, and Welfare, Vocational Rehabilitation Administration, 1962).

5 Melvin Herman, "Reintegration of Handicapped Persons in the Community," in *New Perspectives on Services to Groups: Theory, Organization, Practice* (New York: National Association of Social Workers, 1961), pp. 70–78.

tionalization so that the retardate can begin to develop positive community experiences with some planning according to his needs. The best place to develop and reinforce competence in social skills is within the community rather than the institution alone.[6] This can often best be accomplished through use of small groups. Collective group support can offer additional protection during the period of transition to the community. Current residential treatment programs are so focused on the individual that they may not deal with his group-related needs within and without the institution. Polsky, in analyzing an institution for adolescents with emotional problems, states:

If the goal of therapy is re-integration of the individual into a rational cooperative human community, then we must concentrate on the social relationships in which the resident is integrated as well as on individual psychopathology.[7]

While the concept of using group service agencies for institutionalized retardates is new, these services have long been used successfully for released patients of psychiatric hospitals. Reporting on a resocialization project in Kansas, Morgan noted various gains in healthy functioning, including use of judgment, decision-making, and planning.[8] At the Fellowship Club in San Francisco—a therapeutic social club for post-hospitalized psychiatric patients—meetings were held in a community center because it was felt that social integration could be more easily effected in a social rather than a clinical setting.[9] Individuals can test out a variety of roles in the group. This opportunity to find and restore social roles is consistent with Parsons' description of the therapeutic process. According to him, "The therapeutic process must always have as one dimension the restoration of capacity to play social roles in a normal way."[10]

USE OF COMMUNITY GROUP SERVICES

As the Social Service Department of the Johnstone Center began to revise and extend its social rehabilitation program in response to

---

[6] Gunzburg, op. cit., p. 253.

[7] H. W. Polsky, Cottage Six (New York: Russell Sage Foundation, 1962), p. 41.

[8] Patricia M. Morgan, "A Project on Resocialization of Patients in a Mental Hospital: Use of Group Work Techniques," Social Casework, Vol. 42, No. 2 (February 1961), pp. 60–65.

[9] Dorothea Cudaback and R. Daniel Kahn, "A Therapeutic Social Club for Post-hospitalized Psychiatric Patients," Social Work with Groups 1959 (New York: National Association of Social Workers, 1959), pp. 52–65.

[10] Talcott Parsons, "Illness and the Role of the Physician: A Sociological Perspective," American Journal of Orthopsychiatry, Vol. 21 (1951), p. 453.

the literature and clinical impressions, one development was to initiate co-operative relationships with community group service agencies so that groups of students might actually use community facilities during the period of their institutionalization. This kind of agency is associated with normality and in some measure represents community values. It was believed that through the feeling of belonging and acceptance within the semiprotection of the agency, which provides a means of identification with the community, it would be possible for the institutionalized retardate to reach out even further to less protected community experiences. The social group work method was utilized for this purpose, with the focus set on more healthy ego functioning.

Actually, the center has begun using community resources as a progression toward greater social participation in the community. Starting with selected community experiences for supervised groups of younger, less mature adolescents the program ultimately provides students with opportunities to visit the social agencies on their own. Those presently offered the latter experience are usually day workers in the community. Selection is made jointly by the social service and vocational staffs.

The center staff has been conscious that such experimentation requires frequent review and evaluation to provide information for further modifications and improvements. The development of this program was also perceived as an opportunity to add to the knowledge available from previous studies.

One facet of community experience essentially missing from the data reported in the literature is the first-hand reaction of the retardate to the experience of moving from the institution to the community. Believing this to be of critical import to post institutional adjustment, the center initiated an exploratory study with a focus on the question: "What are the perceptions expressed by institutionalized retardates as they face introductory experiences in the community?"

PROCEDURE OF THE STUDY

Selected for this study, which was conducted during the summer of 1962, were eight young men ranging from 18 to 20. Intellectually they were in the mildly retarded or educable category. Years of institutionalization varied from five to eleven. All were in the final phase of residential training and were conscious that community placement was under consideration. Only one had previously been placed in the community and returned.

Data were gathered from group discussions held in eight weekly meetings at a local "Y." The students had earned their membership through a series of work projects or had paid for it out of earnings. The weekly visit to the "Y" included eating at the cafeteria, swimming, playing pool or ping-pong, and use of the gym. The last part of the evening was the group discussion, which was tape recorded and focused on their immediate reactions and adjustments to the agency and community.

The students were living through similar events, sharing their impressions, and using the social worker and the group in the process of working out adjustments to community living. An essential characteristic of the study is that reactions of the retardates were gathered during a phase of their adjustment to the community, rather than in retrospect or from secondary sources.

Since this was a preliminary, exploratory study, a rather simple approach was taken toward analysis of the content of the discussions. Topics that appeared with sufficient frequency to warrant tabulation are (1) the local YMCA, (2) job placements, (3) the community, (4) the residential institution, (5) the group as a whole or an individual member, and (6) themselves.

The range of topics approximated the authors' projections. There were, however, certain omissions, such as the topic of girls. Although the boys had typically adolescent interest in girls, they evidently did not think the subject was related to the purpose of the group sessions. This suggests that although they were instructed that any topic of interest to them could be covered, they apparently did have some unstated conception of primary purpose. The topics indicated covered well over nine-tenths of the content of the discussions.

The verbatim recordings were reviewed and comments made pertaining to each topic were abstracted and listed as separate items. Each item was then judged on a three-point scale: positive, neutral, or negative.

FINDINGS

A total of 267 comments were identified in the sessions pertaining to the topics listed. The most frequent topic was the group itself, which accounted for slightly over a third of the items. The frequency order of the other topics was self, YMCA, institution, job, and community. The last accounted for less than 7 percent of the comments. When the concentration of discussion topics was examined meeting by meeting, it was noted that the first session was focused primarily on the experience in the "Y." From then on the meetings centered most heavily on discussion related to the group itself.

With respect to the relative incidence of negative and positive comments, 67 percent were on the plus side. The most strongly positive topic was the "Y," which had a response of 90 percent. Next came self, rated as 75 percent positive. Comments about the community and the group were two-thirds positive. Falling below the mean were the job and the institution, with the latter having only 38 percent positive comments.

When the percentages of positive comments during the first four sessions were compared with those in the last four, differences were found according to topics. The comments relative to two topics became more positive: the "Y" from 84 percent to 100 percent and work from 50 percent to 71 percent. Positive comments about the "Y" were concentrated especially in the last session. Comments about the group itself became less positive during the latter half of the discussion, from 80 percent to 69 percent. There was no appreciable shift in comments about the community, the institution, or the self.

The statistical distributions of the subjects discussed are not the most critical findings of this study. The figures on frequency and the proportion of positive to negative expressions are not in any way to be construed as typical of what other institutionalized adolescents express under similar circumstances. To assure that such import would not be ascribed to these figures, the statistical analysis was purposely kept elementary, with no mathematical tests of significance applied.

The data obtained were based on a small, selected group. The staff of the center had reviewed the individuals carefully and had selected those who showed considerable "readiness" for community experiences. Moreover, the introductory work and social experiences were carefully planned and executed. Personnel at the "Y" and the job placements were well oriented to the nature of the individuals involved in the project, all of which undoubtedly tended to influence the positive results attained.

This must be weighed when the highly positive reactions of the group members are noted. There was an absence of any devastating community experiences such as are at times evident in the reports of individuals returning to institutions after placement. Moreover, there was little evidence of strongly negative attitudes toward any aspect of the community. Yet it is safe to say that more negative feelings toward community living (and the other topics) are present within the institution's population. It is reasonable to assume that greater differentiations may be obtained if the number of subjects is increased and the conditions are broadened. This should also afford an opportunity to test out hypothetical questions and predictive conditions in relation to successful community placement arising from practice and available studies.

MAKE COMMUNITY LIFE DESIRABLE

One set of hypotheses is suggested by the comparative reactions toward community and institution expressed by the group in this study. These results appear to have some relationship to experiences at the Johnstone Center, which are not unique to this setting. At times follow-up workers have commented that a student in the community *wants* to come back to the center. The preference for institutional life over community life on the part of some poses a programmatic problem for the field.

The authors believe the central solution lies in making community life more desirable (and desired) than institutional life, not in making the institution an undesirable, unhappy experience. The problem is how to help the residential student realize that life in the community can be rewarding, satisfying, and enjoyable even more than life under institutional conditions. There is a need to reduce the student's ignorance, fears, and anxieties about life in the community.

The exploratory study undertaken suggests that it may be possible to develop an index of readiness for community placement, or at least one aspect of such an index. This might enable testing of such hypotheses as "Readiness for community placement is achieved when reactions of individuals are more strongly positive toward off-campus living than on-campus living," and "Success in community placement is facilitated as positive attitudes toward community living are relatively stronger than those toward residential living."

In the present study, the reactions of the participating group were more frequently positive toward the community than the center. The quality of the reactions become evident when comments about the institution are examined for content. Negative feelings were on the order of "If you don't know something, they'll yell at you," and "They think we need someone to watch over us." This group, moreover, had an appreciation of the major objectives of the habilitation program of the center, as expressed in statements like, "The gold card is a way of training you," and "You learn about good manners in the dining room, the cottage, in class, in work (meaning vocational training) ." Although this still needs validation, the authors would like to believe that this evidences a rather favorable state of readiness for placement—an appreciation of both negative and positive aspects of the residential program without finding it necessary to tear it down to make life in the community appear attractive.

STUDENTS' COMMENTS

One topic not included in the earlier analysis was mental retardation. Actually this term was discussed only in the very first session. When the topic was raised the primary remark made by the boys was, "I was wondering what they thought about me." The group then concerned itself with whether or not they appeared mentally retarded to people in the community, and more particularly to others in the "Y." The conclusion was: "I don't think they thought we were mentally retarded because we certainly didn't show it." However, this was not said with great assurance. Actually, in this session the group *did* stand out considerably in the agency—in dress, manner, behavior, and compliance with procedures.

The basis on which they reassured themselves is contained in the following quotes from the session: "If we were mentally retarded we would be jumping around crazy." "A retarded person is someone who you can't trust." "If we were retarded they would always be watching us and standing around to see that we won't hurt ourselves."

From the position of assuring themselves that they could not possibly be so extremely deviant, they considered in later sessions two other points that had meaning in the process of becoming accustomed to community experiences: they examined how people behave in the community and they considered their own degree of competence. Their observations about persons in the community ranged from such generalities as "Everybody in the world makes a mistake," (IV) [11] to more specific identification of deficiencies, such as "There are plenty of people in this world that can't count money." (IV)

As for their own competence, the following remarks illustrate some of the changes: "I got excellent manners. (II) They can't fire me, I'm a good worker." (II) "At least I prove to people I joined something [the "Y"] that's got some sense to it." (VII)

By the final session of this series they were no longer comparing themselves with the community at large. The content strongly affirmed that they were perceiving themselves as a part of the world

---

[11] Roman numerals refer to the session in which the comments were made.

outside the institution. In this regard they showed both an urge to move in wider circles as well as some appreciation of difficulties they might experience when placed in the community. The desire to go out further varied from a limited suggestion like, "We know the prices at the ["Y"] cafeteria. Let's try some new places," (V) to "Why can't we all get together ourselves and go to Atlantic City?" (V). As for their perception of what living on one's own could mean, here are two samples from the third session: "One problem I'm going to have is living in a room and paying money." "My trouble is going to be facing different people and getting to know them."

Another emphasis obvious from the content of the discussions was the value of the group to the participants. For one, the members were very much conscious of each other's adjustments and behavior. At first they turned to the group leader for direction and correction, but once they realized that this responsibility was theirs, they accepted it with considerable vigor, as evident in the following comments made about each other in the sixth session: "You act like a fool." "He wants everybody to baby him." "He should be big enough to stand up for what he thinks is right." "He will never get out until he gets a good report." Similar comments from a staff person might well have enraged the boy singled out, but getting this barrage from his peers made it acceptable as shown by this comment in the next meeting: "I really feel good about it [the group]. Even though we have had a couple of arguments, I still feel good about it. As long as the boys try to help you when you make a mistake."

SUMMARY

Follow-up studies and impressions of practitioners who are concerned with habilitating individuals in institutional programs identify the period when residents move from institutional to community living as especially stressful. Available results are largely based on retrospective data. Little published material is based on information derived from individuals as they undergo the transition into the community. The project reported sampled the reactions of eight educable, late-adolescent males who were being introduced to work and social experiences in the community while remaining in residence at the center preparatory to placement. Based on the preliminary findings, the field is urged to undertake more extensive study of how retarded individuals feel, think, and cope with extra-institutional experiences.

Exercise for the Reader:
An Assessment of the Parnicky
and Brown Study

CLASSIFICATION

1. What are the specific purposes of the study?
2. What research methods do the authors use to accomplish their purposes?
3. Why is the study classified as exploratory? How does it differ from experimental and quantitative-descriptive studies?
4. How should the study be sub-typed?

EVALUATION

Problem Formulation

1. With respect to the introduction of retardates to the community, what is the practice problem with which the authors are concerned?
2. What assumptions and value judgments do the authors make in regard to preferred procedures for returning institutionalized retardates to the community?
3. How do the authors use the literature for the formulation of the problem for research?
4. How do the authors conceptualize "perceptions" and "introductory experiences" in the community for retardates?
5. In what ways are the community experiences for the retardates different from institutional experiences?

Research Design and Data Collection

1. Was the research design sufficient for developing ideas pertinent to the perceptions of retardates?
2. What sampling procedures were employed in the study with respect to the selection of retardates for the research, the number of meetings, and the content selected for analysis?
3. What kinds of data were collected and by what means?
4. Could the authors have collected other types of data consistent with the purposes of their study?
5. To what extent were potential biases minimized in their collection of data?

282

6. How valid did the data appear regarding perceptions of community experiences as opposed to institutional experiences?

Data Analysis and Conclusions

1. How reliable were the procedures used for classifying the content of group discussions into positive, neutral, and negative responses?

2. What findings were presented, and in what ways could the authors have used their available data for additional analyses consistent with the purposes of their study?

3. Do the hypotheses stem from the findings of the research study or from the initial biases and conceptions of the authors?

UTILIZATION

1. What is the general level of knowledge of conclusions from this study?

2. To what areas of social work practice might the findings be useful, either directly or indirectly?

3. Does the study provide a framework for evaluating practice programs on an exploratory basis?

4. As a function of reading this article, what problems can practitioners become sensitive to?

5. What kinds of detailed studies may be fruitful in this area for further practice utilization, i.e., what hypotheses can the reader develop?

RECOMMENDED REFERENCES

Research Design and Data Collection

BERLSON, BERNARD, "Content Analysis," in *Handbook of Social Psychology: Vol. 1, Theory and Method,* Gardner Lindzey (ed.) (Reading: Addison-Wesley Publishing Company, 1954), pp. 488–522.

Mental Retardation and the Community

HERMAN, MELVIN, "Reintegration of Handicapped Persons in the Community," in *New Perspectives on Services to Groups: Theory, Organization, and Practice* (New York: National Association of Social Workers, 1961), pp. 70–78.

Bibliographic References

AMERICAN PSYCHOLOGICAL ASSOCIATION, *Publication Manual*, 1967 Revision.

ANDERSON, JOHN E., "Methods of Child Psychology," in *Manual of Child Psychology*, Leonard Carmichael (ed.) (2nd ed.) (New York: John Wiley and Sons, Inc., 1954), pp. 52–54.

AYLLON, T., "Intensive Treatment of Psychotic Behaviour by Stimulus Satiation and Food Reinforcement," *Behaviour Research and Therapy, Vol. 1* (May, 1963), pp. 53–61.

BACON, MARGARET K.; CHILD, IRVIN L.; and BARRY III, HERBERT, "A Cross-Cultural Study of Correlates of Crime," *Journal of Abnormal and Social Psychology, Vol. 66,* No. 4 (April, 1963), pp. 291–300.

BARTLETT, HARRIETT M.; KADUSHIN, ALFRED; THOMAS, EDWIN J.; MAAS, HENRY S.; GORDON, WILLIAM E.; and MURPHY, MARJORIE, *Building Social Work Knowledge* (New York: National Association of Social Workers, 1964).

BENNIS, WARREN G.; BENNE, KENNETH D.; and CHIN, ROBERT, *The Planning of Change* (New York: Holt, Rinehart and Winston, 1961).

BERLSON, BERNARD, "Content Analysis," in *Handbook of Social Psychology: Vol. 1, Theory and Method*, G. Lindzey (ed.) (Reading: Addison-Wesley Publishing Company, 1954), pp. 488–522.

BIERI, JAMES; ATKINS, ALVIN L.; BRIAR, SCOTT; LEAMAN, ROBIN LOBECK; MILLER, HENRY; and TRIPODI, TONY, *Clinical and Social Judgment* (New York: John Wiley & Sons, Inc., 1966).

BILLINGSLEY, ANDREW, "The Role of the Social Worker in a Child Protective Agency," *Child Welfare* (November, 1964), pp. 473–79, 497.

BLALOCK, HUBERT M., *Social Statistics* (New York: McGraw-Hill Book Company, Inc., 1960).

————. *Causal Inferences in Nonexperimental Research* (Chapel Hill: The University of North Carolina Press, 1961).

BONJEAN, CHARLES M., "Community Leadership: A Case Study and Conceptual Refinement," *American Journal of Sociology* (May, 1963), pp. 672–81.

CAMPBELL, DONALD T. and STANLEY, JULIAN C., "Experimental and Quasi-Experimental Designs for Research on Teaching," in *Handbook of Research on Teaching*, N. L. Gage (ed.) (Chicago: Rand McNally and Co., 1963), pp. 171–246.

CAPLOW, THEODORE, "Official Reports and Proceedings," *American Sociological Review* (December, 1958), pp. 704-11.

CHEIN, ISIDOR, "An Introduction to Sampling," in *Research Methods in Social Relations* (rev. ed.) by Claire Selltiz, Marie Jahoda, Morton Deutsch, and Stuart W. Cook (New York: Henry Holt and Company, Inc., 1959).

COUNCIL ON SOCIAL WORK EDUCATION, *Manual of Accrediting Standards for Graduate Professional Schools of Social Work* (New York: 1965), pp. 57–58.

DAY, ROBERT C. and HAMBLIN, ROBERT L., "Some Effects of Close and Punitive Styles of Supervision," *American Journal of Sociology* (March, 1964), pp. 499–510.

EATON, JOSEPH W., "Science, 'Art,' and Uncertainty," *Social Work* (July, 1958), pp. 3–10.

EDWARDS, ALLEN L., *Experimental Design in Psychological Research* (rev. ed.) (New York: Holt, Rinehart and Winston, 1960).

————. *Statistical Methods for the Behavioral Sciences* (New York: Holt, Rinehart and Winston, 1961).

FANSHEL, DAVID, "Research in Child Welfare: A Critical Analysis," *Child Welfare* (December, 1962a), pp. 484–507.

———— (ed.), *Research in Social Welfare Administration: Its Contributions and Problems* (New York: National Association of Social Workers, 1962b).

FAUNCE, WILLIAM A. and CLELLAND, DONALD A., "Professionalization and Stratification Patterns in an Industrial Community," *American Journal of Sociology* (January, 1967), pp. 341–50.

FELLIN, PHILLIP; TRIPODI, TONY; and MEYER, HENRY J. (eds.), *Exemplars of Social Research* (Itasca, Ill., F. E. Peacock Publishers, Inc., 1969).

FESTINGER, LEON, "Laboratory Experiments," in *Research Methods in the Behavioral Sciences*, Leon Festinger and Daniel Katz (eds.) (New York: The Dryden Press, Inc., 1953), pp. 136–72.

————, and KATZ, DANIEL (eds.), *Research Methods in the Behavioral Sciences* (New York: The Dryden Press, Inc., 1953).

FLANAGAN, JOHN C., "The Critical Incident Technique," *Psychological Bulletin*, 51 (July, 1954), pp. 327–28.

FINESTONE, SAMUEL, "The Critical Review of a Research Monograph: A Teaching Unit in a Social Work Research Course," in *Selected Papers in Methods of Teaching Research in the Social Work Curriculum* (New York: Council on Social Work Education, 1959), pp. 33–37.

FRANCEL, EDWARD W.; CRANE, JOHN A.; FANSHEL, DAVID; JAHN, JULIUS A.; MACDONALD, MARY E.; and O'REILLY, CHARLES, "Task Force Report on Research in M.S.W. Curriculum," *Social Work Education Reporter* (March, 1968), pp. 13, 20–21.

FRANKS, VIRGINIA L., "Usefulness of Research," Letter to the Editor, *Social Work* (April, 1968), pp. 142–43.

FRENCH, JOHN R. P., JR., "Experiments in Field Settings," in *Research Methods in the Behavioral Sciences,* Leon Festinger and Daniel Katz (eds.) (New York: The Dryden Press, Inc., 1953), pp. 98–135.

GAMSON, WILLIAM A., "Reputation and Resources in Community Politics," *American Journal of Sociology* (September, 1966), pp. 121–31.

GLASER, BARNEY G. and STRAUSS, ANSELM L., *The Discovery of Grounded Theory: Strategies for Qualitative Research* (Chicago: Aldine Publishing Company, 1967).

GOLDSTEIN, HARRIS K., "Criteria for Evaluating Research," *Social Casework* (November, 1962), pp. 474–77.

_____. *Research Standards and Methods for Social Workers* (New Orleans: The Hauser Press, 1963), pp. 303–19.

_____. *Identifying and Maximizing Research Learning Potential for Social Work Students* (New Orleans: School of Social Work, Tulane Studies in Social Welfare, Tulane University, 1967).

GOODE, WILLIAM J. and HATT, PAUL K., *Methods in Social Research* (New York: McGraw-Hill Book Company, Inc., 1952).

GOODMAN, L. A., "Ecological Regression and Behavior of Individuals," *American Sociological Review,* 18 (December, 1953), pp. 663–64.

GOODRICH, D. WELLS and BOOMER, DONALD S., "Some Concepts about Therapeutic Interventions with Hyperaggressive Children: Part I," *Social Casework,* 39 (April, 1958), pp. 207–13.

_____. "Some Concepts about Therapeutic Interventions with Hyperaggressive Children: Part II," *Social Casework,* 39 (May, 1958), pp. 286–92.

GOULDNER, ALVIN W., "Explorations in Applied Social Science," *Social Problems* 3 (January, 1956), pp. 169–81.

_____. "Theoretical Requirements of the Applied Social Sciences," *American Sociological Review,* 22 (February, 1957), pp. 92–102.

_____. "Explorations in Applied Social Science," in *Applied Sociology: Opportunities and Problems,* Alvin W. Gouldner and S. M. Miller (eds.) (New York: The Free Press, 1965), pp. 5–22.

_____. and MILLER, S. M. (eds.), *Applied Sociology: Opportunities and Problems* (New York: The Free Press, 1965).

GREENWOOD, ERNEST, "Social Science and Social Work: A Theory of Their Relationships," *Social Service Review,* 29 (March, 1955), pp. 20–33.

_____. "Social Work Research: A Decade of Reappraisal," *Social Service Review* (September, 1957), pp. 311–20.

_____. *Lectures in Research Methodology for Social Welfare Students,* University of California Syllabus Series No. 388, University of California (Berkeley, 1960).

_____. "The Practice of Science and the Science of Practice," in Warren G. Bennis *et al.* (eds.), *The Planning of Change* (New York: Holt, Rinehart and Winston, 1961), pp. 73–82.

HERZOG, ELIZABETH, *Some Guidelines for Evaluative Research: Assessing Psychosocial Change in Individuals,* U.S. Department of Health, Education, and Welfare, Social Security Administration, Children's Bureau (1959).

_____. *About the Poor* (Washington: Children's Bureau, 1967).

HIRSCHI, TRAVIS and SELVIN, HANAN, *Delinquency Research: An Appraisal of Analytic Methods* (New York: The Free Press, 1967).

HOLLINGSHEAD, AUGUST B. and REDLICH, FREDERICK C., *Social Class and Mental Illness* (New York: John Wiley and Sons, Inc., 1958).

HYMAN, HERBERT, *Survey Design and Analysis* (Glencoe, Ill.: The Free Press, 1955).

JANSYN, LEON R. JR., "Solidarity and Delinquency in a Street Corner Group," *American Sociological Review* (October, 1966), pp. 600–14.

KADUSHIN, ALFRED, "Assembling Social Work Knowledge," in *Building Social Work Knowledge* (New York: National Association of Social Workers, 1964), pp. 16–37.

KAHN, ALFRED J. (ed), *Issues in American Social Work* (New York: Columbia University Press, 1959).

————. "The Design of Research," in Norman A. Polansky (ed.) *Social Work Research* (Chicago: The University of Chicago Press, 1960), pp. 48–73.

KATZ, DANIEL, "Field Studies," in Leon Festinger and Daniel Katz (eds.) *Research Methods in the Behavioral Sciences* (New York: The Dryden Press, Inc., 1953), pp. 56–97.

KENDALL, PATRICIA L. and LAZARSFELD, PAUL F., "Problems of Survey Analysis," in Robert K. Merton and Paul F. Lazarsfeld (eds.), *Continuities in Social Research: Studies in the Scope and Method of "The American Soldier"* (Glencoe, Illinois: The Free Press, 1959).

KERLINGER, FRED N., *Foundations of Behavioral Research: Educational and Psychological Inquiry* (New York: Holt, Rinehart and Winston, 1967).

KNOP, EDWARD, "Suggestions to Aid the Student in Systematic Interpretation and Analysis of Empirical Sociological Journal Presentations," *The American Sociologist* (May, 1967), pp. 90–92.

KOGAN, LEONARD S. (ed.), *Social Science Theory and Social Work Research*, National Association of Social Workers (New York, 1960a).

————. "Principles of Measurement," in Norman Polansky (ed.), *Social Work Research* (Chicago: The University of Chicago Press, 1960b), pp. 87–105.

KRASNER, LEONARD and ULMANN, LEONARD P. (eds.), *Research in Behavior Modification* (New York: Holt, Rinehart and Winston, 1965).

LAZARSFELD, PAUL F. and ROSENBERG, MORRIS (eds.), *The Language of Social Research* (Glencoe, Illinois: The Free Press, 1955).

————, SEWELL, WILLIAM H.; and WILENSKY, HAROLD L. (eds.), *The Uses of Sociology* (New York: Basic Books, 1967).

LEVINGER, GEORGE, "Continuance in Casework and Other Helping Relationships: A Review of Current Research," *Social Work* (July, 1960), pp. 40–51.

LEWIN, KURT; LIPPITT, RONALD; and WHITE, R. K., "Patterns of Aggressive Behavior in Experimentally Created Social Climates," *Journal of Social Psychology*, 10 (May, 1939), pp. 271–99.

LEWIS, OSCAR, *The Children of Sanchez* (New York: Random House, 1961).

LIKERT, RENSIS and LIPPITT, RONALD, "The Utilization of Social Science," in Leon Festinger and Daniel Katz (eds.), *Research Methods in the Behavioral Sciences* (New York: The Dryden Press, Inc., 1953).

LUNDBERG, G., *Social Research* (New York: Longmans, Green and Company, 1942).

MAAS, HENRY A., "The Young Adult Adjustment of Twenty Wartime Residential Nursery Children," *Child Welfare* (February, 1963), pp. 57–72.

_____ (ed.), *Five Fields of Social Service: Reviews of Research* (New York: National Association of Social Workers, 1966).

MACDONALD, MARY E., "Methods of Teaching Research in the Social Work Curriculum," in *Selected Papers in Methods of Teaching Research in the Social Work Curriculum* (New York: Council on Social Work Education, 1959), pp. 5–9.

_____. "Social Work Research: A Perspective," in *Social Work Research,* Norman A Polansky (ed.) (Chicago: The University of Chicago Press, 1960).

_____. "Reunion at Vocational High: An Analysis of Girls at Vocational High: An Experiment in Social Work Intervention," *Social Service Review* (June, 1966), pp. 175–89.

MAIN, MARJORIE W. and MACDONALD, MARY E., "Professional Functions and Opinions of Social Group Workers," *Social Service Review* (December, 1962), pp. 421–32.

MALINOWSKI, BRONISLAW, *Crime and Custom in Savage Society* (New York: Harcourt, Brace and World, 1926).

MARKS, RACHEL, "Research Reporting," in Norman A. Polansky (ed.), *Social Work Research* (Chicago: The University of Chicago Press, 1960), pp. 187–200.

MERTON, ROBERT K.; BROOM, LEONARD; and COTTRELL, JR., LEONARD S., *Sociology Today: Problems and Prospects* (New York: Basic Books, Inc., 1959).

MEYER, HENRY J.; JONES, WYATT; and BORGATTA, EDGAR F., "The Decision by Unmarried Mothers to Keep or Surrender Their Babies," *Social Work* (April, 1956), pp. 103–09.

_____. BORGATTA, EDGAR F.; JONES, WYATT C., *Girls at Vocational High: An Experiment in Social Work Intervention* (New York: Russell Sage Foundation, 1965).

_____. "An Experiment in Prevention Through Social Work Intervention," in *Behavioral Science for Social Workers,* Edwin J. Thomas (ed.) (New York: The Free Press, 1967).

_____. LITWAK, EUGENE; THOMAS, EDWIN J.; and VINTER, ROBERT D., "Social Work and Social Welfare," in *The Uses of Sociology,* Paul F. Lazarsfeld, William H. Sewell, and Harold L. Wilensky (eds.) (New York: Basic Books, Inc., 1967), pp. 156–90.

_____. "Social Work," *International Encyclopedia of the Social Sciences* (New York: MacMillan Co. & Free Press, 1968).

MILLER, ROGER R., "An Experimental Study of the Observational Process in Casework," *Social Work* (April, 1958), pp. 96–102.

MORGAN, MARGARET; GOODGLASS, HAROLD; FOLSOM, ANGELA; and QUADFASEL, FRED A., "Epilepsy and Social Adjustment," *Social Work,* 12 (April, 1967) pp. 70–76.

MOSER, C. A., *Survey Methods in Social Investigation* (London: Heinemann Educational Books Ltd., 1958).

NAGEL, ERNEST (ed.), *John Stuart Mill's Philosophy of Scientific Method* (New York: Hafner Publishing Company, 1950).

NORRIS, MIRIAM and WALLACE, BARBARA (eds.), *The Known and Unknown in Child Welfare Research* (New York: National Association of Social Workers, 1965).

NORTHCUTT, TRAVIS J., JR.; LANDSMAN, THEODORE; NEILL, JOHN S.; and GORMAN, JOANNA F., "Rehabilitation of Former Mental Patients: An Evaluation of a Coordinated Community Aftercare Program," *American Journal of Public Health* (April, 1965), pp. 570–77.

ORCUTT, BEN A., "A Study of Anchoring Effects in Clinical Judgment," *Social Service Review* (December, 1964), pp. 408–17.

PARNICKY, JOSEPH J., and BROWN, LEONARD N., "Introducing Institutionalized Retardates to the Community," *Social Work* (January, 1964), pp. 79–85.

PAUL, GORDON L., *Insight vs. Desensitization in Psychotherapy: An Experiment in Anxiety Reduction* (Stanford: Stanford University Press, 1966).

————. "Insight Versus Desensitization in Psychotherapy Two Years after Termination," *Journal of Consulting Psychology*, 31 (August, 1967), pp. 333–48.

POLANSKY, NORMAN A. (ed.), *Social Work Research* (Chicago: The University of Chicago Press, 1960).

POLLAK, OTTO, "Worker Assignment in Casework with Marriage Partners," *Social Service Review* (March, 1963), pp. 41–53.

POSER, ERNEST G., "The Effect of Therapists' Training on Group Therapeutic Outcome," *Journal of Consulting Psychology*, 30 (August, 1966), pp. 283–89.

REIK, THEODOR, *Listening with the Third Ear* (New York: Farrar, Straus and Cudahy, Inc., 1948).

RILEY, MATILDA WHITE, *Sociological Research* (New York: Harcourt, Brace and World, Inc., 1963).

RIPPLE, LILIAN, "Motivation, Capacity, and Opportunity as Related to the Use of Casework Service: Theoretical Base and Plan of Study," *Social Service Review*, 29 (June, 1955), pp. 172–93.

RIPPLE, LILIAN, and ALEXANDER, ERNESTINA, "Motivation, Capacity, and Opportunity as Related to the Use of Casework Service: Nature of the Client's Problem," *Social Service Review* (March, 1956), pp. 38–54.

ROBINSON, W. S., "Ecological Correlations and the Behavior of Individuals," *American Sociological Review*, 15 (June, 1950), pp. 351–57.

ROETHLISBERGER, F. J. and DICKSON, W. J., *Management and the Worker* (Cambridge: Harvard University Press, 1939).

ROSENBLATT, AARON, "The Practitioner's Use and Evaluation of Research," *Social Work*, 13 (January, 1968), pp. 53–59.

SARRI, ROSEMARY C. and VINTER, ROBERT C., "Organizational Requisites for a Socio-Behavioral Technology," in Edwin J. Thomas (ed.), *The Socio-Behavioral Approach and Applications to Social Work* (New York: Council on Social Work Education, 1967), pp. 87–99.

SCHWARTZ, EDWARD E. (ed.), *Manpower in Social Welfare* (National Association of Social Workers, 1966).

SCOTT, W. RICHARD, "Reactions to Supervision in a Heteronomous Professional Organization," *Administrative Science Quarterly*, 10 (June, 1965), pp. 65–81.

SELLTIZ, CLAIRE; JAHODA, MARIE; DEUTSCH, MORTON, and COOK, STUART W., *Research Methods in Social Relations* (rev. ed.) (New York: Holt, Rinehart and Winston, 1959).

SHULMAN, LAWRENCE, "Scapegoats, Group Workers, and Preemptive Intervention," *Social Work*, 12 (April, 1967), pp. 37–43.

SHYNE, ANN, "Casework Research: Past and Present," *Social Casework* (November, 1962), pp. 467–73.

————. "Social Work Research," in Harry L. Lurie (ed.) *Encyclopedia of Social Work*, (New York: National Association of Social Workers, 1965).

SILVERMAN, MARVIN, "Knowledge in Social Group Work: A Review of the Literature," *Social Work*, 11 (July, 1966), pp. 56–62.

Stein, Herman D. and Cloward, Richard A., *Social Perspectives on Behavior* (Glencoe, Ill.: The Free Press, 1958).

Stollak, Gary E.; Guerney, Bernard G.; and Rothberg, Meyer (eds.), *Psychotherapy Research* (Chicago: Rand McNally and Co., 1966).

Suchman, Edward A., *Evaluative Research: Principles and Practice in Public Service and Social Action Programs* (New York: Russell Sage Foundation, 1967), pp. 51–73.

————. "The 'Hang-Loose' Ethic and the Spirit of Drug Use," *Journal of Health and Social Behavior*, 9 (June, 1968), pp. 146–55.

Sussman, Marvin, "Experimental Research," in Harold T. Christensen (ed.), *Handbook of Marriage and the Family* (Chicago: Rand McNally and Co., 1964).

Thomas, Edwin J., "Field Experiments and Demonstrations," in Norman Polansky (ed.), *Social Work Research* (Chicago: The University of Chicago Press, 1960), pp. 87–105.

————, and McLeod, Donna B., *In-Service Training and Reduced Workloads: Experiments in a State Department of Welfare* (New York: Russell Sage Foundation, 1960).

————. "Selecting Knowledge from Behavioral Science," in *Building Social Work Knowledge* (New York: National Association of Social Workers, 1964), pp. 38–48.

———— (ed.), *Behavioral Science for Social Workers* (New York: The Free Press, 1967a).

———— (ed.), *The Socio-Behavioral Approach and Applications to Social Work* (New York: Council on Social Work Education, 1967b).

Tripodi, Tony and Miller, Henry, "The Clinical Judgment Process: A Review of the Literature," *Social Work* (July, 1966), pp. 63–69.

Use of Judgments as Data in Social Work Research (New York: National Association of Social Workers, 1959).

Webb, Eugene J.; Campbell, Donald T.; Schwartz, Richard D.; and Sechrest, Lee, *Unobtrusive Measures: Nonreactive Research in the Social Sciences* (Chicago: Rand McNally and Co., 1966).

Weinberger, Roslyn and Tripodi, Tony, "Trends in Types of Research Reported in Selected Social Work Journals: 1956–1965," University of Michigan School of Social Work, mimeographed (May, 1968).

Whyte, William Foote, *Street Corner Society: The Social Structure of an Italian Slum* (Chicago: The University of Chicago Press, 1943).

Zald, Mayer N. (ed.), *Social Welfare Institutions* (New York: John Wiley & Sons, Inc., 1965).

Zander, Alvin, and Newcomb Jr., Theodore, "Group Levels of Aspiration in United Fund Campaigns," *Journal of Personality and Social Psychology* (June, 1967), pp. 157–62.

Zetterberg, Hans L., *On Theory and Verification in Sociology* (New York: The Tressler Press, 1954).

————. *Social Theory and Social Practice* (New York: Bedminster Press, 1962).

Name Index

Subject Index

Types of research
  see research
Types of knowledge, 100-101

Utilization of social research, 13-14, 94-130
  experimental studies, 126-127
  exploratory studies, 130
  first steps, 125-126
  frameworks, 95-99
  guidelines, 107-124
  in social work, 96-99
  level, 112-114
  potential relevance, 110, 111
  problems in, 105-107
  quantitative-descriptive studies, 127-129

research methods, 96
social work purpose, 114-115
types of use, 121-123
value perspective, 111

Validity, 36, 118
Value perspective, 111
Variable manipulation, 77-78
Variable relationship studies
  see searching for variable relationships
Variables
  accessibility, 120
  feasibility of use, 120-121
  identifiability, 119
  manipulability, 13-14, 73, 120
  potency, 118

BOOK MANUFACTURE

The Assessment of Social Research: Guidelines for the Use of Research in Social Work and Social Science was typeset and printed by offset at Webb Publishing Company. Cloth binding was by A. J. Dahl Company. The paper is Perkins & Squier Company's Glatfelter Old Forge Wove. Internal design was by the F. E. Peacock Publishers, Inc., art department. Cover design was by Earl E. Hilland. The type in this book is Baskerville with Bodoni display.